Frontiers of Faith

Frontiers of *Faith*

Bringing Catholicism to the West in the Early Republic

JOHN R. DICHTL

THE UNIVERSITY PRESS OF KENTUCKY

Editorial and Sales Offices: The University Press of Kentucky
663 South Limestone Street, Lexington, Kentucky 40508-4008
www.kentuckypress.com

12 11 10 09 08   5 4 3 2 1

Library of Congress Cataloging-in-Publication Data

Dichtl, John R., 1965–
  Frontiers of faith : transplanting Catholicism to the West in the Early Republic /
John R. Dichtl.
     p. cm.
  Includes bibliographical references and index.
  ISBN 978-0-8131-2486-5 (hardcover : alk. paper)
  1. Catholic Church—United States—History—19th century. 2. United
States—Church history—19th century. I. Title.
  BX1406.3.D53 2008
  282'.7709034—dc22   2007043776

This book is printed on acid-free recycled paper meeting the requirements of the
American National Standard for Permanence in Paper for Printed Library Materials.

Manufactured in the United States of America.

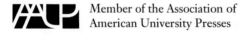 Member of the Association of
American University Presses

For
Joan Lottie Smith Dichtl
and
Rudolph John Dichtl

Contents

Acknowledgments

This book began as a doctoral dissertation at Indiana University, and I thank current and former faculty there—particularly Stephen J. Stein, Bernard W. Sheehan, Robert A. Orsi, and Peter F. Guardino—who provided direct and indirect guidance. Professor Stein, most of all, as dissertation adviser and friend, has been a constant source of intellectual enthusiasm. I am also indebted to the late Paul R. Lucas who planted the inklings of ideas that became this project. Numerous colleagues read parts of earlier versions of these chapters. Scott Stephan, Patrick Ettinger, and Steve Warren read most everything and generously offered crucial suggestions. Scott, in particular, has my deep gratitude. Peter W. Williams, Stephen Aron, and other, unnamed, reviewers, as well as Linda K. Kerber, offered valuable comments at various stages. Additional thanks to Peter Carmichael and the University Press of Kentucky editor-in-chief Joyce Harrison for bringing this work to publication, and to Liz Smith for her careful attention.

I also am grateful for the use of the archives at the University of Notre Dame, the Filson Historical Society, the Kentucky Historical Society, the Historical Society of Western Pennsylvania, and the convents of the Sisters of Charity of Nazareth in Nazareth, Kentucky, and the Sisters of Loretto in Nerinx, Kentucky. Each collection was a well-kept treasure, cared for and made accessible by individuals in whose debt I remain.

My final words of grateful acknowledgment go to Dana and Annika, whose love and encouragement made the completion of this book meaningful.

Introduction

Father John Carroll saw great promise in the nation's future, particularly in its lands to the west. In the spring of 1785, two years after the Treaty of Paris had ended war with England and only months after his appointment as head of the missions of the Roman Catholic Church in the United States, Carroll described for a European colleague the rich forests and potential farmlands spread between the seaboard states and the Mississippi River. He asked his friend to convince American Catholics training for the priesthood abroad to return home, where the shortage of clergymen was acute. Not only were older parishes growing rapidly, particularly in Pennsylvania and Maryland, Carroll wrote, but thousands of Catholics were moving westward; "nothing withholds them but the dread of wanting the ministrations of Religion." In fact, Carroll added, there were "repeated offers of liberal grants of land for the support of Clergymen there." Most surprising, said Carroll, was that "indeed some protestants, with a hope of having their lands speedily settled, have been induced to give their bonds for the conveyance to a Catholic priest of very ample property."[1] Protestants willing to supply land to attract Roman Catholic priests—the situation was as astonishing as it was promising. Catholic-Protestant relations had been improved by the French alliance during the American Revolution, and John Carroll and his clergy were attuned to the increasing spirit of toleration.

Yet experience taught caution. Only weeks earlier, Carroll himself had ended a three-month delay by accepting the Vatican's offer to appoint him to lead the American church. His superiors knew about the hostility of Protestant and republican Anglo-Americans toward bishops. They cautiously offered him the title of prefect apostolic of the United States—an office without episcopal authority. Carroll appreciated this discretion, but he was more concerned that by not holding the office of bishop with a diocese grounded in the United States, he would be seen by Americans as a mere agent of Rome, by way of the Sacred Congregation for the Propagation of the Faith. He feared the semblance of foreign interference in a nation that had just won its independence.[2]

As Carroll glanced backward across the Atlantic toward the source of his authority and looked ahead to the future of his church in the West, he knew he could not avoid considering the opinion of America's non-Catholics. Unlike the more populated East where Catholics might have been a minority easily ignored, in the sparsely settled countryside and small towns in the early West even small concentrations of Catholics stood out. Carroll's reign and those of his successors would involve constant negotiation with American Protestants and other non-Catholics.

Catholics living in the trans-Appalachian West interacted with non-Catholics at a variety of religious and social contact points during the early republic. Time and again Catholic clergy and laity successfully pursued strategies of growth in frontier regions, in the midst of Presbyterians, Baptists, Methodists, Episcopalians, deists, and others of different religions or of no belief. For forty years Catholics and Protestants contested the trans-Appalachian frontier with a degree of fluidity not possible earlier because of the insignificant Catholic population, and not likely later because of worsening sectarian relations. Most important decisions made by Catholic clergy and the episcopacy during these middle decades were shaped by, or at least deliberately considered closely against, the shadow of Protestant opinion.

Despite this rich period of sectarian interaction, the Catholic Church and the various Protestant denominations have been treated by historians as though they developed in isolation or, at best, along parallel tracks.[3] When historians have considered Protestant-Catholic interaction in early America, they have tended to concentrate on the colorful friction of anti-Catholicism before the American Revolution or in the antebellum period.[4] It is clear instead that from the Catholic perspective, the growth of the church in frontier areas in the intervening period of the early republic took place in a context both of cooperation and of competition with American Protestantism prior to the hardening of sectarian animosities in the 1830s. In fact, Catholicism in the new West had more in common with the quickly spreading evangelical Protestant denominations so famous for their triumphs than scholars of early American religion have recognized.[5] Catholic clergy did not simply keep to their own and quietly work to expand the church. Like many of their Protestant peers, Catholic leaders aggressively established congregations, enforced church authority, ministered to the faithful, sought converts, and otherwise attempted to display the distinctive features of their religion that would inspire the hearts of their own people as well as those of other faiths or of no faith at all.

The early Midwestern frontier, like other backcountry and borderland areas, was not a dividing line but a meeting place, in which "multi-sided negotiations of power" took place between cultures and peoples, typically Native American and European. Emphasizing religious differences over ethnic and cultural, this study examines the interaction of Catholic and non-Catholic primarily from a point of view within the Catholic community looking outward, and most frequently through the eyes of Catholic clergy. Although not treated here, other points of view existed, for even within a single geographical zone of interaction there can be many "frontiers," each a "variant perspective" on the same set of encounters.[6]

Because of the focus on religion that follows, the framing of the term "frontier" will be somewhat broader than that used by most historians who study the late eighteenth- and early nineteenth-century trans-Appalachian West. Some scholars, borrowing from Leonard Thompson and Howard Lamar's useful 1981 definition of the frontier, time the closing of a frontier period at the point "when a single political authority has established hegemony over the whole area." In the case of Kentucky, the frontier era as a time and place of European, American, and Indian interaction might be said to end with statehood in 1792. Nevertheless, for people establishing religious institutions, communities, and traditions in the trans-Appalachian regions of western Pennsylvania and northern Kentucky, no single authority could ever be said to have exerted hegemony over all churches and denominations. Even within one religious group, such as the Catholics, authority was not firmly established until well into the nineteenth century, after the Bardstown diocese received its first bishop in 1811, or after that bishop was able to build institutions—such as a convent, seminary, and schools—that made the diocese self-supporting. Moreover, the conditions of the frontier life persisted as well. Extreme scarcities of priests, scattered parishes and missions, an absence of supporting institutions (e.g., convents, seminaries, schools), and persistently short supplies of financial resources and devotional, liturgical, sacramental, and catechismal materials beset the Catholic Church into the early decades of the nineteenth century. The trans-Appalachian region was a "frontier" for at least as long as the Holy See considered the U.S. church to be a mission under the control of the Congregation for the Propagation of the Faith.[7]

The open wilderness of Kentucky and other peripheral areas to which Catholics migrated in the first years of nationhood fostered enthusiasm and optimism, as well as a more assertive and outward orientation. But although the frontier was a cultural meeting ground open to adaptation, innovation, and deviance, it also strengthened traditional features of Catholicism. Many priests, for example, surprised their parishioners and superiors by their lax regard for episcopal authority, yet they ultimately were reined in as the church retrenched. Likewise, frontier shortages of cash and material goods might have fostered innovation in church construction and decoration or the creation of liturgical items, yet Catholics in the West cleaved to a European aesthetic and imported religious items with great enterprise. Difficulties of frontier life pressed Catholics to use familiar methods of establishing institutions, proselytizing, defending the faith, and inculcating piety and devotion. Catholics were invigorated by the problems and possibilities of the frontier and responded by emphasizing their traditional distinctiveness.[8]

The trans-Appalachian frontier of the 1780s to the 1820s was not a crucible that remade American Catholicism but a contested space in which, for a time, Catholics mingled with non-Catholics more freely and with more optimism than they had during the eighteenth century. In this zone of interaction, Catholics encountered non-Catholics on more equal terms than in urban or eastern communities and assertively displayed Catholicism, tried to enlighten fellow settlers, and hoped to attract friends and converts.[9] At a variety of "contact points," there took place "kinetic interactions" between Catholics and non-Catholics, laity and clergy. The present study approaches these primarily through the viewpoints of Catholic priests and bishops, and traces slowly narrowing options and possible outcomes as the situation polarized into a Catholic versus anti-Catholic standoff.[10]

The story that follows traces Catholic-Protestant relations during the 1780s through the 1820s, from backcountry Pennsylvania and Maryland to the far edges of Kentucky and Indiana. Chapter 1 outlines the scope of the project cast at the feet of westward-moving Catholic clergy, who began with high hopes and remained generally optimistic about building churches, encouraging Catholics to populate frontier regions, ministering to the needs of settlers already dispersing across the West, and carving out a place for Catholicism.

Chapter 2 emphasizes the central importance and authority of the priest, both internally, within the Catholic communities of trans-Appalachia, and externally, as an authority figure between bishop and laity and as the focal point of public relations. The proximity of neighboring non-Catholics, as well as frontier conditions (i.e., long distances, few clergymen, scattered Catholic communities, and a lack of church buildings and other materials) and frontier opportunities (i.e., new settlements and new lands to develop) created pressing demands on Catholic priests. Responding to these challenges, priests gained power that made them difficult to control, by bishop or by lay parishioners. Yet bishops did find ways to exert authority, knowing that a functioning ecclesiastical system required it and that non-Catholic Americans were watching them closely.

Chapter 3 explores the controversies surrounding those priests who found ways to exploit the underdeveloped power structure of the western Catholic Church. Problematic priests, or "renegades," became a serious concern for the church in the 1790s to 1810s, especially as Catholic leaders, highly conscious of the history of anti-Catholicism in America, hoped to legitimize their denomination's place within the new nation. The magnitude of problems caused by troublesome priests suggests a reevaluation of the heavy stress placed by other historians on trusteeism—i.e., the republican-influenced system of lay trustees controlling church property—and the discord it caused in parishes of the early republic. Clashes with renegade priests, complicated by interaction with Protestants, sapped the energy of the parish and diocese, delayed the church's growth, resulted in strict application of episcopal authority, and fostered a dependence on Rome.

Physical representations of Catholic community and identity are the subject of chapter 4. Here the analysis turns to efforts to build and furnish churches and obtain religious materials, such as sacred objects, devotional items, and simple adornments. In claiming sacred ground and expressing cultural distinctiveness, Catholics in the trans-Appalachian West created sites for worship, connected themselves to European aesthetic traditions that in turn strengthened their own sense of legitimacy, attempted to inspire wayward Catholics, and created contact points through which to awe and instruct non-Catholics. Rather than withdrawing inward defensively, Catholics established their churches in the new western settlements with open enthusiasm, often seeking non-Catholic assistance and approval.

Moving outside church walls, chapter 5 looks at more intimate points of contact: Catholic conversion of and intermarriage with non-Catholics. On new ground, sparsely settled, clergy hoped to bolster Catholicism in trans-Appalachia while at the same time to prevent the loss of Catholics and their descendants to laxity, unorthodoxy, or Protestantism through mixed marriages. Clergy tried to win over non-Catholics in a variety of ways, most directly through conversion. Yet priests and bishops discussed their efforts in vague and symbolic terms that belied a general disappointment with the meager numbers of actual converts. Attempts to limit mixed marriages also proved frustrating. By the 1820s, the colloquy of conversion rang flat, issues of intermarriage persisted, and clergy fretted over ever more complex questions of religious and social contact with non-Catholics.

Chapter 6 addresses more formal means by which Catholics attempted to persuade non-Catholics. Through religious processions, targeted preaching, and verbal as well as written arguments, priests and bishops contested public and religious space in western settlements. Distinctive spectacles of religious identity grew more elaborate over time, indicating Catholic success in legitimizing its presence on the land. Opportunities to preach to non-Catholics also seemed to become more frequent in the second and third decades of the nineteenth century. Nevertheless, Catholic success provoked a response. In the process of promoting the faith outside their own churches, clergy exacerbated worsening relations with Protestant America as anti-Catholic and nativist sentiments took hold of the nation. By the end of the 1830s, Catholicism had become a defensive and insular immigrant church.

Chapter 1

The View to the West

Moving away from the east coast to find opportunity, some Catholics settled in or immediately across the Appalachians in the southwest part of Pennsylvania, near Pittsburgh. Others traveled down the Ohio River to Kentucky, where new lands were opening up in the 1780s. Few settled in between, preferring the company of their fellow religionists at either the eastern or the western end of the Ohio River valley. Although they tended to group together, Catholics in the trans-Appalachian frontier found themselves in the midst of Presbyterians, Baptists, Methodists, nonbelievers, and others.

Careful Beginnings

The climate of public opinion during the 1780s was uncertain, requiring Father John Carroll, superior of the American missions, to keep an eye on what he called the Protestants' "extreme circumspection" toward Catholicism in America. He would continue to do so throughout his episcopacy. Assessing Catholic/non-Catholic relations at the time he assumed command of the church in 1784, Carroll's conclusion was somewhat sobering: "To dissipate these prejudices will take time." The clergy, he believed, should be attentive to not giving "pretexts to the enemies of Religion to deprive us of our actual rights." Carroll believed Catholics should treat the Protestants' "circumspection" by proceeding cautiously, or else face a legal and political backlash. Given their minority position, American Catholics also were in danger of being overrun. During his first sermon as bishop (December 12, 1790), Carroll outlined his own obligations as prelate in this regard, emphasizing his role in preserving the faith "untainted amidst the contagion of error surrounding" Catholics "on all sides," and amid the "fatal and prevailing indifference" toward the dissimilarities among religions. Nevertheless, Carroll remained assured about sectarian relations. In the same inaugural sermon the new bishop pledged to help Catholics "preserve in their hearts a warm charity and forbearance toward every other denomination of Christians."[1]

Still, by the mid-1790s, Bishop Carroll perceived a broader spectrum within which the Catholic Church could operate with regard to non-Catholic opinion. This range extended from a cautious sensitivity to not offend on the one hand, to a commitment of directly engaging Protestants and other non-Catholics on the other.

In 1793 Carroll wrote to Cardinal Leonardo Antonelli, prefect of the Congregation for the Propaganda of the Faith, seeking permission to change the words in the oath used when consecrating new bishops in the United States. Carroll's duties had burgeoned in the Baltimore diocese, and he wanted to share the burden by appointing Lawrence Graesl or Leonard Neale to be his coadjutator (a co-bishop who would become his successor). Specifically, he wanted to discard any reference in the text of the bishop's oath to the word "heretics, etc." Otherwise, Carroll thought, "the heterodox" non-Catholics would probably use it "to arouse ill will towards our religion," since they tended to "decry" it "as so opposed to the religious liberty to which we Catholics in the United States are so indebted." American Protestants, he asserted, should not be given any reason to think that Catholics were a threat. Being outspoken about a new bishop's responsibility to counter heresy would be counterproductive in America. So Carroll asked that the reference to heretics be dropped as it had been in consecration oaths in other countries, such as Ireland. Otherwise, "without a doubt," explained Carroll, "non-Catholics in great numbers will witness the ceremony of episcopal consecration; they will weigh everything, and they are apt to interpret unfavorably." As one historian has put it, "Carroll and his co-religionists understood that the very survival and growth of the Catholic Church in the United States depended upon its ability to accept and become a part of the American way of life."[2] Carroll realized blending in was essential.

Finding the optimal point between avoiding unnecessary conflict and maintaining open channels of contact with non-Catholics would be difficult, however. Carroll and his mainly European clergy had no models to follow in a post-revolutionary nation trying to build itself anew in contradistinction to Europe. In 1795 Carroll wrote to the new prefect of the Congregation for the Propaganda of the Faith thanking him for the Congregation's willingness to be flexible and for approving efforts to deal with the special conditions in America. "The peculiar form" of the U.S. government, "the frequent contacts of Catholics with sectaries in the discharge of public duties, the contacts too in private affairs, the need to conform with others whenever it is possible without detriment to the faith and the precepts of the Church"—these, wrote the bishop, required "care, watchfulness, and prudence." A bishop's responsibility, moreover, as Carroll characterized it, was not simply to avoid offending Protestant opinion, but to interact with non-Catholics, and to do so in a manner that preserved Catholic faith and orthodoxy while laying a foundation for harmonious relations. The church could not simply hope to withdraw and to isolate itself. Catholics would have to engage while insulating themselves only as necessary. Catholic Americans "must be on guard lest the faithful be gradually infected with the so-called prevailing indifference of this country," said Carroll; "but they must likewise take care lest unnecessary withdrawal from non-Catholics alienate" those outside the church "from our doctrine and rites." Such caution was warranted. Non-Catholics, said Carroll, "outnumber us and are more influential, [and] they may, at some time, be inclined to renew the iniquitous laws against us."[3] The trick was to remain cautious while not withdrawing so far from view that Catholic doctrine, ritual, and display would ever appear foreign to American Protestants.

Errands into the Wilderness

Other than John Carroll of Maryland, who would lead the church as its first bishop and archbishop, the most visible characters in this story of westward movement and constant negotiation with Protestant America were European priests. Their journals, letters, and reports provide a wealth of information about how they perceived their duties in the frontier region and how they felt Catholic and

non-Catholic settlers perceived them. From Maryland and Pennsylvania westward to Ohio, Kentucky, and beyond, certain early
priests stood out in their work because they embodied an assertiveness, optimism, and conservative traditionalism elicited by the trans-
Appalachian frontier.

The French émigré Father Stephen Theodore Badin, the first
priest ordained in the United States, floated down the Ohio River
on a flatboat from Pittsburgh to the shores of Kentucky to establish a mission church in 1793. He was beginning a long career of
traversing the open wilds like other missionaries and circuit riders,
covering hundreds of miles a week, caring for small groupings of
the scattered faithful. And Catholic communities were spread over
huge distances. In 1789, the diocese that Bishop Carroll maintained
and in which Badin traveled was the size of the entire American nation. It included thirty thousand to thirty-five thousand Catholics
intermixed with almost four million others. Like Carroll, Badin understood that Protestant America had been unforgiving soil for the
seeds of Catholicism. Through overt persecution, by siphoning off
church members, and by more subtle forms of influence, Protestant
denominations had stunted the growth of Catholicism in the British
colonies. Although Catholic leaders at the time were not aware of
the actual numbers involved, it has since been estimated that there
were 240,000 Irish, German, Dutch, French, and English Americans of Catholic ancestry in 1790 who had fallen from the faith.[4]
Badin would always be uneasy about the influence of Protestantism
on his flocks. The way to protect them was by emphasizing religious
orthodoxy, his own priestly authority and that of the bishop, and the
sacramental basis of Catholic life.

Father Demetrius Augustus Gallitzin, the son of a Russian prince,
and the second priest ever ordained in the United States, worried
even more than Badin or Carroll about the effects of Protestantism
on Catholics, and particularly about its more subtle and insidious
influences. On the lookout for signs of declension, he emphasized
orthodoxy and submission to his authority among parishioners. But
Gallitzin also relished the economic opportunities of the frontier.
In 1799 he settled at a small community in the Allegheny Mountains, optimistic about the church's future in the region. Soon after
arriving in western Pennsylvania, Gallitzin wrote to Bishop Carroll that the "country is amazing fertile, almost entirely inhabited

by Roman-Catholics"; and, he noted, its economic prospects were so propitious that it would certainly become an important Catholic refuge. Over the years he purchased twenty thousand acres for re-sale to worthy parishioners and used thousands of dollars of his own money to encourage economic development. He hoped to estab-lish a purely Catholic community in which his parishioners would not be adversely influenced by what he considered the laxities and heresies of the Presbyterians, Baptists, Methodists, Lutherans, and German Reformed groups in the area.[5]

Father Gallitzin had cause for concern. Catholics had an early foothold in Pennsylvania and were moving westward rapidly, but they remained vastly outnumbered in the late eighteenth and early nineteenth centuries. European settlers had begun trickling into this region after October 1784 when the Iroquois, Wyandots, and Delawares gave up their remaining lands in the western part of the state. Settlement started in earnest after the defeat of the Indian alliance at the Battle of Fallen Timbers in 1794. Catholics began ar-riving primarily from the missions of Goshenhoppen near Philadel-phia and from Conewago, both of which had been established in the 1740s. The major Protestant denominations each had at least one church in the western reaches of the state prior to the first Catholic one at Sportsman's Hall in 1790, for a total of ninety Protestant buildings before the Catholics constructed their first sacred place. In 1800, the Pennsylvania counties west of the Appalachian divide were home to 174 Protestant and only three Catholic churches and three permanent priests. When construction of the Pennsylvania Canal (Philadelphia to Pittsburgh) started in 1826, immigrant Cath-olics flooded into the state and across the mountains. Still, Catholics remained a minority among denominations, with the Presbyterians being the predominant Protestant group. Gallitzin's relationship with his Protestant neighbors, particularly the Presbyterians, would remain chilly throughout his tenure in Cambria County. Occasion-ally he counted a few of them his friends when factions within his own congregations opposed him.[6]

Meanwhile, at Gallipolis in southern Ohio there landed in 1790 a faltering colony of French settlers, which included the first Catho-lic presence in the state since the Jesuits abandoned their missions in the aftermath of the French and Indian War. Father Badin and Vicar-General Michael Bernard Barrieres visited in 1793, en route to Kentucky, and baptized approximately forty children. According to Badin, "The entire village revived at the sight of these two priests, their fellow countrymen, at the singing of the sacred canticles, and the celebration of the Holy Mysteries." Badin's reinvigorated Catholics were the remnants of the failed Scioto Colony, victims of a poorly administered speculative land scheme. Their own priest, Father Peter Joseph Didier, had moved to St. Louis, reportedly on finding the majority of the settlers bitter about their losses and cold toward religion. European American settlement across the rest of Ohio remained hampered by the struggle among Native Americans, the British, and the United States around the Great Lakes until the mid-1790s, when General Anthony Wayne's victory at Fallen Timbers and the British withdrawal to Canada in 1796 opened the region. Father Edmund Burke arrived in 1794 but returned to Canada with the British two years later. When Father Badin visited the area again a few years later, he "found still a spark of faith," although the French colony had "much declined" since he had last visited.[7]

In 1805, Catholicism in Ohio received new energy when thirty Catholics near Lancaster began petitioning Bishop John Carroll for the services of a resident or at least a visiting priest. The cleric they ultimately would receive, Father Edward Fenwick, first passed through in 1808, on his way from Kentucky to Maryland, and then made regular visits as an itinerant missionary once or twice a year until he was permanently transferred to Ohio in 1816. Fenwick's charges in Ohio were more scattered than Catholics were in Kentucky. Rather than settling as groups and as whole communities, the faithful in Ohio dispersed themselves as individuals and families.[8]

Despite its slow start, Ohio became a populous state within two decades, and this increased Father Fenwick's burden. For the five hundred thousand inhabitants in 1818, noted Fenwick, there was not a single priest other than himself, "travers[ing] vast and inhospitable forests." By 1819, there were three churches erected (Somerset, Lancaster, and Cincinnati), for close to three thousand Catholics spread across the state. In 1821 Cincinnati would become an episcopal see and Edward Fenwick would be consecrated its first bishop by Kentucky's Bishop Benedict Joseph Flaget, with responsibilities stretching from Ohio to Michigan and the rest of the Northwest Territory.[9]

During these same decades, downstream along the Ohio River

grew a larger garden of Catholicism in north-central Kentucky. Individual Catholics first entered the area in the 1770s to take up residence. A group from Maryland made a major settlement in Nelson County in 1785 and grew into a strong, conspicuous presence in twelve central counties by 1807. In 1788 Father Charles Maurice Whelan, an Irish friar, was the first missionary sent to assist Catholics in the region and to establish the first parish. Whelan was replaced by Vicar-General Barrieres and Father Badin, who arrived in 1793 to care for approximately three hundred Catholic families, the majority of whom had migrated from Catholic settlements in Maryland and Pennsylvania. These pioneers were of English descent, and they were joined by increasing numbers of Irish and Germans. Catholics tended to cluster together in Nelson and Washington counties at the center of the state. This served their religious needs by situating them near church and priest, but left the impression that they had settled for "2d & 3d rate-lands," while non-Catholics, it was believed, bought up the best properties because they were more willing to put economic concerns ahead of settlement patterns along denominational lines. Wherever they laid down roots, Catholics were arriving in ever greater numbers, too often ending up far from the nearest priest. In 1807, Badin wrote to a colleague about a journey from Kentucky back to Baltimore: "Almost every day and in every settlement through which I passed, I have found catholic families of every nationality—French, Italian, Irish, German, and American. . . . Nothing but catholics all along the road! God only knows how many live in the backwoods, and not one priest!"[10]

Like many of the clergymen who would join him in Kentucky, Badin was a European émigré, pitched on American shores by the turmoil of the French Revolution. He and his fellow priests were joined by Trappist monks from France in 1805, Dominican priests from England in 1806, and, in 1811, by the Frenchman Benedict Joseph Flaget—first bishop of the American West—whose expansive new diocese of Bardstown swept from the Appalachian Mountains to the Mississippi.

By 1815 there were more than ten thousand Catholics and nineteen church structures in Kentucky alone, and two orders of nuns had established themselves there: the Sisters of Loretto in Marion County and the Sisters of Charity of Nazareth in Nelson County. A third order, the Dominican Sisters, was founded in Washington

County in 1822. Upon his arrival, Bishop Flaget had the help of eight priests to minister to more than a thousand Catholic families spread throughout thirty congregations. By 1818 Kentucky boasted eighteen priests, only three of whom were American by birth. As Father Charles Nerinckx reported to Catholic patrons in the Netherlands in 1815, the western states "expand unbelievably every year to such a degree—through immigration from other regions and through their own natural growth—that it can be said with truth that the work [for the church] increases every year by at least one priest."[11]

In 1821, Badin announced there were twenty-five priests, thirty-five churches or chapels, and forty thousand Catholics out of a population of two million in the whole diocese. In addition, Catholics had opened a number of fine schools in the state that served non-Catholics as well as members of the faith. Soon after building a church near Springfield, Kentucky, Dominican fathers established St. Thomas Aquinas College, the first Catholic institution of higher education in the West and a school open to Protestant and Catholic students alike. The Sisters of Loretto and the Sisters of Charity were dedicated to educating children, including orphans, and by 1824 the former group ran six schools. By 1830 there were five Catholic academies for young women in Kentucky. Catholics were expanding in numbers and in resources with which to propagate their faith.[12]

This growth was rapid growth for Catholics, who were relative latecomers to the region. Presbyterian and Baptist clergy were ministering already to their congregants in Kentucky before 1786, when the first two Methodist ministers arrived. By 1824 there were almost 50,000 church-going Protestants in Kentucky: 21,680 Baptists; 20,850 Methodists; 3,700 Presbyterians and Cumberland Presbyterians; and 500 other Protestants.[13]

An Anti-Catholic Context

The successful spread of Catholicism was not without setbacks and obstacles, however. Strong strains of sectarian intolerance persisted. America's Protestant roots and long-standing identification with the British imperial cause against Catholic France and Spain and their designs in the New World meant that anti-Catholicism was ingrained. John Adams's biases may have been typical of the time, especially among the rationalist leaders of the young nation. During the First Continental Congress in Philadelphia, in the autumn of 1774, the future president attended a Catholic Mass. He described the members of the congregation as "poor Wretches, fingering their Beads, chanting in latin, not a Word of which they understood." Most of what he witnessed struck him as odd: "Their holy Water— their Crossing themselves perpetually—their Bowing to the name of Jesus."[14] Adams's bemusement and condescension were representative of many Americans' feelings toward Catholicism.

Such attitudes were maintained in the trans-Appalachian West. Although religion, and things Catholic in particular, were rarely mentioned in the *Kentucky Gazette* during the 1790s, the church built at Loretto drew attention in 1797 for being "a most curious piece of priestcraft," an example of that "which has long been imposed upon the votaries of the Romish church." During Kentucky's second constitutional convention in 1799, for example, a former Presbyterian minister attempted to get the other delegates to adopt a provision blocking Catholics from holding state office. When Father Badin reported in 1805 that non-Catholics in trans-Appalachia were generally friendly, he had to add that "We have nine or ten printers . . . which do not fail to turn their ridicule . . . on the true religion." Two years later Father Nerinckx reported that although the number of Catholics settling in the region was growing, so was the number of non-Catholics who moved away as a result. Catholic laymen petitioning Archbishop Carroll of Baltimore on behalf of two local priests defended the harsh measures of their clerics who daily had to face many difficulties in the wilderness. Most painful, these men indicated, "We are surrounded by Protestants that laugh at Our weakness and reproach our Church with the folly and wickedness of the few." And speaking from the Protestant side, John Mason Peck, a Baptist missionary widely respected for his kindness, rationality, and tolerance in the West, commented in 1819, "The Catholick religion is the same in its spirit and tendency as in the fifteenth century . . . it is still a *beast*, though in the United States without horns." Such strains of anti-Catholicism never disappeared from the frontier, and, in fact, became more frequent and strident in the late 1820s, eventually developing into an urgent refrain among Protestant missionary societies and nativist politicians and editors focused on the West.[15]

During the first decades of the early republic, however, Catholic leaders were encouraged. The religious climate in the nation seemed to be improving, especially when compared to the treatment of Catholics in England and Canada. In 1800 John Carroll noticed a "virulence against Catholicity" in English publications over the past decade, which he attributed both to Protestants' millennial preoccupations and to the envy of clergy who, unlike Catholic priests, had not stood the "fiery trial" of persecution in revolutionary France. In 1807 the superior of the Trappist community in Kentucky relayed complaints from the bishop of Quebec, who was writing about the "pitiful condition" of religion in Canada, "owing to the harshness of the English government toward catholics." Within the United States, tolerance seemed to be on the rise. Catholic churches were appearing in places where Catholicism "was unknown a few years ago," Carroll wrote in 1803, even in Boston, that former "hotbed of the most rancorous Calvinism." The "protection of the law" was for both Catholics and all other denominations in the United States, wrote Father Badin. He reported to the cardinals of the Congregation for the Propagation of the Faith in 1805 that "there are no distinction of religions" in America, "the Constitution protects us in the exercise of our sacerdotal functions—a thing which was unheard of before the American Revolution." Several years later, Nerinckx found a reason for further hope in reading the latest work of a non-Catholic scholar, Benjamin Davis, whose book *Geography* (Philadelphia, 1813), had just been published. The author described Maryland and its Roman Catholic majority in neutral terms and complimented Archbishop Carroll's "very respectable character and connections." This was more than Nerinckx ever expected from a Protestant. Even slight glimmerings of better relations were seized upon as a sign that Catholics need no longer fear persecution in America.[16]

Catholic leaders felt sanguine specifically about sectarian relations in the trans-Appalachian West. In 1805, writing from Kentucky, Badin reported to Rome that "the non-Catholics who live among the Catholics are less under the influence of prejudices, and they treat us generally as brothers." In 1811 when Bishop Benedict Joseph Flaget assumed command of his new diocese, which stretched from Canada to the southern border of Tennessee, and from the Appalachians to the Mississippi, he also noted that Protestants living near Catholics were less bigoted: "Most of the Protestants [in Lexington] are well-disposed in our favor, not that they are inclined to be Catholics, but they do not seem to have prejudices against Catholics, which is a great deal in this section." Indeed, Catholics reaching western settlements were surprised by the openness of the Protestants they met. David Barrow, a Baptist minister journeying from Virginia to central Kentucky in 1795, had observed, according to his diary, "allmost all denominations" on the frontier, including Roman Catholics, "disputing their points without giving any general disturbance." Bishop Flaget and Fathers Badin and John Baptist David each remarked on their own favorable reception in the West. "[We have] perfect freedom of conscience and worship," said Badin; "we go in procession [and] preach in the town halls, and even in the Protestant meeting-houses where we have no chapels, and all sorts of sectaries come in crowds to hear us. . . . We are also surprised to find non-Catholics sometimes taking up the defense of the dogmas of our belief." In 1816 Father David noted that "the world . . . lets us alone, which even esteems and favors us. For Monseigneur [Bishop Flaget] has gained the confidence not only of the Catholics, but of all the other religions." Recalling old persecutions in Europe and pre-revolutionary America, Catholic leaders felt encouraged by the potential for workable relations with non-Catholics in the new West.[17]

Chapter 2

A Central Role for Priests

Passing through the southwestern corner of Pennsylvania in the fall of 1807, traveling along rough roads and trails, Father Badin "found Catholics almost every where," not only those he saw with his own eyes, or with whom he talked and prayed, but "many more . . . known or scattered about" in between the Ohio and the Monongahela rivers. In reporting to Bishop Carroll about his trip through a region that remained a frontier for the Catholic Church, he described the hazards, burdens, and obstacles the faithful faced. Unfortunately, he observed, some of the Catholics he encountered "do but faintly acknowledge what they are, others sink into heresy or latitudinarianism." The problem, Badin noted, was that they were without clergy; "there is no rallying point, or priest to commune with."[1] These conditions were familiar after his fourteen years missionizing in the West. They would remain typical for several more years in Pennsylvania, as well as in Ohio, Kentucky, and Indiana, and then be repeated in the western states beyond. What was needed was evident—more priests. Badin knew it, Bishop Carroll and later bishops and archbishops struggled to address it, and settlers in the backcountry dealt with it year after year.

But what kind of priest would suffice in the West? Getting the right kind was another perennial problem. Badin had an answer during his journey through Pennsylvania in 1807. After years of working alone in Kentucky, putting up with all kinds of privations, he outlined for Bishop Carroll the most important characteristics a frontier priest should possess, particularly in a place like southwestern Pennsylvania where there were already many active Protestant churches. The successful backwoods missionary must be "indefatigable," "dexterous," and extremely hardy, resistant to "disagreeable weather, cross-rides, disappointments, and even insults," exhibiting an outward assertiveness able to subdue troublemakers, both within the Catholic community and from outside. This latter point he stressed. Rather than masking their Catholic identity or avoiding confrontations and riding past potential trouble, Badin urged his brethren "not to be backward in acknowledging anywhere or rather in making known their sacerdotal character." Frontier priests, in "the spirit of the ancient Jesuits," he concluded, "should be always ready to give a sermon an exhortation or a controversial speech publicly or privately."[2]

Priests in trans-Appalachia had a central role in Catholic community, not only as spiritual leaders, but in other spheres as well. Frontier clergy tried to control access to the sacraments, foster piety and spirituality, and provide religious instruction, but they were influential figures for additional reasons. In some cases they sought to guarantee the general moral and political order of settlements. Clergy also could be entrepreneurs in land development and business, and focal points of sectarian controversy or cooperation. They worked to make themselves crucial to the Catholic march inland and to become the central points of interaction with non-Catholics—organizing parishes, helping to establish schools, raising money for churches and building them, collecting decorative and devotional items for these houses of worship, and even traveling to Europe to gather additional support.

Central as they tried to be, clergymen often felt overstressed by the demands placed on them in ministering across such extensive areas to lay Catholics who were often either too poor or too parsimonious to assist the clerics make anything but a meager living. Priests, however, were not completely at the mercy of their parishioners. They were mobile and could be recalled to the East or transferred farther west. They were empowered to provide or withhold sacraments, and this helped to structure the lives of lay Catholics. In an environment of short supply and high demand for sacraments, therefore, clergy readily found opportunities to adopt more welcoming parishes farther into unsettled regions of the West. Moreover, priests in frontier areas took on multiple roles as social, economic, and sectarian leaders in their communities, which strengthened their position. Seeing the needs of their parishioners, priests tried to answer them in ways that sustained their personal authority and that of the Catholic Church.

Few Good Men

Because Catholic clergy, like their Protestant and evangelical Protestant counterparts, were in short supply in the trans-Appalachian West, they were often separated from their colleagues and superiors for long stretches of time. As a result, missions and parishes on the recently settled frontier were exhausting, dangerous, and lonely. In April 1796 Badin wrote from Washington County, Kentucky, to Baltimore, begging Bishop Carroll for help: "In my present abandonment I am utterly incapable, my lord, of fulfilling the heavy charge of the ministry. I have neither the virtue nor the bodily strength necessary: If I had at least one priest to consult with me, to advise and encourage me! I once more beseech you, my lord, to look with an eye of pity on the poor priests of Kentucky."[3]

Badin eventually received help in the person of fellow priest Father M. Fournier, sent to assist him in 1797. Still, Badin noted the two of them would "be insufficient to serve the multitudes which are in, & every day flock into Kentucky" near their home, which they called "Priestland"—a name indicating the two priests understood their cabin and few acres to be a sort of refuge of fellowship in the vast wilderness. Judging the near hopelessness of keeping up with the numerical onslaught and geographical spread of incoming Catholic settlers, Fournier and Badin decided it was most important for them to stay together in one spot, for mutual support and their "spiritual welfare," on which their congregations depended. Life in undeveloped regions remained arduous for the missionary priest. An observer in 1810 indicated the persistence of this problem for frontier priests: "One of the greatest difficulties to be encountered, and experience alone can make it understood, is that one is left completely alone, and sometimes at a distance of twenty, fifty, a hundred miles and more from any other priest."[4]

In 1805, on a journey from Kentucky to Ohio, Father Charles Nerinckx observed from another perspective the effects of the continued shortage of priests in the West. "A woman rushed toward me out of the woods, thinking I was a protestant minister," he wrote to his parents in amazement. "When I informed her that I was a catholic priest she wept for joy, and entreated me to stop at her house, as she was catholic herself, and had not seen a priest for four years." In her desperation for religious sustenance, she had approached an unfamiliar clergyman, whom she had assumed was a Protestant clergyman. Nerinckx learned from her there were more Catholics about, some "scattered in the woods." Some "feared they would die without consolation of receiving the rites of the church," and others had already "given up all practices of religion."[5] Such were the dangers to the church: low morale among missionaries, laity without regular access to the sacraments, and gradual religious declension or even adoption of Protestant values.

A scarcity of priests would persist for the next several decades. Demographic trends worked at cross purposes to those of the Catholic hierarchy. Clergy, already in short supply at the institutional founding of the American Catholic Church in the mid-1780s, were not being produced in sufficient proportion to laity emigrating from Europe to America, and moving westward from the seaboard states to trans-Appalachia. In 1790 only thirty-four priests in the United States served some 30,000 to 35,000 Catholics (one holy man per 1,000 lay persons); there was one priest for every 12,270 square miles of U.S. territory. By 1810, the situation was perhaps more daunting. There was only one priest per 1,350 lay Catholics, and each clergyman, in an abstract sense, was responsible for 8,693 square miles. By the 1830s, the trans-Appalachian frontier was conquered, though the increase in Catholic immigration from Europe left the average priest even more inundated. In 1830 there was one priest for every 1,370 Catholics, though now there were only 3,781 square miles for each ordained priest.[6]

St. Mary's Seminary in Baltimore for years was the sole institution set up to train new priests, and it was slow to alleviate the chronic shortage of clerics. It had been founded in 1791 by members of the Society of St. Sulpice (a French group whose primary purpose was to operate seminaries and train diocesan clergy), whom Bishop Carroll invited to seek refuge in America from the chaos of revolutionary France in 1791. During its first ten years, when Carroll perhaps needed the most clergymen to help establish the fledgling church, St. Mary's Seminary produced only four priests for service in the United States: ten others quit their studies, one died, and one was ordained but went back to his home in Canada. Part of the problem was the school at Georgetown in the District of Columbia, which was supposed to be preparing youths for the seminary. During the seminary's first ten years, Georgetown provided only one candidate and called away four seminarians to be teachers. In its next decade, 1800–1810, production swelled. St. Mary's accepted forty-six students, of whom twenty-three became priests. This still was barely enough to maintain the status quo, due to the increasing numbers of Catholics arriving in the United States and the spread of settled parishes. Scarcity and attrition, as well as delays inherent in building institutions to produce priests, plagued the church's efforts to supply enough clergy.[7]

Bishops, archbishops, and visitors from the Vatican agreed the lack of reliable men was the most serious obstacle to Catholic expansion in America, especially as the faithful moved across the continent. In his report to Cardinal Antonelli of the Congregation for the Propagation of the Faith in 1785, John Carroll outlined three closely related problems facing the infant American church. First was the "lack of fervor" among the faithful resulting from their infrequent contact with priests—typically once a month or every two months. The second problem, "want of priests," was another side of the first. And the third difficulty, the "distance of congregations from each other," was merely an aggravating factor with regard to both of the others. The country needed clergymen. Father John Grassi, a Jesuit visiting the United States in 1810, highlighted in a report to Rome the same desperate need for priests. The primary obstacle to the spread of Catholicism had not changed in twenty-five years. Bishop Michael Egan of Philadelphia, touring the distant corners of his diocese near Pittsburgh, wrote to Archbishop Carroll on a similar note in 1811. "I have been highly gratified with the rapid increase of Religion in the different congregations," he said, though noting that all were in desperate need of more priests. Egan determined that "without some timely aid from Europe, particularly from Ireland," he would not be able to "provide for the necessities of this diocese."[8]

Prelates, priests, and visiting clergy were not the only observers to feel the absence of priests. Catholic settlers raised the issue often. For example, it was not unusual for a western community to petition

Bishop Carroll or his successors in later years to designate a pastor to come and organize religion in their area. A German farmer representing thirty Catholics in Lancaster, Ohio, humbly asked for a bishop or priest to drop by at least en route to Kentucky, his backwoods settlement being "on their way to that country." Carroll's papers contain many other examples of requests for him to station a priest permanently in a western community, or at least to send one temporarily to perform baptisms, marriages, and other sacraments. Petitioners were conscious of the vital role a man of the cloth could play. Some claimed a priest's presence might be the key to future growth and prosperity for their settlement. "I expect we will be daily getting more numerous especially if we had a priest," wrote Connel Rogers in May 1803. He appealed to Bishop Carroll on behalf of the ninety-five Irish Catholic families of Buffalo and Slippery Rock in Butler County, Pennsylvania. The congregation wanted a resident priest so they would not be dependent on the German Father Peter Helbron, who lived more than fifty miles to the south at Sportsman's Hall, or on another German, Father Demetrius Gallitzin, who seemed to be trying to keep the parish open for a priest-in-training, who would not be available for two more years. To sharpen his plea, Rogers added, "The sectaries here of all denominations have their preachers," yet "we are the only people left desolate of a pastor." Rogers reasoned in the same vein as a Kentucky priest who was "convinced that there are nearly as many more families . . . scattered among unbelievers" on the frontier as appeared visible. In other words, half of all Catholics were hidden "among [the] infidels" because they had "had no priest to guide them and are ashamed to own up to their belief." Balancing the image of the itinerant minister who might or might not have been welcome in a particular settlement was the potential resident pastor that Catholic communities craved.[9]

Connel Rogers's first petition was unsuccessful, and his second, in November 1804, rang with resentment. It also revealed what he and his neighbors considered to be the crucial burden priests carried in preserving the social order. "Why," asked the group, "cannot we get . . . [a] disinterested priest on a visit who would fix matters and establish rules among us that we could go by?" Apparently the Catholic frontier community wanted much more than access to sacraments. "We cannot do any more in the case of ourselves, seeing we have no leading person among us that will undertake to do anything but what we have proposed to do."[10] Rogers and friends wanted not just religious guidance, but rules to go by; not simply a paragon of piety, but a "leading person" to organize the community for all it hoped to accomplish. They needed a leading citizen, a virtuous man disinterested enough to resolve differences of opinion, respectable enough to inspire trust; one who would bring stability and purpose to their settlements.

These frontier families had been deeply frustrated after months of delay and no sign of their own pastor arriving anytime soon. Rogers's second petition, therefore, also contained a veiled threat for Carroll. If "a priest cannot be got here," some in the settlements would "make our situation known to our Bishop in Ireland." (Most of these backwoods Catholics had emigrated from adjoining parishes in a single Irish county.) Using rhetoric loaded with meaning for an Irish American writing only six years after the uprising led by the United Irishmen that had rocked the Emerald Isle in 1798, Rogers asserted that "if we do not get a Priest the people will go in rebellion and will be a scandal to the communion." In a sense, he was threatening that he and his neighbors had the upper hand in this contest of wills with the bishop; they wanted a priest and were likely to misbehave until they received one. Rogers and friends knew their actions could embarrass the church. The petitioner certainly did not mean the Butler County Catholics would have an organized, political uprising. Rather, they might continue to wallow in the ferment of social and political disruption resulting from pure egalitarianism. The situation reeked of the excesses that frightened Federalists and that eighteenth-century political philosophers saw as the result of too much democracy. Rogers's petition then continued on a different tack. He turned his line of reasoning and asked for a priest to come and exert a firm hand on the congregation. Figuratively repositioning himself and his neighbors under the yoke of obedience to priest and bishop, he explained that small disturbances already had been a source of embarrassment before non-Catholics in the area. At the previous "spring court for this county," near the time when he had made his first petition for a pastor, "there was no less than 44 state warrants returned against Catholics for riot whereas if a priest was among us we would put a stop to the like." Here was an additional role for the Catholic priest, exerting overt social control—both simply to bring order and to prevent the faithful from scandalizing the church in the eyes of non-Catholic neighbors.[11]

In Scott County, Kentucky, two years later, another set of petitioners pleaded with Bishop Carroll to send a permanent priest they could call their own. Father Badin had ministered to them from the fall of 1793 until the summer of 1795; then Father John Thayer took up the office of pastor at St. Francis parish, from February 1799 to March 1801, until he was removed by Carroll for his troublesome behavior. In 1806, members of the parish petitioned the bishop and offered $150 to pay for the horse and traveling expenses of anyone Carroll might send. They declared that without a priest they labored under "great evils . . . which threaten the total anihilation [sic] of faith and morals in our congregation." Clearly the settlers believed a priest was their principal hope for normalcy. Occasional visits by other, distant Kentucky clergymen, such as Badin and Nerinckx, in the subsequent years had "fallen very short of stemming the overflowing current of immorality and vice." Alone, the petitioners could do nothing about the growing list of outrages occurring in their corner of Kentucky: "Improper and irregular marriages have been contracted, persons have died without the last offices or any spiritual assistance, the negroes of all ages are without spiritual instruction, and unchecked in the progress of sin and vice, and the youth amongst us are growing up without having their habits formed to the usages and institutions of holy religion, and to regular compliance with church duties, and even many grown persons amongst us are in a state of great laxity."[12] A resident priest, therefore, was a necessity. His presence ensured more than leadership in extra-ecclesiastical activities of the community, and more than protection from humiliating behavior before Protestant denominations. A strong, permanent pastor, it was believed, even could restore the fabric of society damaged by "improper marriages" and growing depravity among the slaves and young people. He could ensure the future moral health of society by preventing illegitimate marriages and by monitoring the character of the lesser members of the community.

To convince Bishop Carroll further, the petitioners pointed out how important a contribution a priest in their community could make to "the course of religion in general and the saving of souls." They tried to tempt the bishop with a rich harvest of Catholic souls in their area, as well as with the sundry Protestants nearby, ready for the picking. Catholics were scattered in Shelby County, Lexington, and elsewhere, noted the petitioners, and "At all those places, many conversions, we believe, might be made." What began at Cane Ridge swept evangelical Protestants along in a storm of camp meetings across Kentucky. "At this particular time," asserted the St. Francis parishioners, "the surrounding people are weary of their own extravagances and might, by the divine grace, be disposed to seek refuge and rest in the bosom of the true church." Without pastoral influence, potential Protestant converts would turn infidel, for if "an opportunity not be afforded them of embracing the truth, they must, as many have already done, sink into deism."[13] Whether or not the Catholics of Scott County believed a priest would successfully convert many backcountry Protestants, the petitioners added the possibility to their train of reasons for having a permanent pastor. Perhaps they knew this was the kind of rhetoric used by church leaders in discussing the West as a fertile ground for expansion. They certainly defined the Catholic pastor's role as being fundamental to the healthy future of their sylvan community.

In 1806 Fathers Badin and Nerinckx traveled to another distant congregation in dire need of a priest, taking four weeks to make the journey. Vincennes on the Wabash in the Indiana Territory, like St. Francis parish in Scott County, had earlier had its own priests—a sequence of four Jesuits before 1763, then Father Pierre Gibault, Father Benedict Flaget, and finally Father Jean F. Rivet. But for the past several years the river town had been dependent on the infrequent visits of missionaries from Kentucky or elsewhere. Nerinckx reported to Bishop Carroll that he and Badin found the more than eighty Catholic families at the post and in its environs to be "like sheep astray and almost perishing," with "their total destruction . . . certain, unless a helping hand be extended to them." Nerinckx judged them to be "a very bad people, . . . unmindful of the commandments of the church," yet wanting "very much to have a priest who would help them in their distress." Father Gibault had discovered this same paradox of sinners desperate to be saved by a priest when he first visited the river town in 1770. Little had changed after Gibault's departure, or with the visits of later missionaries, and the inhabitants seemed to be incorrigible. Unfortunately for the congregation and for whoever might be appointed their pastor,

Nerinckx decided, "They are a lazy voluptuous set, and the position of a priest among them will necessarily be trying, desolate, and sad." Two years later the border town of Vincennes was still "much in need of a pastor." Father Badin warned his bishop in Baltimore that he and Father Jean Olivier, who visited Vincennes occasionally from Illinois, could not "but regret that the establishment made by . . . [Father] Flaget and . . . [Father] Rivet is likely to disappear from the capital of that Territory." Adding insult to injury, he continued, "The itinerant ministers preach in Town, even in the house of a Catholic, and a Presbyterian clergyman will be stationed there, next Fall, to create and attend an Academy—*Galli, cavete in ferments.*" "Be on your guard," he warned Bishop Carroll.[14]

Pastors and the People

When a community did receive regular visits from a priest, the relationship between pastor and parishioners could be intense. From the clergyman's perspective, his presence was vital to any western Catholic community. For him, the relationship between priest and parish might become, literally, a matter of life and death, and he would be reluctant to make long trips lest his congregation fall apart or a single soul pass away without the last sacrament. In theory, each Catholic's chance for eternal life was imperiled were he or she to pass away without benefit of extreme unction, or the "last anointing" of the sick or dying. This sacrament was crucial because, as the Council of Trent had proclaimed in 1551, it completed the cycle of anointings that began with baptism and ultimately "fortifies the end of our earthly life like a solid rampart for the final struggles before entering the Father's house." Unable to tell if a loved one was with or without sin, family members and friends could only assume that a dying Catholic desperately needed last rites and the absolution of sin that this final sacrament offered. A Catholic who died without benefit of ultimate forgiveness for serious or mortal sins was doomed to hell; he or she not absolved of less serious sin would spend years in purgatory. Understandably then, family members, fellow Catholics, and priests were devastated when a parishioner died unprepared for eternity. Indeed, when Father Pierre Gibault first visited Vincennes in 1770, several years after the last Jesuit had been forced to abandon it, a common heartbreaking complaint he heard was, "Ah, Sir, why did you not come a month ago, then my poor wife, my dear father, my loved mother, my poor child would not have died without the sacraments."[15]

Thus, Fathers Badin and Gallitzin both were hesitant to leave their flocks for long. Their caution and their devotion to their core parishes made it even less likely they would visit the distant, priest-less congregations or settlements in need of their services. Badin was never one to let bad weather or other obstacles keep him from making his rounds of visits. But in June 1796 he wrote his bishop about delaying a requested trip to Father Rivet at Post Vincennes. "I should not hesitate a moment about" making the journey, said Badin, "were it not that upon my return I might find a number of my parishioners in their graves." The way to Vincennes was long, and certain lay members were not well. In the end, the Kentucky priest concluded he would have to make the trip: "I must sacrifice myself." At the beginning of August that same summer, Badin was back in Kentucky, but not at his home parish in Washington County. He felt he was falling behind in his missionary work, struggling to reach sick Catholics before they died. From the Salt River he wrote, "I have to leave to-morrow morning by the same route for Scot Co[unty] to see another sick man whom I shall perhaps find dead. It costs me much to leave those in Washington." Badin wondered whether much of his effort to help Catholic families and communities scattered across the region simply hurt his parishioners waiting at home. He worried that "before my return some one else may be deprived of the last sacraments"; yet not to go "would be to cast almost into despair those of Scot [County] whom I have not visited for nine months." On August 24, Badin lamented to Carroll that he had made his return journey from Vincennes and then Scott County as fast as possible, spending "twenty-two days . . . continuously on horseback, sometimes day and night," yet found upon returning "my fears realized—one of my parishioners had died without assistance."[16]

Father Demetrius Gallitzin—the son of a Russian prince, a product of an Enlightenment education at the Hague, a young man who converted to Catholicism and became the second priest ordained in the United States—also felt utterly responsible for his small mountain community of Catholics in southwestern Pennsylvania. Originally he had been sent on a sick call from Conewago in the eastern portion of the state to a huddled group of houses whose inhabitants called themselves "McGuire's settlement" in 1796. Enamored with the secluded community, he returned the residents' petition for a resident priest to Bishop Carroll, and gratefully accepted appointment there in March 1799. He would devote his life and substantial sums of money to making the settlement, which he later renamed Loretto, into his vision of an ideal Catholic corporate body.

When his father died in 1803 and his mother implored him to return to Russia only long enough to secure his inheritance, Gallitzin refused to go. Troubled by debt in the United States, he needed to make the long voyage. And his mother, a patroness of the Catholic Church as well as a princess with many important connections, pressured Bishop Carroll to convince her son to return. Gallitzin told the bishop and his mother he would not leave, since "he was the cause of a large number of Catholic families settling in a wild, uncultivated region, where they formed a parish of considerable extent." Gallitzin gave many other reasons. He said he hated to lose even one soul by his absence and was too interconnected in his parishioners' daily affairs, finances, and business concerns to leave. Moreover, he knew the legislature was considering a new county in the area and wanted his Loretto to be its seat. Besides the state's growing interest in the region, he feared land speculators and lawyers were beginning to infiltrate, and no one but he was prepared to counter their wiles. Gallitzin also worried his absence would invite trouble from neighboring Protestants, who he thought set a bad example for the nominal Catholics and recent converts in the area. Without his vigilance, he thought, "A wolf in the clothing of a sheep or a sectarian preacher might have crept in among them." Gallitzin felt so integral to the life of Loretto that in 1823 he refused Archbishop Ambrose Maréchal's offer to appoint him bishop of Detroit, saying that to leave the mountain community, "one of the most important in the United States . . . would ruin it, and ruin me."[17]

Unfortunately, such pastoral dedication often was unrequited. A complaint common among frontier missionaries was that too often they did not believe their congregations cared sufficiently for them. Pastors had many reasons to feel this way over the years. Most congregations became embroiled in some kind of clergy-laity conflict over behavior inside or outside of church. Points of contention might include what the priest interpreted as excessive revelry, flagging morality among young people, or laxity in religious practice. For priests and bishops, however, a clear indicator of a parish's allegiance to its pastor was the character of financial support it provided. In part, the parsimony of the laity was a universal difficulty for American Catholicism. In 1791 Bishop Carroll and his fellow clergy at the first diocesan synod agreed that the nation's Catholics must be asked explicitly to help carry the church. Carroll's pastoral letter in 1792, therefore, explained that Americans were obligated to give, even though they might find it initially unfamiliar. Carroll and his colleagues discussed how Catholicism had been limited to Maryland and Pennsylvania for so long, and that few priests were needed for the relatively contained numbers of Catholics. Funds for support had been independent of gifts from congregations. Now that religion was spreading to all the states, and church numbers were rising, Carroll and his fellow clergy were establishing no less than five statutes regarding "this backwardness of the faithful to contribute" for support of priests, a problem that they declared one of the greatest obstructions to the practice of Catholicism in the United States.[18]

In fact, the first Catholic laity/clergy controversy in Kentucky to embarrass Catholics publicly before Protestants occurred because of a disagreement over remuneration for a priest. In 1788 Father Charles Maurice Whelan complained to his parishioners about their tardiness in paying him. Bishop Carroll, whom parish folk had petitioned to send Father Whelan, had negotiated with the six leading men that they would provide one hundred pounds per year. Upon Whelan's complaint, two of the six took him and their contract with Carroll to a civil court to dissolve the agreement. They lost their case. It was the court's decision, however, that the lay people could provide the priest's income in the form of produce. When Father Whelan continued to complain, they took him to court for slander, where a jury decided in favor of the parishioners, forcing Whelan to pay five hundred pounds or go to prison. The rebellious parishioners paid his bail, forced him to negate his contract, and sent him packing back to Baltimore.[19]

In western Pennsylvania, one disgruntled priest named Francis Fromm discovered the fiscal hardship of ministering to frontiersmen who seemed so ungrateful. Fromm had adopted the parish in 1791, against Bishop Carroll's orders, in part because it provided a somewhat secure income. Yet after three years with the Sportsman's Hall congregation, out of a sense of frustration, Fromm hyperbolically suggested that he was "determined to hire myself to a farmer or to follow a trade or to become a teacher to make a decent living. In this locality a priest without some other occupation cannot live properly." The Dutch pastor also complained to the bishop that "the people do not even contribute the most necessary things; they either refuse or are not able and at times glory in the fact that they can deceive the pastor." He explained how he had been duped: "At the priest's first visit the Catholics here show themselves very polite, they promise and subscribe generously but at the end of the year, when the payment is to be made, they have either left for Kentucky or for Spanish territories or for other regions."[20] Bishop Carroll, in any case, had little sympathy for Fromm because he had been trying to remove the priest from the parish for other reasons.

In Kentucky, Father Badin and three of his earliest colleagues, M. Fournier, Anthony Salmon, and John Thayer, who joined him between 1797 and 1799, felt the poverty of backwoods society as soon as the Kentucky ranks of clergy expanded from one to four. Sole priest in the region for six years, Badin had not had difficulty soliciting financial support from local Catholics. With the arrival of Fournier, and then Salmon and Thayer, resources were stretched. It became apparent that the laity had a weak tradition of support. Father Salmon complained in May 1799 about the vast distances between communities, the scarcity of money, and "the backward dispositions of the individuals" of Kentucky, reporting to Bishop Carroll that he could not say when any of his congregations would build a first church. Even worse, Salmon was unable to extract enough support from his parishioners for the most basic necessity of a wilderness priest—his horse. Any "in this remote country" who have money, he said, "are very hard to part with it." "Our people," Salmon determined, "have no idea of generosity and are quite strangers with the disposition of making any sacrifice." "They are mean [and] narrow minded."[21]

The four priests decided on a European convention, tithing, to establish a dependable economic support for themselves. Gifts of land were rare, and occasional monetary payments were not enough. When Thayer arrived as the new pastor in Scott County, Badin wrote that summer to Bishop Carroll about the new man's intention to secure a source of revenue. Badin "agreed with him that his salary would more easily be raised by receiving a tythe," which in this case would be one-twentieth of each family's produce. "Money being very scarce in this State I see no surer or easier mean [*sic*] to obtain a salary for Priests," Badin decided. Asking support of any kind was frustrating work; "Mr. Fournier meets with much difficulty in order to obtain the payment of nine shillings from every head of family & many will not acknowledge his services by so modest a sum." The zealous and hardworking Father Salmon, noticed Badin, had such trouble obtaining a salary from the "backward" people of Bardstown that he and Salmon would probably have to continue to live together. "Being satisfied with the little moneys that did occasionally pass through my hands & were soon spent for the use of the congregations as much as for my own," said the French priest, was the best he could expect unless the bishop would grant the formal request of the four Kentucky priests to establish a modest tithe.[22]

In October, Badin again complained to the bishop about the "ingratitude of the Kentuckians" toward priests and explained the trouble he, Fournier, Salmon, and Thayer faced in trying to eke out salaries from their congregations: "The demand of a salary has given great offence to Mr. John Lancaster the Kentuckian Robespierre who has been elected to the Assembly by the influence of Priests, as well as Robt Abell who would plainly associate themselves to rob the Church of Kentucky of its land as the Jacobins have plundered the Gallican church."[23] Apparently, establishing a secure cure for a priest did not play well with certain elements of the Catholic community. As Badin's conflict with Lancaster and Abell suggested, some had, or claimed to have, ideological reasons for opposing priestly salaries. But generally parishioners gave unwillingly, as the clergy observed, because there was little excess capital available in the West, especially in the form of cash; and because typically there was no convention of giving support. American Catholics, especially in trans-Appalachia, were used to occasional visits by clergy during which they might be asked for food, lodging, or small monetary fees or gifts. Clergy in most places and decades have claimed trouble in collecting money from the laity, but in the western fringe of the early republic, Catholic priests believed they had found poor parishioners who were most concerned with acquiring wealth, and who generally thought priests should look out for themselves. Because lands were continually opening farther west, parishioners could migrate before their priest had had an opportunity to inculcate in them the custom of giving.

Several years after the four priests' trouble collecting remuneration, there continued to be problems in Kentucky with parishioners unwilling to support priestly standards of living. In October 1805 Badin discovered that certain church members were circulating false stories about him. He became eager to turn over church lands to a group of Dominican priests, in part to counter their rumors that he opposed the arrival of other clergy who might diminish his personal salary. In 1807 Father Nerinckx wrote to his parents across the Atlantic that his parishioners were still unusually reluctant to support their pastor. Kentucky Catholics, he alleged, were being lured away to distant frontiers before he could train them to make donations. "The largest number of settlers, although not over pious, wished to live near the priest. This is the case when they are poor. When, however, they begin to hunt for wealth, they go to more distant regions, without any further care for religion, and so they avoid contributing for church purposes."[24] Thus, twelve years after Father Fromm claimed that his recalcitrant parishioners in Pennsylvania were leaving "for Kentucky or for Spanish territories or for other regions" rather than pay what they had promised him, Nerinckx believed his own flock was cheating him and heading farther west, from Kentucky to Spanish Louisiana.

In the end Nerinckx decided it was an American dilemma. All western settlers were affected "with the complaint commonly called money-fever, which is very endemic," he wrote. Moreover, the Catholics in Kentucky were impoverished because they had settled the poorer lands over time by following the footsteps of the original Catholic pioneer community of 1785 and by choosing to live near each other and near priests rather than selecting the best acreage. "Protestants who become converts to our holy religion and are as a rule in better circumstances because occupying the best lands," and who might be expected to be more generous, were, according to Nerinckx, "few in number and less accustomed to these small duties." The Belgian priest added in disgust, "I can truly say that I alone have contributed more to the church, than the four or five hundred families under my care taken together; and that during my two years' residence here, I have not appropriated three dollars of the salary to my own use."[25]

Problems between clergy and laity over compensation continued. After fifteen years of missionary experience and thousands of miles itinerating in Kentucky, Indiana, Illinois, and Tennessee, Father Badin began placing strong prerequisites on making sick calls. Word circulated that he was brazenly charging one dollar to make such calls, thereby capitalizing on the Catholic's fear of dying without benefit of extreme unction. Several parishioners wrote to Bishop Carroll and told him that Badin had even ordered other priests to refuse to hear the confessions of any who complained against him. The beleaguered cleric informed his superior that the accusations were false and based on a simplification of his old policy on sick calls. Disgruntled parishioners, he asserted, were saying "Mr. Badin, with a view to make money, has prescribed that one Dollar shall be his fee to visit the sick." Badin stated his actual policy had been fairer, though admittedly firm. "As I am the only Priest in Kky, and cannot conveniently obey the unnecessary & vexatious applications frequently made to me to visit the sick," he announced, "as a check . . . I shall not visit the sick, unless one Dollar be paid for the service of the Altar: excepting however the negroes & those who are too poor."[26] In a letter sent a few days later to Bishop Carroll's coadjutator, Bishop Leonard Neale, Badin further described his position on sick calls. Father Salmon had died in November 1799, Father Thayer was ordered to return to the east coast in March 1801, and Fournier passed away in March 1803, leaving Badin alone for seventeen months to care for "at least 6000 individuals, white and black, occupying 800 square miles . . . all liable to die with sickness, and likely except for infants to send for me . . . at any time of day or night, by all seasons and weathers." Far too often, Badin observed, he had made a long journey "in the greatest anguish of body . . . to visit persons less sick than myself." To make a sick call, therefore, Badin required that one dollar be paid not to himself as alleged, but to parish trustees "for the service of the altar"; that a horse be brought by the sick person's messenger, so as to spare his only mount; and that a physician should certify the gravity of the patient's condition. He felt this protected his interests as well as those of the parishioners who might fall seriously ill. In addition, Badin noted, he had always made exceptions to the stated policy, and he had, of course, ended it when Father Nerinckx arrived in the summer of 1805 to assist him in his duties. As much as Badin wanted to settle down, the continuing sparsity of clergy in trans-Appalachia meant that his pastoral responsibilities were scattered over an expansive area. Even when additional priests arrived, Badin felt stretched in too many directions.

Diverse Duties

The demands on clergy were immense and varied, and they strengthened the priest's position at the heart of western Catholic communities. Called to the frontier by eager petitioning and expected to bring religious and social order, priests found themselves awash in the travails of wilderness living and the persistent material, cultural, and political needs of parishioners. In addition to their role in controlling access to the sacraments, priests maintained power and authority because of the exigencies of life on the frontier in the early republic. Communities needed leaders. Catholic clergy thus acquired consequential roles as economic entrepreneurs, educators, and ethnic mediators in their communities, which further bolstered their standing. Priests exercised more than the power of the church and had other means to maintain authority. At the same time, clergy were at the forefront of Catholic expansion into trans-Appalachia. As public figures they were responsible for reclaiming wayward Catholics and setting the tone for how a Catholic community as a whole might interact with Protestants.

Further, clergy were extremely difficult to replace, and their scarcity in the trans-Appalachian West was chronic, just as it had been for the Spanish and would be for the Americans in the trans-Mississippi West. Like the money-hungry parishioners who might move away in part to avoid paying their share of a priest's salary, Catholic clergy felt the pull of the West and could be lured to the Mississippi or beyond, creating more of a shortage in the near West. Parishioners might lose their priest if they burdened him too much, and bishops, particularly those who were hundreds of miles to the east, were not always able to control the emigrations of individual clergymen.

If settlers could pack up and move farther down the trail, so could the wandering missionary or the afflicted parish priest. Father Badin, in fact, was abandoned by his co-missionary and superior Father Barrieres, with whom Badin originally had been sent to Kentucky in 1793. After only four months, Barrieres, appointed by Bishop Carroll as vicar-general for the West, fled to New Orleans in April 1794 because he was dissatisfied with his life in Kentucky. After being captured by the Spanish, Barrieres became a missionary to the Indians for twenty years. Bishop Carroll later decided that he had discerned in earlier correspondence with Barrieres "a design not to remain long in Kentucky, formed even before he arrived at that country." Barrieres had agreed to follow another group of emigrating Catholics from Baltimore, across the Mississippi. "The most unexpected and distressing resolution of Mr. Barrieres, to forsake his post almost as soon as he was placed in it, filled me with the utmost concern," Carroll lamented. What really rankled was the situation of the "good Catholics of Nelson county," whose "patience . . . had been tried for many years." Carroll had sent Barrieres to them "with the utmost exultation of heart," promising "he would be everything to them; when, instead of answering the expectations he had raised, he leaves them." Disheartened but not defeated, Carroll confirmed Badin as the new senior clergyman until further notice, with authority over any others who might arrive.[27]

Because none of them had the fortitude of Jesuit missionaries, Badin once noted, two of the first four priests sent to Kentucky had deserted their posts—Father Barrieres and Father Whelan. The latter served only two and a half years before returning to the east coast. The third priest suffered from alcoholism. Although this Father William de Rohan was comfortably ensconced in Kentucky upon Badin and Barrieres's arrival in 1793, Badin reported that the troubled Irishman "ought to have" fled his post. It would have been in the best interest of Catholicism, said Badin, if Rohan would have left the frontier parishes on his own accord.

Badin himself thought about deserting. Admitting the fact to Carroll in 1796, Badin may have been overstating his position for the effect it might have in getting some assistance. He wrote that when he pondered leaving, he was "tempted to do it." He had good reason to look westward. During the period in which he was the sole Catholic missionary in Kentucky, Badin witnessed groups of Catholics being enticed to move to Illinois, which was under the control of the Spanish. In August 1796 he reported that French American settlements in Illinois had "nearly reached the point of dissolution ... because the inhabitants are emigrating to the Spanish side where they are very welcome." As a result, "the services of a priest would probably not be desired there in a few years."[28]

Trouble also stirred in Badin's backyard. One of his Scott County parishioners, Joseph Fenwick, scouted for suitable land in Illinois that would be in the vicinity of a priest. Like other westerners, he was the target of Spanish efforts to win over Americans disgruntled by the economic difficulties of living under U.S. control. The Spanish crown had closed the Mississippi as a trade route for Americans in 1784, but by 1787 it had realized how upset the frontiersmen were and how easily they might be turned from their loyalty to the federal government in far-away New York City. Westerners hinted broadly to Spanish officials that they might be persuaded to migrate to lands under crown control, or even to deliver themselves and American territories over to Spain, in return for more security from Indian raids or for economic access to the Mississippi and the port of New Orleans.[29]

Joseph Fenwick returned after obtaining "from the Spanish governor a grant of six thousand acres of good land for himself and his family, and more than 20,000 acres for such persons as wish to accompany him," noted Badin. "A number of Catholics, discouraged in Scott county, will undoubtedly follow him." Because he was a Catholic himself and the Kentuckians were searching for religious security as well, the Spanish governor also promised to build a chapel and provide an English-speaking priest for the prospective settlers. "What Mr. Fenwick has done," concluded Badin, "I should gladly have done myself were I a simple layman and my faith as great as his and his wife's." The grass had looked greener to priest and laity alike, though two years later the situation changed and the land beyond the Mississippi no longer appeared to be such a haven for Catholicism. Badin conveyed the following in March 1798: "The emigrations from Kentucky to the Illinois have been considerable, but are entirely stopt, as sickness and mortality have caused great ravages among them last summer. I have seen many Americans since their return; they are also much displeased with the quality & situation of the lands, with the vicinity of the Indians, the rudeness & irreligion of the generality of the inhabitants, & the pamphlet of Mr. Jos. Fenwick who must also be displeased with himself [for enticing them there]." However discouraging the situation in Illinois for the Kentucky emigrants, Badin recalled the emigration, ten years later, as a golden opportunity he had foregone. In 1808, at the height of troubles with certain members of his parish who had petitioned the bishop to discipline Badin for, among other things, charging a fee for the sacrament of communion, the French priest noted resentfully in a 32-page letter, "If money had been my object, I would have yielded to the invitation of the Spanish Government made to me twelve years ago, to remove from Kky, and exchange my truly pitiful situation for a salary &c. worth nearly 1000 $."[30]

Enough priests in this early period moved farther and farther west, without authorization, that Bishop Carroll recognized it to be a singular obstacle to the good of the Catholic church. From his vantage point it appeared that priests whom he had stationed in communities near the Mississippi River were succumbing to lay pressure to provide pastoral functions to Catholics on the other side. But to cross the Mississippi was to go beyond the bounds of Carroll's diocese. He had the power to provide these semi-itinerant priests with temporary official papers, though none were asking for them. They simply abandoned the old and took up new parishes on the river's opposite bank. In October 1798 Carroll raised the issue with Luis Penalver, bishop of the diocese of Louisiana, who had authority over Catholics west of the Mississippi. Carroll's intention was not to recall or punish Father Dominic Lusson, the most recent case of trans-river migration. Rather, Carroll said, "I bring this to the attention of your Lordship . . . so lest others, influenced by his example, and attracted by larger stipends, leave their parish and their diocese, and deprive the souls committed to their care of all spiritual help."[31] If roaming priests were enough of a problem to become the focus of an agreement between the continent's two prelates, obviously individual clergy were in high demand. This in turn indicates they retained significant personal power. If unappreciated or maltreated in one community, clergy might look for another.

Indeed, when priests in the far West decided to move on to better prospects they affected the lives of fellow clergymen who stayed behind in trans-Appalachian areas such as Kentucky. If the draining away of clergy worsened the working circumstances of the remaining missionaries, at least it made them rarer commodities with increased personal authority. As the western colleagues of Gallitzin in

Pennsylvania, Badin and others in Kentucky, and the French priests along the rivers of the Northwest and in Detroit moved onward toward new opportunities, they created even greater demand for priests in the trans-Appalachian region. In 1805 Father Donatian Olivier, in charge of the French mission of Kaskaskia in Illinois, wrote Father Badin a disheartening letter in which he informed the vicar-general of the West that after news of the Louisiana Purchase spread, "all the priests who were on the banks of the Mississippi, who received their salary from Spain, had deserted their parishes and followed the Spanish officers to Peru or Mexico," where they would receive the same rate of pay. In Badin's analysis of the situation, he and Olivier were the only priests in "a country 800 × 400 miles . . . whereas six years ago, we were at least twelve." The nearest other priests, he reminded his superiors, were in Quebec to the north or New Orleans to the south.[32]

The missionary's desire and opportunities to relocate, however, were hypothetically under the control of his superior. He could not move at will, although, as the next chapter shows, some priests ignored the needs and commands of the church and did as they pleased. In general, however, clergy were as stuck with laity as the laity were with them. The prospect of losing their pastor entirely was enough of a threat in the early years of the church to keep the parishioners in line. Father Charles Nerinckx, the Belgian priest sent to assist Badin in the wilds of Kentucky, tried to be transferred soon after arriving. Carroll had once refused his request to move to what was known as Upper Louisiana, or Missouri, yet Nerinckx attempted again in 1809, once the Spanish ceded the territory and religious responsibility of the Louisiana Purchase. Now that Kentucky was the center of the new western diocese, Nerinckx thought the state would soon have an "abundance of laborers" to provide for the religious needs there so that "the necessity of my remaining any longer in this region completely disappears." On the other hand, wrote Nerinckx, in Missouri the "extreme want and penury call most emphatically for any priest who can be spared," for the territory was "entirely destitute of workers, over one hundred and fifty miles away from a priest; it counts hundreds of families—catholics, or rather to be made catholics over again—scattered in divers settlements." Offering to act as an anchor of Catholicism on the far fringe of the United States, the type of place where experience taught that religion and morals drifted, Nerinckx wrote, "Many new families are continually going out there, and will emigrate in greater numbers when they see me or any other priest settled there."[33] Carroll had been trying for two decades, however, to secure Kentucky and was not ready to lose a proven parish-builder like Nerinckx. He would not release him to go farther west until 1824, and then only after Nerinckx's presence in Kentucky had become problematic.

Providing for the General Welfare

Trans-Appalachian clergy also strengthened their personal authority in other ways in the western communities they served. Often they fulfilled secular roles demanded by the material conditions found in the sparsely settled regions of the young nation. In certain cases, clergy felt compelled to deal in land development to benefit religious and secular goals, start or otherwise foster new businesses, engage in politics, and establish schools for the betterment of Catholic and non-Catholic youth.

At his growing Dominican convent and college at Rose Hill in Washington County, Kentucky, Father Edward Fenwick found himself almost too busy for spiritual matters, "having my hands and head all full." He had built a spacious brick church and was beginning a large chapter house that would double as an academy. In addition, the three companies of laborers, carpenters, and bricklayers had just completed a new sawmill and a gristmill. Rose Hill was serving the local community as a center of religion, commerce, and education.[34]

Fathers Fenwick, Demetrius Gallitzin, Stephen Badin, Charles Nerinckx, and Benedict Flaget—as well as Father Gabriel Richard, their colleague in the Michigan Territory—all participated in land development, cultivated local industries in some cases, and encouraged the economic prosperity of the faithful. Such efforts ensured the survival and stability of Catholic settlements and fostered moral development.

Sent to the far western boundary of the United States in Illinois only five months after arriving from France, the zealous missionary Benedict Flaget was unprepared for what he interpreted to be the indolence of French and Anglo-American, Native American, and Métis lifestyles along the Mississippi. Escorted the last miles by

Colonel George Rogers Clark himself, Flaget reached Vincennes in December 1792. There he found a stagnant economy and impoverished inhabitants. The decrepit church structure signaled the seriousness of the religious and economic situation. Of the seven hundred Catholics he discovered there, only twelve would take communion. Flaget's response was spiritual invigoration, religious exercise, and European American style economic development. He worked to improve living conditions and productivity in several ways. He urged local farmers to plant more crops, accumulate surpluses, and sell them for cash. He bought a farm and used it as a hands-on trade school for boys. He made weaving equipment for women of the town and monitored their work. And Flaget preached the doctrine of self-sufficiency through home manufactures, particularly the making of one's own clothing. Industry would replace idleness, self-sufficiency would become self-discipline.[35]

Far to the north, in the outpost that was Detroit, Father Gabriel Richard, a French émigré, similarly led his parishioners by industrious example. Richard arrived in 1798 and worked vigorously to reform the secular and spiritual lives of the town's inhabitants. In 1801 he arranged for the bishop of Quebec to provide the sacrament of confirmation to more than five hundred of his people, and a few years later he had established a girls' academy and a seminary. A terrible fire in June 1805, however, incinerated the town, leaving only two out of approximately three hundred houses and other buildings standing. Richard, already a respected community leader, led the town's recovery efforts and used his bilingual ability to coordinate assistance from nearby French and English farmers up and down the river for the Americans in Detroit. In the next few years, Father Richard found diverse ways to serve his community. He became a volunteer fireman and chaplain to the local militia, mediated between the French majority and the English-speaking Protestants in Detroit, and brought the town's first printing press in 1809. When one of his parishioners used the press to launch a newspaper and it soon failed, Richard began a venture printing blank business and legal forms. Later, Richard is reported to have managed a fishery on the Detroit River, attached to his town lot, and used his profits to accelerate the construction of a Catholic church. The priest also became politically active, adding his name to petitions for various purposes, including land titles sent to Congress. In 1823, Father

Richard's broad experience and numerous business and political contacts helped him win election as the Michigan Territory's delegate to the United States Congress.[36]

Southeast of Richard, in Pennsylvania, Father Demetrius Gallitzin similarly took a broad view of his responsibilities toward his parish. Economic development, he believed, would make his Catholics self-sufficient and religiously pure. After a few years in the early missions of eastern Pennsylvania and Maryland, Gallitzin had chosen a small settlement in the Allegheny Mountains. The village that he eventually would name Loretto became his experiment in creating the ideal Catholic community. In 1800, soon after arriving, Gallitzin wrote to Bishop Carroll, "The prospect of forming a lasting establishment for promoting the cause of religion is very great." In addition to the high concentration of Catholic settlers, the ambitious priest observed that the land was so fertile and "so advantageously situated with regard to market" that he had "no doubt but it will be a place of refuge for a great many Catholics." Propitious economic prospects already had drawn forty Catholic families, with many more on their way. "I try as much as I can to persuade them to settle around me." Gallitzin knew the supply of priests in America was short. Over the next decade, the priest directed and helped pay for the construction of a sawmill, tannery, and other rudimentary industries. Gallitzin also would purchase twenty thousand acres to sell in smaller parcels to incoming Catholic settlers, and it is estimated he ultimately spent at least $150,000 of his own money to encourage settlement and economic development. Gallitzin was the only son of a Russian prince, whose death in 1803 should have left Gallitzin a very wealthy man. When he chose not to return home to claim his inheritance, however, his father's properties were absorbed both by the Russian state and by the young prince's sister and her husband. Instead, the prince-priest drove himself deep into personal debt buying mountain lands on credit from Philadelphia financiers. He resold the land on easy terms to other settlers.[37]

Gallitzin hoped to attract fellow Catholics and to transform Loretto into a prosperous Catholic village. But there was more to his reasoning. In 1823, Gallitzin explained to his archbishop what he had intended for Loretto, "one of the most important" missions in the United States. "When I established myself here in 1800 the entire County of Cambria was but an immense forest and almost impenetrable." Yet "by force of labor and expense (expenses which already reach to more than forty thousand dollars)," he continued, "I have succeeded, with the help of God, in forming an establishment wholly Catholic, extending over an immense extent of country, which is rapidly augmented by the annual accession of families who come here from Germany, Switzerland, Ireland, and from different parts of America." When asked near the end of his life why he had ventured into the wilderness as a young man, Gallitzin clarified, "to get away" and "to begin something new," to avoid the "universal tendency to imitate the Protestants." In particular he disliked the "trustees and pew-renting and all the other evils" that lay Catholics seemed to borrow when establishing new parishes. Gallitzin had labored to create a Catholic settlement that would be insulated from the sway of Protestantism in his adopted country.[38]

In addition, a colleague of Gallitzin's reflected that the Russian prince-priest had had a republican perspective on how the propagation of Catholicism would best be achieved. The key to successfully rooting religion in the United States was land ownership. According to Badin's colleague, he "bewailed the fatal custom of immigrants stopping in Eastern cities" where acculturation might erase Catholic traditions and Protestantism could be overwhelming. They should head for "the interior of the country" to become "independent owners of the soil." Economic self-sufficiency would help ensure religious orthodoxy and the centrality of authority necessary in the Catholic Church.[39]

In a like manner, Father Badin in 1798 had given the role of the priest in settling the frontier an economic cast. Besides concerns of spiritual well-being, a community's religious leader had to forward the cause of material sufficiency. When members of Badin's parishes began to consider moving outward and onward to new lands, he not only cautioned them to stay concentrated so as to be within reach of priestly visits and to have "hope of church services," but he began to weigh the importance of economic pragmatism. If parishioners were to move away from the small, early Catholic settlements, at least "a clergyman should be at their head in order to rally them & [thus] a large tract of land might be bought on better terms." Badin went on to elaborate the material circumstances that would strengthen Roman Catholic community in Kentucky. He wanted to see new Catholic settlements along the Ohio River where the situation was "favourable to trade & fishing & the conveniency of the new-comers that would not have any land carriage." In other words, the economic promise of town life along the river and the ease with which new Catholic emigrants could find their way there would be an improvement over the hasty and arbitrary settlement patterns of Catholics who, so far, were "scattered about" the state.[40]

Two years later, in 1800, Badin wrote to Bishop Carroll that he could no longer contain the material ambitions of his parishioners and that he needed the assistance of another priest who could lead the next wave of settlement rippling outward from central Kentucky. Like Father Gallitzin in his alpine community of Loretto, Pennsylvania, Badin imagined this priest would provide priestly, spiritual guidance, as well as the leadership necessary to focus the economic impulse of lay Catholics. Send a priest to replace the late Father Salmon, Badin asked, because "we are too thickly settled and the 2d & 3d rate-lands are impoverishing fast & great many people are very uneasy and they are by turn exploring the unsettled parts of the state." Only the likelihood of losing regular contact with the region's few priests prevented their "emigrating from the two counties of Nelson & Washington."

Perhaps Badin could not have imagined another priest like Gallitzin who had the personal resources to broker major land deals to benefit lay Catholics and the church. But he knew economic leadership could be an important responsibility of the local priest. If a clergyman would not rally resources himself, he could at least—as Badin did—advocate that a lay Catholic leader do this: "I wish there might be found among Catholics a man of wealth and moderate ambition to purchase at once a considerable tract of land and parcel it out on reasonable terms to Catholics only." It was the church's responsibility to overcome the tendency of random settlement in the West, to reformulate the way Catholic communities arose, because new patterns in material concerns would benefit the growth of the Catholic Church. As soon as a few Catholics would settle together, Badin noted, nearby land increased in value by 50 to 100 percent, and this made it difficult for other Catholics to settle in the vicinity, which in turn could make the priest's job ever more difficult. This was "another hardship that we labour under and [that] obstruct[s] the expansion of the church."[41]

Yet the increase in the value of lands surrounding a settled

Catholic pastor and community signaled a process that was working to the benefit of the individual priest. If the Catholics already owned land in an area and a priest arrived, pastor and parishioners thereafter might benefit from the sale of nearby parcels at increased prices to newcomers. Pastor and parish could grow wealthier together. In addition, the rise in land prices would be due to the arrival of like-minded families, Catholic settlers, hoping to have access to religion. As John Grassi, a visiting Jesuit, reported in 1810, this was still the model on the frontier: "For people prefer to settle in places where they can easily procure the helps of religion, and hence the lands increase in value. . . . Add to this, that the settlers in newly opened sections are most anxious to have churches and missionaries." Therefore, the number of offers of free lands to the Catholic Church was remarkable: "many landholders also, even Protestants," Grassi exclaimed, "offer hundreds of acres gratis for this purpose, not through any special zeal for religion, but simply as a matter of speculation." Free land donated because of the presence of priest and church, particularly that which was provided by non-Catholics, strengthened the status and economic power of the pastor. He could be seen marshaling resources, focusing settlement efforts, and even attracting the attention of Protestant benefactors. Moreover, Grassi suggested, through such land speculation the church could reap the rewards of converting new members. "Missionaries who should establish themselves in such places," said Grassi, "would have the consolation of seeing the whole neighborhood embrace the Catholic faith."[42]

Propagating the Faith

The Catholic Church faced many obstructions to expansion in the trans-Appalachian West, though none proved debilitating enough to slow growth significantly. Ubiquitous however, even on the landscape of the frontier, was the problem of dealing with Protestantism, from its subtle influences on lay Catholic perceptions of religion to its overt doctrinal challenges to Roman Catholicism. Whatever the level of opposition from Presbyterians, Baptists, and Methodists, it was the priest who was expected to be the primary bulwark against encroaching Protestantism and the figure most responsible for the Catholic image in the non-Catholic eye. As Connel Rogers and his fellow petitioners in Butler County, Pennsylvania, had threatened in 1803–1804, without a priest they could not help continuing to be a "scandal to the communion."[43] As the man on the spot, often surrounded by active evangelical denominations and by numerous Protestants with only tenuous adherence to any church, the frontier parish priest or missionary, with ecclesiastical superiors dozens to hundreds of miles away, held the line against Protestant criticism and conducted a public relations campaign.

As Father Badin had observed about the ideal characteristics for frontier priests in 1807, the clergyman should not be afraid of revealing his identity as a Catholic priest. In "the spirit of the ancient Jesuits," said Badin, the priest would need to be ready to give impromptu sermons and speeches, especially on controversial, sectarian topics, either "publicly or privately." He could not be shy or even modest about displaying his faith, nor should he permit his parishioners to be so. The western priest needed to set an example for lay Catholics, particularly, as Father Nerinckx observed, those "scattered among unbelievers," everyday Catholics who, without a "priest to guide them," were "ashamed to own up to their belief among infidels."[44]

On the frontier, especially, priests had the added duties of restoring backsliding Catholics, as well as winning over Protestants or the irreligious. Writing about his journey through the backwoods of Maryland and West Virginia in September 1812, Bishop Flaget calculated a huge number of Catholics who "forget their religion" due to "the lack of zeal of the priests who have charge of these congregations." Each day en route, he claimed, he and his companions found "strayed sheep" who had become "Baptists, Methodists, etc., or at least nothingists." Reporting on parishes in the Illinois Territory, the far fringe of his Bardstown diocese in 1815, Flaget informed Pope Pius VII, "The Americans who inhabit these regions, are for the most part heretics, and are generally without ministers of their own sects and could be brought into the Catholic faith with little difficulty if there were missionaries who joined to their zeal and doctrines a knowledge of the language of these people." Writing in the same year, also to an audience in Europe, Father Charles Nerinckx explained what held Catholicism back from its full potential in the United States. It was, in part, old persecutions. More significant, however, was that there had been for thirty years too few priests to "look for old Catholics and who would bring to the Church those who want to pass from a foreign religion to the true one." In the Catholic mind, the American wilderness held potential for Catholic settlement, but also for reclaiming wayward members of the faith and for converting heretics and heathens. And the crucial variable for success was a sufficient supply of clergymen.[45]

The priest, often with the encouragement of his parishioners, saw himself at the very core of community life in western settlements. His roles might vary from maintaining Catholic identity and religious practice amid a sea of Protestants and other non-Catholics, to leading economic development, providing for the educational welfare of frontier youth, and bolstering the social and moral cohesion that held together Catholic communities. Early groups of Catholic settlers typically felt their communities were incomplete without a resident clergyman and petitioned aggressively for clerical assistance in the late eighteenth to the early nineteenth century. Still, Catholic priests were present in barely sufficient numbers on the trans-Appalachian frontier. This scarcity made them difficult to replace and thereby gave them an advantage when in conflict with the laity. Priests were known to abandon communities and move farther west. This ready mobility, along with the multiple leadership roles they fulfilled, made western Catholic priests formidable figures in trans-Appalachian settlements.

Chapter 3

"Presumptuous Renegades"

Controlling Priests and Congregations

Father John Baptist Causse wielded substantial authority and fulfilled the many roles expected of a frontier priest. He also used his position for personal gain. In sowing dissension and defying his bishop, the immigrant cleric typified a pattern of behavior that would plague church officials in the early republic. Given the national shortage of trained priests, the church's inchoate structure, and the overwhelming problems of a rapid expansion in the urban East and especially into the trans-Appalachian West, American congregations attracted a large number of inept, misguided, or combative clergy from the 1780s through the 1820s. These were not necessarily men of heretical bent, but they tested the limits of episcopal authority, encouraged factions within their congregations to cement their own positions, and otherwise caused public controversies that damaged the integrity and reputation of American Catholicism.

Responding to these problem priests, however, reinforced the central authority of the church and entrenched its traditional European ways. Crisis discouraged innovations or adoption of American models of organization. Crisis fostered reliance on what was familiar, tested, and conservative. "Presumptuous renegades," clerical imposters, and deserters temporarily slowed the growth of Catholicism, but in curbing these rogue individuals, church officials strengthened hierarchical control. Other denominations similarly attempted to

centralize authority and limit the latitude of clergymen, both itinerant and settled. Like Protestantism in the early republic and the
West, American Catholicism was undergoing centralization and authoritarian cohesion rather than declension or democratization.[1]

Arriving in Philadelphia from Mainz, Germany, in 1785, after
six years' experience in a French parish, Father John Causse seemed
an answer to Bishop Carroll's repeated prayers for help in his burgeoning diocese. Despite Causse's unintelligible English and his reported proclivity for "roving," Carroll sent him to the mission at
Lancaster, Pennsylvania. The brief stay in Philadelphia, the bishop
believed, had helped the immigrant German to become "better settled" and sufficiently proficient in English to be of service in rural
America. Eventually Carroll appointed him as assistant at the Conewago, Pennsylvania, mission.

Yet Causse did not stay at his post; there were complaints that he
traveled to the western reaches of the state without permission. In
the autumn of 1790, Causse attended the bedside of a dying priest,
Father Theodore Brouwers, who had established a parish in Westmoreland County, two hundred miles west of Conewago. On hand
for a month before Brouwers's death, Causse allegedly refused him
the comfort of last rites until the Dutch priest bequeathed his mission and private estate to the priests at Conewago. This brazen attempt to commandeer the congregation and its pastor's lands ran
afoul of the local county registrar, whose protests prevented Causse
from taking complete control of the situation. Still, he did not give
up. When Brouwers finally died, Causse sent to Conewago for
horses to transport back east the frontier priest's belongings. Meanwhile, he remained in the parish until he had persuaded the skepti-
cal parishioners to entrust him to withdraw Brouwers's savings of
$1,146 from a Philadelphia bank. The executors of Brouwers's will
had reason to be suspicious, but Causse insisted that he had to go to
Philadelphia on other business in any case, and that he would never
return to provide the sacraments if they would not trust him. Causse
received their authority, returned east to Conewago to spend the
winter, and then withdrew the money in Philadelphia in the spring
of 1791. Tempted by the sudden access to cash, Causse spent the
money on himself—oddly enough, to purchase and manage a traveling theatrical production called "Jerusalem."

For abandoning his duties, misappropriating parish funds, practicing deceit, and humiliating the church in the public eye, Carroll suspended Causse from exercising any sacerdotal functions. Causse's response was to sow dissension among his fellow disgruntled German Catholics in Baltimore, proceeding almost "to set up a schismatical church, using the pretence that the Germans" were being neglected by the Anglo-American episcopacy. In early 1792, when Causse began telling his coconspirators he belonged to a religious order and "did not need episcopal authorization to act as a pastor of souls," Carroll finally excommunicated the belligerent man.[2]

A year later the somewhat humbled priest wrote to Carroll asking for forgiveness: "If after absolution you would allow me to go behind in the Back parts of the country and settle a mission about Red Stone [south of Pittsburgh], I would sell the show." Carroll welcomed Causse back into active church membership, while preventing him from representing the faith in the wilderness where he might be beyond the reach of bishop, vicars-general, and even fellow priests. Carroll told him any such posting would come only after a long, long period of probation, "for reasons which your own reflections will suggest easily to you."[3] Bishop Carroll, however, barely could afford to put the priest on probation. The most critical problem was to find priests, any trustworthy ones, to assume leadership in far-flung congregations and missions.

The seemingly indefatigable Causse was symptomatic of the fragile ecclesiastical system and nascent episcopal authority in the early republic. Finding enough priests at home or abroad to keep up with the expanding Catholic population was a primary obstacle while priests were in short supply and the seminary in Maryland was not able to train clergy quickly enough to satisfy demand. Moreover, many of the few clergy at hand would prove themselves unfit for service. While the church slowly established structure, organization, and policies to meet the new demands of American life, rogue priests sought personal power, financial gain, or simply a new start free of episcopal scrutiny. Some rebellious clergy like Causse caused major disturbances, while others defied authority in less significant ways. All challenged the church in a time of structural weakness.

Father Causse's adventures also illustrate how individuals could take advantage of the thinly applied church discipline in the trans-Appalachian West. As priests followed emigrating Catholics, hierarchical control over these men of the cloth was tested by the miles and weeks of travel between bishop and frontier missions. Geographical distance, unfamiliarity, and a desperate need for clerical assistance made it difficult for the hierarchy to control clergy, assess new arrivals, and test them over time. Once a new pastor was in position, he could be difficult to remove—whether the laity or the bishop wanted him ejected. The same social conditions of settlement that empowered the priest and made him central to the local community also made the pastorate a position that could be twisted by unfit candidates—such as Father Causse who had tricked the Westmoreland County parishioners into trusting him with their deceased pastor's life savings.

Frontier conditions made it difficult to control troublemakers, although each clash with men such as Causse forced church officials to exert traditional structures of control. The church hierarchy began to counter the rebelliousness of Causse and other dissident clergy, a slow and frustrating process. Carroll and his fellow bishops eventually stressed the importance of screening all volunteers more thoroughly, testing them under supervision for as long as possible, and shifting to domestic sources of priests. Bishops also worked more readily at first with lay trustees in congregations to crack down on clergy, and then sought to deplete the power of the lay trustees themselves, who proved to be adding to the problem of discipline. All such provisions reinforced episcopal power.

Controversy within a congregation or between a priest and his bishop was threatening for many reasons, including the negative public attention it attracted. Scandal before the watching eyes of Protestants and other non-Catholics became an omnipresent concern for a church with an undeveloped ecclesiastical structure in a nation in which it carried outsider status. Every controversy with an incompetent or quarrelsome priest acquired extra drama because of its potential for eliciting an anti-Catholic public response. Carroll learned this soon upon becoming bishop. In May 1784 Charles Wharton—a former fellow Jesuit, a Marylander, and Carroll's friend—left a chaplaincy in England, returned to Philadelphia, abandoned Catholicism, and published a pamphlet hostile to the Roman faith. Carroll answered with his own booklet in that same year, though he refrained from responding to a second from Wharton because he did not want to upset the state of inter-sectarian relations. Wharton's attempt to ignite American anti-Catholicism taught Carroll the necessity of downplaying internal dissension and handling such public embarrassments as quickly and quietly as possible. Such caution, however, sometimes allowed problems to mushroom and made the removal of the guilty party more difficult and even more public. Eventually church leaders would conclude that sharp action was appropriate to end scandal. They would also discover that some non-Catholics would condone their attempts to demand orthodoxy and obedience, for both Catholicism and Protestantism were undergoing a centralization of authority in this period. In the matter of ecclesiastical discipline, Catholic officials realized they shared common ground with some Protestant churches.

Renegades versus Trusteeism

Catholics soon discovered something in common with Protestant churches in another area: a tendency among the laity to challenge church hierarchy. Lay trustees elected by Catholic congregations to manage church affairs and administer church properties increasingly attempted to control the parish priest or defy the will of the bishop. Such "trusteeism" seemed suspiciously akin to the Protestant use of presbyteries and other lay institutions to control the minister. It also appeared to incorporate other Americanisms into the Catholic ecclesiastical structure, such as republican ideology and a democratic spirit, as well as the inheritance of an English "antipathy . . . to the claims of Roman and canon law."[4]

Trusteeism was a significant problem, especially because it exacerbated ethnic divisions within dioceses and parishes; nevertheless, historians have emphasized it at the expense of the equally chronic crisis of troublesome priests. Several serious trustee crises occurred in the 1780s to the early 1800s in New York, Boston, and Baltimore, and particularly during a near-schism in Philadelphia caused by Father William Hogan and his trustees; but the solution was clear. In 1822 Pope Pius VII issued an apostolic brief, *Non Sine Magno*, instructing American trustees and laity to accept the bishops' ultimate control over church property and the employment of priests. In 1829 the problem lingered, and it elicited a response in the pastoral letter from America's First Provincial Council of bishops. The pastoral pronouncement, however, also underscored at length the problem of rebellious priests.

Nevertheless, at the heart of most major trustee scandals, from 1785 through 1830, was a priest encouraging fractious behavior and defiant stances toward episcopal authority. Historian Thomas W. Spalding has claimed, "As often as not . . . the crisis was provoked by a problem priest who encouraged rebellion as a shield for his own aberrant behavior." Facing trusteeism and unruly priests, the church chose an ever more conservative and traditional stance. "Because of the internal battles over lay trusteeism," says historian Patrick Carey, "these years in particular were crucial for the gradual institutional transformation of the Catholic church from a loose confederation of local congregations under minimal, and at times ineffective, episcopal supervision to a nationally organized denomination under forceful episcopal leadership."[5] Trusteeism remained primarily a dilemma for eastern, urban congregations where it frequently was both cause and symptom of existing ethnic divisions. In western missions and parishes the situation was different; priests typically were better able to monopolize power and were freer from episcopal oversight. Hence it was to the West that renegade clergy often found their way.

Two of Carroll's earliest crises, in the mid-1780s, as well as the famous Hogan schism, in 1819, involved rebellious priests scheming with lay trustees. In 1784 Charles Maurice Whelan, an Irish friar and former chaplain in the French navy during the American Revolution, became New York City's first resident priest. Whelan was reputed to be a dreadful preacher, and his simple demeanor, complained the genteel French and Spanish merchants and diplomats who dominated the parish, was unacceptably unrefined. When a second Irish friar, Andrew Nugent, arrived in 1785, important persons in the congregation and certain of the lay trustees wanted to oust Whelan. Carroll, who did not want to surrender completely to the whims of the laity, appointed both priests "joint chaplains." Father Nugent, however, encouraged the trustees in ousting Whelan. Nugent continued to stir controversy, and even some supporters had soured on him by 1787 when he again tried taking over the parish. As prefect apostolic, Carroll dismissed him and revoked his faculties (i.e., the powers conferred on him to supply the sacraments and minister to the laity). Attempting a show of authority by appearing in Whelan's New York Church of St. Peter, Carroll found himself physically prevented by Nugent and his followers from entering the church. Nugent continued to preach defiance against Carroll and the pope, with fealty only to Jesus Christ and the civil authorities of New York. The controversy came to a climax in a New York courtroom when Nugent was convicted for disturbing the peace. The court ruled he should not hold any office in the church because he did not accept its fundamental doctrines. Throughout the affair, Carroll was worried about what Protestants might think. Writing to two parishioners within Nugent's faction, the bishop expressed his consternation on having learned that members of the congregation had seized the collection made one Sunday "in a tumultuary manner." He found this "peculiarly mortifying" for the division it caused and the "very disadvantageous impression to the prejudice of the Catholic cause" it had in New York, a city in which the Catholic public worship was still so new.[6]

Father Nugent's disgraceful behavior toward the Catholic hierarchy and the rift within his congregation have been described by historians as the first of the many trustee problems to rack the American Catholic Church in the late eighteenth and early nineteenth centuries. Nevertheless, this affair and other incidents of trusteeism in eastern cities were instigated, manipulated, and exacerbated by a resident renegade priest. Carroll's next major public embarrassment, for example, was also caused by a man of the cloth, Father Claude Florent Bouchard de la Poterie, who arrived in Boston in 1788 and immediately defied episcopal authority by neglecting to notify Bishop Carroll of his presence. Later, when Poterie's individual style proved to be too pretentious, flashy, and alienating for his parishioners, the prelate suspended him. Poterie defied Carroll until the end, publicly ridiculed him, and caused chaos in the congregation, maintaining his temporary grasp on power only by dividing the laity and lay trustees into factions.[7]

Twenty years later the problems of trusteeism and troublesome priests were still intertwined in the East. During the notorious schism launched by Father William Hogan in Philadelphia in 1820—what historian Sydney Ahlstrom called "the *cause célèbre* of trusteeism"—the rebellious priest ended up discharged from his pastorate for publicly mocking his superior, Bishop Henry Conwell. Hogan retaliated by asking the archbishop to call a council to rule in his favor, then forged a letter from Bishop Conwell and encouraged the trustees to publish an attack on the hierarchy as a call for an independent Catholic Church. When he found himself excommunicated, the pugnacious Hogan concluded the affair by becoming a lawyer and getting married. He later made a career as an anti-Catholic polemicist.[8]

What these crises in New York, Boston, and Philadelphia revealed was not simply the church's great difficulty with "trusteeism" or democratization and Americanization of the laity, but an organizational difficulty in asserting episcopal authority. Scattered and isolated priests on whom the church and lay Catholics were dependent, in areas far from direct scrutiny by church leaders, found themselves nearly autonomous representatives of Catholicism. Under such conditions, priests had the advantage in the occasional struggles for control waged between clergy and lay trustees, lay trustees and bishops, and bishops and clergy. Indeed, if scandals could brew in New York, Boston, and Philadelphia, unscrupulous clergy in trans-Appalachia could have even freer rein in their distant abodes.

Renegades in the West

Whether they built factions within congregations or simply created disturbances and controversy on their own, belligerent and incompetent clergy would plague the trans-Appalachian church well into the nineteenth century. Bishop Carroll feared this immediately upon his rise to power. In 1785 his initial report as bishop on the state of religion in America informed his superiors in Rome that he had at hand fifteen hundred Catholics in New York without a pastor, and that afar he was responsible for the many Catholics in the Mississippi Valley who were also "destitute of priests." East and West he desperately required more clergy. Despite the clear need to send ministerial help westward, Carroll brooded about bad priests setting a poor example. With regard to Catholic-Protestant relations in the context of a predominantly Protestant nation, "the Catholic faith would suffer less harm," Carroll told Rome, "if for a short time there is no priest at a place, than if living as we do among fellow-citizens of another religion, we admit to the discharge of the sacred ministry, I do not say bad priests, but incautious and imprudent priests." The new bishop feared such men would tarnish the image of Catholicism, which he continually struggled to improve.[9]

His colleagues agreed. In 1796, shortly after his co-priest had abandoned him and their Kentucky post, Father Stephen Badin addressed the same problem. Badin noted it was "foreign and volunteer priests," some of whom "seek their own interests as much if not more than they do the cross of our Lord," who were retarding efforts to spread Catholicism. He agreed with his bishop, concluding that "the priests have done more harm to the Church here than its declared enemies." In 1815 Father Charles Nerinckx observed the "deplorable miserie" of how the West continued to draw troublesome priests, whom he called "presumptuous renegades." "It has been the misfortune to these regions," he wrote, that on several occasions he had met priests who "being more concerned with themselves than with Jesus Christ, have travelled here, to their own great detriment," and, more significantly, "without any benefit to religion or to their fellow-man." Referring to Hogan in Philadelphia, Bishop Benedict Flaget in 1821 wrote from Bardstown to a colleague that "it is lucky Hogan had not entered this diocese as the vastness of the territory might have resulted in victory for the priest [since] I would not have been able to have visited that man." Flaget earlier had written to Conwell, chastising him for having recommended Hogan for reassignment to the sprawling Bardstown diocese. If such damage could be done under the noses of bishop and archbishop in the East, what was the potential for disaster on the frontier?[10]

Certain priests saw the new nation, particularly the frontier, as a place to test the limits of church authority. And they were attracted to frontier regions and newly inaugurated dioceses where they might find more latitude than in eastern urban centers or in Europe. Priests were so scarce and scattered that it was extremely difficult to administer discipline, or even monitor their behavior. As lay Catholics moved toward the nation's unsettled edges, contumacious priests followed them, hoping to carve out spaces for themselves. Problematic priests headed for the frontier to escape episcopal scrutiny. An all-too-common pattern was for troublemakers to sail from Europe, cause headaches in a coastal city, and then move successively farther and farther west, making it more difficult for Carroll or other bishops to monitor their actions.

Like other border regions, the trans-Appalachian West was perceived to be a haven for misfits, criminals, and dissemblers. One Scottish traveler called the Ohio River "the greatest thoroughfare of banditti in the Union," an escape route for horse thieves, debtors, and runaways who were attracted to an area "where so many are continually moving . . . without property, without acquaintances, without introductory letters, and without the necessity of support- ing moral character." Individuals, good and bad, blended together. New communities were burgeoning, and often only time would tell whether the new schoolmaster could teach, the new gentleman was honorable, or the new minister was the man of God he promised to be. Beyond the network of family, friends, and close neighbors lay a world of mendacious possibilities, with little social structure in place to check deceit. In 1806 the Ohio and Mississippi valleys would be- come the scene of such uncertainties played to their fullest in the international intrigues of Aaron Burr and James Wilkinson. These co-conspirators exploited the difficulties of long-distance commu- nication, cross-border suspicions, and the credulity of frontiers- men to build western support as they played Britain against Spain and both against the United States. Their ill-fated plan was to steal New Orleans and other Spanish territories for themselves and their followers. As a region, trans-Appalachia in the late eighteenth and early nineteenth centuries seemed to be a haven for disingenuous characters, including renegade priests.[11]

Concurrent with the beginnings of the Catholic mission to Kentucky, for example, was a series of problems with priests. Fa- ther Whelan, the Irish Capuchin who had competed with fellow Capuchin Father Nugent for control of the New York City parish in 1785–1787, eventually was sent to Kentucky. He established the first parish, stayed for two and a half years, and then left in 1791. Five years later, Father Badin complained to Bishop Carroll that Whelan's colorful descriptions of frontier privation and controversy in Kentucky were scaring off potential missionaries for the region. "For the glory of God and the advantage of the Church," said Badin, he "ought not to recall the scandals in Kentucky except to deplore and remedy them if he can." Unfortunately, Father Whelan was do- ing the opposite. He was busy in eastern communities endeavoring to "dissuade priests from ever setting foot" in the western lands so desperately in need of clergymen.[12]

Bishop Carroll next sent Fathers Badin and Michael Bernard

Barrieres in 1793. The first was newly ordained, the second "a man of experience." In April 1794, however, the older priest, whom Carroll had appointed as vicar-general for the entire West, abandoned his post in Nelson County, leaving Badin alone at his station near Frankfort. Barrieres's departure left many frontier Catholic families destitute of moral leadership, said Badin, and took its toll on the parish, with "charity & faith . . . cooling there by degrees." Bishop Carroll interpreted it as a personal betrayal, for he had "promised" himself that Barrieres "would be everything" to the patient parishioners who had waited years for spiritual assistance. A suspicion gnawed at Carroll later that summer: Barrieres had been ruminating about abandoning his mission even before arriving on the frontier. He had allowed himself to be stationed; yet he had been planning since Pittsburgh eventually to continue down the river to New Orleans. Complicating the situation was the deserter's outstanding financial debt to the Catholics of the region, as well as his failure to deliver a breviary and other books, which he had purchased in Vincennes, for Badin's use on the Kentucky missions. Adding insult to the injury, claimed Badin, was the fact that Barrieres had written in 1797 to the man sent to replace him and to assist Badin, Father Fournier, "to entice him by the basest motives to abandon me."[13]

When Badin and Vicar-General Barrieres first floated down the Ohio in 1793, however, they quickly learned that they were not the only priests to have arrived since Whelan's departure in 1791. The two new Frenchmen discovered yet another priest, Father de Rohan, "who had intruded without any authorization" from Bishop Carroll of Baltimore, and whom Carroll described as an unreliable, "rambling Irish" priest. Settlers demanded pastors; the rivers provided access; and the bishop beyond the mountains was too distant to fully regulate the influx of clergymen, especially those who did not seek his permission. Consequently, Badin and Barrieres found an indolent priest, a former chaplain from the French navy, "exercising the sacred ministry during two years while living in public and habitual drunkenness." To Barrieres the bishop confided that he and Badin should be "very cautious" in using the man for any ecclesiastical purpose, until they had time to observe in him an "entire reformation" of character. De Rohan most likely had drifted from Virginia to North Carolina, from there to Tennessee, and then up into Kentucky.

After Barrieres had absconded to New Orleans in 1794, Badin, who then became vicar-general, removed de Rohan's faculties. Yet he was stuck with the man, his only colleague until Father Fournier arrived in 1797. And de Rohan, it seems, was not much help. Badin complained in 1796 that de Rohan, the only person in Kentucky who could share his problems, "makes himself incapable of doing so"—presumably because of his inebriety. By the spring of 1797, de Rohan had limited himself to teaching school near Bardstown, having moved there after giving up a school in a small community on the Salt River. Badin was thankful for the move and for de Rohan's willingness to "not pretend to ministerial functions" and "not give any scandal," yet he wished the problematic priest would move or be transferred back East, under the watchful eyes of either Carroll or "some other superiors near the Episcopal See." A decade later Badin would again regret de Rohan's presence; a group of Badin's enemies in the parish "associated to themselves a worthy member in the person of Mr. Rohan, who has not forgiven me as yet the trespass of having suspended him." De Rohan ultimately proved to be rather harmless, though he had wandered without permission into a frontier region that desperately needed priestly help he could not provide, had been a source of deep concern for the overburdened vicar-general, and had been a potential embarrassment for the church.[14]

More serious problems occurred with priests who set out to escape episcopal control and who intentionally caused scandal to strike at the authority of the bishop. Early troublemakers in Kentucky, such as de Rohan, Barrieres, and Whelan, were by comparison easy to deal with. One of the most vitriolic attacks on John Carroll's character, in fact, came from an Irish immigrant, one Father Dennis Cahill, who slipped into the backcountry of western Maryland in 1788. Carroll had not authorized his missionary work; indeed, the bishop knew little about the man or his background. One historian characterized the Irish priest as "a recent arrival of uncertain antecedents." Out of the blue, in 1795, Cahill announced to Carroll that he had organized congregations at Hagerstown, Martinsburg, Shepherdstown, and Cumberland, Maryland, and Winchester, Virginia, as well as Chambersburg, Pennsylvania. Carroll undoubtedly was pleased with the news, though dismayed at not knowing more about the backwoods priest. A year later, when Cahill thought Carroll was attempting to turn over the Hagerstown church to a Father Bodkin, Cahill snapped. He wrote that Carroll was jealous, wanted to perpetrate a "cruel injustice," and was trying "with venemous breath to blast the fruits of my labor." Worse than these personal insults, however, were Cahill's continued threats to publicize scandalous rumors: Carroll had bribed his fellow Jesuits in order to be made bishop; a fellow priest had had an illicit affair; and Carroll himself had sired children. When Cahill attempted to extort $300 and the right to keep the Hagerstown congregation in return for silence, the controversy degenerated further, simmering until 1803 when he finally offered a lukewarm apology.[15]

Efforts to Control

Given the difficulties Bishop Carroll and his colleagues had in finding suitable clergy for western settlements, it is understandable that they required extensive personal written character references for new candidates. Priests who developed problems or those who arrived intending mischief were usually the same ones who had appeared before the bishop without credentials. Letters of reference and introduction became increasingly important, particularly for introducing new clergymen from the East to the West and from Europe to the United States. Only young men trained in domestic seminaries, under the eye of one's close colleagues, might be trusted.

During the first controversy involving a renegade priest, Carroll had learned to question even the best letters of reference from Europe. Of the Irish Capuchin friar Andrew Nugent, who scandalized New York City in the late 1780s, Carroll wrote: "he shewed me good credentials, when he first arrived, and amongst others, a strong recommendation from Fr. o Leary. I have reason now to suspect, that it was forged; for Nugent has been detected to be a most infamous fellow; & there is no excess of which he does not seem capable." In the same letter, Carroll went on to ask his English friend to look into the background of an Irish priest named Smyth, whose "manner of coming, & even his discourse at times has something mysterious." Clues in his letters of reference indicated the Irishman had some unstated, underlying objective that smacked of intrigue. Preventing the arrival of undocumented immigrant priests thus became an objective of the church hierarchy. In fact, when Carroll formally authorized Father John Thayer to minister to Catholics in Boston, he also specifically instructed him "to prevent transient priests from exercising any functions of the sacred ministry before you have examined their documents, and satisfied yourself in respect to their faith and morals." If such questionable fellows persisted in trying to circumvent his authority, Thayer was to gather information on them and forward it to the bishop's office. It had become necessary, with regularity, to question the legitimacy even of the priest who carried documents.[16]

Letters of reference from individuals on whom Carroll regularly depended also could be suspect. Given the great distances involved, sometimes the bishop might come to depend on third parties who were themselves recommended by friends. In 1789, a man whom Carroll apparently trusted for general information about the West, news of Catholics in the Illinois region, and personal evaluations of priests who visited settlements along the Mississippi demonstrated how unreliable such long-distance reports could be. The French trader boasted to a friend how Carroll "assures me of all the confidence he has in me" due to the "testimony of some mutual friends." Barthelemi Tardiveau mocked Carroll's trust, relating to the friend how he single-handedly had blighted the career of a priest, Mr. de la Valinie're, who had crossed him, and raised up an incompetent Mr. Ledru to preach in his place. With a long letter "assuredly . . . not loud in his praises," Tardiveau dispatched de la Valinie're. Despite Ledru being a "wretched scribbler," a "dryasdust schoolmaster," and a "Jacobin by profession" in Tardiveau's opinion, Tardiveau managed to give Carroll enough misplaced confidence to secure the priest a one-year assignment in Illinois and Vincennes. More amazing still, gloated the French trader, Carroll had already asked for a report after Ledru's first year, and about other priests in the area as well. Clearly the bishops were at a tremendous disadvantage.[17]

Part of the problem was the ease with which priests emigrated, and, once in the United States, moved from location to location without a bishop's approval. Over time, Carroll, his successors and fellow bishops, and other trusted clergy laid out a careful system of providing and checking a clergyman's papers. Carroll, for example, wrote to his fellow bishop, Luis Penalver of the Louisiana diocese, in 1798 to request help in preventing American priests from crossing the Mississippi to take up new pastorates whenever they felt like it. Exactly one year later Carroll returned to the subject in correspondence with his fellow bishop and named three of these priests: Charles Leandre Lusson, Michael Bernard Barrieres, and John McGuire. Lusson had arrived from the island of St. Domingo, and Carroll had trusted him with a parish near Baltimore, though a scandal forced his transfer to Kaskaskia. Lusson soon abandoned that post and crossed the river to begin anew west of St. Louis. In a similar fashion, Barrieres and McGuire had abandoned their positions in Kentucky, floated downstream to New Orleans, and never repaid the traveling expenses for their trips from the east coast, which had been supplied by Kentucky parishioners.

Carroll hoped to prevent future embarrassments by formalizing a system of central control. He told Penalver he would write letters for those who wished to leave his diocese, should they properly request to depart; "And to the letter by which such permission is granted I shall add such details," he told Bishop Penalver, "that you may judge whether these priests are of such a character that the care of souls can be safely entrusted to them." Without it, all dioceses would be in danger of receiving each other's failures. "I solemnly assert that among those who hitherto have gone to Louisiana there were some who will be a source of scandal rather than edification unless their superiors are very vigilant." Indeed, Carroll added, some of the priests who left the trans-Appalachian for the trans-Mississippian West had probably done so "because they feared the attention of their superiors" and were seeking a new start.[18]

Even official church documents, however, could be misused, particularly when they traveled far from the administrator who had written them. For example, a straightforward *exeat*, an episcopal permission to move from one diocese to another, might be presented instead as a personal letter of recommendation. Bishop Carroll at one point had given up trying to reform a troublemaker named Father Flynn and had granted him a letter of *exeat* for leaving the country. The document noted the priest's behavior had been publicly, at least, acceptable. Instead of departing the United States as told, however, Flynn traveled about "availing himself of the favourable expressions" in the *exeat*, using the document to gain credibility with various Irish congregations, and creating headaches for their legitimate pastors. Several years later in 1809, when Flynn passed through Kentucky for a third time, the vicar-general, Father Badin, guessed the fellow priest might have changed for the better. Badin convinced himself and Flynn that the Irishman could help with the work of the Kentucky mission. Badin became cautious, however, when Flynn asked for faculties to say Mass. He reviewed the priest's letters of reference from Bishop Carroll and then conversed with Flynn about his "propensity to exceed in drinking." Despite Flynn's promise of "total abstentiousness" and Father Nerinckx's advice to give the man a small congregation at least, Badin decided to put him on probation instead, to see if he could be trusted. Two months later Badin reported that he stationed Flynn in his own residence so as to keep an eye on him. In the meantime, without having been granted faculties to do so, Flynn said Mass once before the people of St. Rose's Church. Badin disapproved of this impropriety, increasingly thinking Flynn unsuited for taking charge of a congregation.[19]

Badin had his hands full. Following years of solitary service in frontier communities, the Vicar of the West enjoyed at last the assistance and collegiality of fellow clergy in Kentucky, Ohio, and other western territories. But troublesome priests and imposters were a frequent worry, especially as they might be used to divide a parish against itself. In the autumn of 1810 Badin found lay leaders in the congregation were building a rebellion around the person of an imposter priest. Badin reported with obvious repugnance that there was "so much ignorance and carelessness about religion" in Vincennes that the troublemakers thought they would be successful. They made the pretender take "an oath before two magistrates" to "discharge [the] said functions to the best of his abilities." Thankfully, Badin noted, no one had taken action on the petition for incorporation he himself had outlined three years before. If the trustees or the "artful new-comer" had thought of it, they might have twisted the meaning of Badin's petition to the territorial government and instituted a "Calvinistical not . . . a Catholic Congreg."[20] Vigilance seemed necessary lest a false priest turn an entire parish away from the true church.

Facing so many problems at home, particularly in the West, Bishop Carroll and other members of the hierarchy grew cautious in accepting help from overseas. Letters of reference were especially crucial when the carrier appeared in the American diocese after traveling from afar. Father Charles Nerinckx of Belgium, for example, carefully introduced himself in 1803 to Bishop Carroll by way of letter and notification that two cardinals and a bishop were willing to act as his references. Precautions were necessary, Nerinckx hinted, "because to be unknown is to be unloved, as the proverb goes." Understanding the vicissitudes of the mail, Nerinckx explained he would be carrying a copy of the introductory letter he was writing, and he would be sending the original and another copy by different routes. Accompanying each would be a testimonial letter from his former vicar-general. "May [it] thus be clear that there is no suspicion of trickery, which cannot be sufficiently guarded against in these days of mounting wickedness."[21] Facsimiles verified documents; and documents authenticated the clergyman. Yet even vigilance and scrutiny sometimes failed.

Recognizing the torrents of extra correspondence, the years of trouble, and the scandal they generated, the bishop would be ever less likely to trust suspicious credentials. And he eventually resolved to take a hard line with errant priests. Carroll's long battle with an Irish priest named Simon Felix Gallagher convinced the prelate he long had been too lax in accepting new clergy because of the diocese's manpower shortages, and that he had been too slow in removing troublemakers. At the end of his spat with Gallagher in 1807 he wrote, "I am determined to discard from the service of the altar and the care of souls every intemperate priest. My past forbearance has perhaps increased the evil." Gallagher had arrived in 1793 with a laudatory letter of introduction from Archbishop John Troy of Dublin. Carroll, still desperate for able-bodied priests, ignored his suspicions of the "jejune character of the documents" and appointed the Irish priest to Charleston, South Carolina. Two years later the bishop heard reports that Gallagher was an alcoholic and a Freemason, had participated in a duel, and had had an affair with a married woman. Carroll wrote Gallagher that several people said "you have given offence or scandal often," appearing obviously drunk even in church and using "profane oaths." No progress toward building a church in the affluent city of Charleston had been made, he added, and all the materials used around Gallagher's altar showed "total inattention" to their "sacred uses." Moreover, Carroll noted, "I scarce ever hear you mentioned, by a Catholic or a protestant, especially the latter, who, tho they give you credit for your uncommon talents, do not add some remarks on [your] intemperance." Gallagher's ignominy was made worse by the attention it garnered from non-

Catholics. Overlooking the Irish émigré's dubious credentials in 1795 led to an intractable, thirteen-year problem.[22]

The Persisting Problem

A decade and a half later, long after established farms, brick churches, bustling towns, and even cities dotted the trans-Appalachian West, frontier circumstances of long distances, scattered parishes, immense dioceses, and insufficient numbers of clergy endured. Roving renegades still confounded Catholic authorities, and a dearth of able clergy and the geographic vastness of dioceses kept their attention stretched thin. Even after Bishop Benedict Joseph Flaget became the first western bishop and formed a diocese at Bardstown in 1811, with clergy, a seminary, convents, churches, and a cathedral, he struggled with clerical pretenders and malcontents. Trying to maintain order and authority was all the more difficult, he reported to Pope Pius VII, in a "country where the principles of liberty and independence are carried to such extremes," and where the schismatic priest "finds support and protection in the very Constitution of the Republic and has unbridled liberty to write and say whatever he pleases."[23]

Flaget knew the problem was larger than any one diocese, that a solution required closer cooperation between bishops. Unfortunately, these prelates were not closely linked. Flaget would remark on the isolation and distance between American bishops, explaining to the archbishop of Baltimore, "[We are] as strange to one another as we are with the bishops of China." Sadly, there "is so little correspondence" that each "has no knowledge of that of his neighbor."[24] Questionable or even insidious characters still could slip into respectable positions, shifting from one diocese to another, playing bishop against bishop.

Following his appointment as archbishop in 1818, and after making an extensive tour of his archdiocese, Ambrose Maréchal reported to Rome that the American church still had not established a native clergy. Most serious of all its many problems was the extreme shortage of priests. Maréchal conceded his continuing need for English, French, Belgian, German, and Irish clergy. Three years later, while in Rome, Maréchal submitted a report to the Propaganda outlining major problems facing the church in America. First on the list were the many problematic priests from Ireland. Maréchal asked the Propaganda to reprimand the Irish bishops who permitted them to travel. He also requested clear and strict rules for dismissing such unworthy clergymen in his archdiocese. In response, the Propaganda ordered Irish bishops to give letters of transfer only to priests actually invited by American bishops. Maréchal also complained that priests were abusing their right of appeal to the Holy See and that Rome was remiss in not reprimanding them. The cardinals' response indicated Rome would tend to back Maréchal more in the future.[25]

Maréchal and his bishops needed all the help they could get. Even clergymen with letters of reference and coming from the archbishop's cathedral itself might not prove dependable or even passable as priests. In the winter of 1820 Flaget explained to Archbishop Maréchal how one Mr. Roddy had arrived with sufficient letters of introduction, yet with other "extremely doubtful papers." Worse still was "his manner of saying Mass," which left Flaget and company "in a well-founded doubt that he was a priest." When the Kentucky bishop pointed out that Roddy had "neglected to say several prayers, even some words of the consecration," the so-called priest "had the impudence to tell me, in the presence of Msgr. David, that the intention supplied for everything." Insulted, Flaget put his pen to paper, reporting Roddy's misdeeds and observing that he was nothing if not a conceited, foolish dandy, as well as a "potens potator liquoris." Flaget added that he had rebuked the intemperate man and sent him away, taking the precaution, however, to write "to my neighbors to beware of the wolf in sheep's skin."[26]

In the 1820s the supply of priests in the trans-Appalachian West finally began to catch up to the demand created by growing parishes and emigrating families. Bishops Benedict Flaget in Bardstown, Joseph Rosati in St. Louis, Edward Fenwick in Cincinnati, and others were in a stronger position from which to evaluate the unfamiliar priests who traveled from the east coast. Flaget established a seminary, St. Thomas, in 1811 and a college, St. Joseph's, in 1819 to train his own clergy at Bardstown. During its first decade, however, St. Thomas Seminary met delays in producing priests. One-fourth of the seminarians in 1816, for example, a group of young men accepted into the Kentucky institution after arriving from France, were difficult to handle. One Mr. Millet was kept on hand only because Bishop Flaget admitted being desperately short of new priests. Another, Mr. Ganihil, aroused Flaget's suspicions enough for him to write to Ganihil's original diocese in France for background information and references. And a third vexatious seminarian, Mr. Grandchamp, made frequent, public complaints, calling the seminary nothing but "a hole." Father John Baptist David, who directed the seminary, was so determined to be rid of the ungrateful Frenchman that he gave him a horse and the supplies required to ride the several hundred miles back to Baltimore. David also sent word ahead, warning that Grandchamp should not be enrolled in any seminary there.[27]

When a questionable character named Father Carroll arrived in Louisville in 1822 and presented himself to the wary bishop, Flaget finally had enough manpower on hand, as well as enough experience, to put the new priest on probation. Even though Louisville was in need of a resident pastor, the bishop chose to send Father Carroll to "spend some weeks" in the seminary, to "make a spiritual retreat, and be able to note all . . . [the] ways of eating, drinking, dressing, praying, etc." of the Bardstown clergy. Flaget pointed out to the young man that clergy and "some Catholics of respectability" in Louisville had already reported their "great surprise" and "true scandal" at seeing the priest's gold ring, ruffles, and otherwise unpriestlike garb. The bishop ordered him to either comply or immediately cease exercising all functions in the diocese other than private Mass. Given this choice, Father Carroll instead skulked away, farther along the Ohio River, out from under the bishop's watchful eye. According to Flaget's second-in-command, Father David, after Father Carroll fled, "the reports that [came] concerning him from different quarters [did] not make us regret him."[28]

The following year, 1823, Flaget complained to Archbishop Maréchal in Baltimore about a young priest sent under letter of reference from Maréchal himself. Flaget had "positively refused" to accept the priest because his trusted friend, Father Nerinckx, had warned him about certain character flaws. Much to Flaget's surprise, the young clergyman, Father Van Vichel, appeared in Bardstown unannounced. "He was quick to show me his dismissorial which represents him as a priest of upright morals, of an eminent piety, &&," which came from Maréchal's hand. Desperate for priests in the growing diocese, Flaget gave the young man a chance to preach twice in the seminary. "Instead of drawing tears he made everyone laugh," because no one could understand a word of his attempt at English. After nine months of training, Flaget explained, he and his clergy had agreed that Van Vichel would be useless either for preaching or catechizing. Because the western bishop "had no other priests at . . . [his] disposal," however, he gave Van Vichel the chance to prove himself by ministering to the dying in Louisville. He failed there, too. "Impelled by a cupidity unseemly in a layman and unworthy of a priest," Van Vichel would press his "expiring penitents" with demands for donations to the church and payment for himself. Then he would push their families to fulfill their often unrealistic promises. Flaget had to chastise Van Vichel severely when it became apparent the young priest was "scandalizing the Protestants as he did the Catholics." Skills and character flaws might matter differently in the West than they had in the eastern states. In small trans-Appalachian communities, Catholics were in close contact with Baptists, Methodists, Presbyterians, and other groups. Preaching to a crowd was a crucial skill, highly valued in Protestant denominations and increasingly among Catholics. A clergyman lacking the ability was of little use. One who managed to alarm neighboring Protestants as well as lay Catholics was a liability.

If a priest recommended by the archbishop could fail so utterly in the West, the arrival of an unknown priest, or one with suspect credentials, was cause for even greater concern. In February 1825, one Patrick McGuiligen, a young priest who had departed from Bishop Rosati's St. Louis bailiwick, asked to be employed by Flaget in Kentucky. The bishop was suspicious even of the name the youth was using. In addition, McGuiligen's only papers were proof of ordination and an *exeat*, which in this case noted the holder must eventually be returned to Rosati. Apparently McGuiligen was a liar, and not a very adept one. He claimed he had left St. Louis because Rosati wanted only priests of the Lazarist order on hand, yet Flaget found this strange because he knew of other non-Lazarists in Rosati's diocese. "I do not know him from Eve or Adam," sputtered the frustrated bishop. "I have never heard of him" and only want to "learn all the truth of the story and especially the line of conduct that I must take with this young man" who is only practiced in "begging in a sneaking and ignoble manner."[29] McGuiligen's evasiveness and deceit were not given the chance to play themselves upon a parish. Quickly checked while still an internal matter, McGuiligen's behavior did not blossom into a public scandal.

Protestant Complications: Three Cases

Over the many errant clergy who went uncorrected, however, loomed the shadow of public scandal. Catholic leaders were apprehensive that internal disagreements about clerical discipline, control of parish life, and parish-episcopal relations would eventually attract negative attention. They worried most about stoking the low-burning fires of anti-Catholic sentiment. Officials weighed most major policy decisions, particularly those involving controversy and divisiveness, by asking themselves what non-Catholic neighbors and critics would believe, what they might say, how they could use the situation against Catholic interests, and to what extent the context of Protestant influence had caused or exacerbated the situation. Such concern affected not just their own perceptions but actual policies, decisions, and behavior.

Three serious crises involving unruly priests were exacerbated by church officials' concern for what Protestants were thinking and how they might react. The bishops' fear that abrupt disciplinary action could trigger a larger conflict involving non-Catholics in fact weakened their responses and resulted in lengthy controversy and greater scandal. In addition, church leaders generally chose to leave open the possibility that their renegades might repent and reform. This seemed to protract the scandals. For example, in 1799 Bishop John Carroll had to confront a German priest, Father Frederick Cesarius Reuter, who cast aspersions on Carroll, cultivated dissension among German Catholics in Baltimore, and then traveled to Rome and tried convincing the Holy See to partition the U.S. diocese and make him a bishop for German Americans. Reuter falsely claimed Carroll permitted no church business to be conducted in German and had threatened to excommunicate Germans who defied his rules. The beleaguered bishop, despite his frustration with Reuter, hoped the priest would see the error of his ways. Carroll's paramount concern remained that "all the disputes which [Reuter] ... stirred up will be quieted" and for something to be done "to preserve the Catholic faith in the estimation of heretics" in the United States.[30] Bishop Carroll was guiding myriad efforts to expand the church, the immediate success of which depended on good relations with the Protestant majority in America.

Charles Coomes

Father Charles Coomes's scandalous relationship in 1827 with a former woman religious, for instance, acquired added meaning both because local Protestants condemned it and because other Protestants relished his degradation and his divorcement from the church. In many ways, the controversy was highly charged because the improprieties involved seemed to fit Protestant stereotypes of priests and nuns as unnatural individuals ultimately doomed to some form of corruption. Church officials strove not only to discipline the errant priest but to preserve the image of Catholic institutions and personnel. Bishop John Baptist David, coadjutator to Bishop Flaget at Bardstown, struggled to describe the seemingly unprecedented situation of "the unfortunate priest whose horrible misdeeds wound us terribly and create a great scandal in the Church in Kentucky."

Only fourteen years before the scandalous affair, David, who had been in charge of the Bardstown seminary, described Coomes, a promising young seminarian, as "my son, my very dear son . . . my delight and consolation here." But in 1827, Coomes ran off with a young member of the Sisters of Charity whose preliminary vows had expired. His fellow clergy recognized trouble in his unusual "attachments" to the nuns, over whom he had been given a special charge; he repeatedly was warned, and he repeatedly sought forgiveness.[31]

Coomes then asked for an *exeat* to transfer himself to the settlements of Missouri. Upon receiving it, he raced back to the Sisters of Charity and convinced them he would escort the young woman in question back to her parents, since she was so unsuited to and unhappy with the convent. In Missouri he received Bishop Rosati's permission to place her with the Sisters of Loretto. Coomes later asked to have her placed in his own household as housekeeper. This being refused, the errant priest and his love went back up the Ohio to Louisville and then to Bardstown, said David, "to the great scandal of the people." Still seeking acceptance, the two arrived at his parents' home, only to be turned away. Despite Bishop Flaget's intervention and offer to arrange a respectable separation, Coomes again went back on his penance and eloped with the woman. According to

David, they found a means of "seducing" her father, "who for many years had only the name Catholic," and he helped them arrange a marriage. Immediately Coomes and the woman were excommunicated, and Bishop Flaget with Fathers Francis Patrick Kenrick and Guy Ignatius Chabrat officially denounced the two, first in the Bardstown cathedral, then ten days later at the church in Union County, in the far western portion of the state, where Coomes had settled.[32]

The Coomes affair was not solely a Catholic one. Protestants participated in the story and gave it shape. It was a Methodist preacher who finally performed the marriage ceremony that united the priest and former Sister of Charity. Protestant opinion also added a layer of opprobrium on their heads: after denouncing Coomes in his home parish in Union County, Bishop Flaget wrote to Father David that the man was "despised very much by all the people, Protestant and Catholic" in the area. And Protestant influence as well as the historical context of poor sectarian relations in the country gave the affair a grander meaning. Every Catholic loss might be a Protestant gain. Father David worried about both the shame of too much publicity before non-Catholics and the danger of allowing Coomes to disappear from view. With the former priest in hiding, worried David, we "do not know what he is doing, although it is very certain that he is doing harm." Coomes stayed away from the Union County church but, at the "persuasion of some Baptists, who triumph in his defection," he visited the local courthouse during a day of public events there. His Baptist supporters "advised him to speak up in his defense," to clear his name before the crowd, but Coomes "barely raised his head and kept a profound silence."

In the end, the Kentucky clergy felt Coomes received what he deserved and pointed to his fall as a morality tale. The renegade priest and spouse ended up in a cabin on the Ohio River, selling wood to passing steamboats. One clergyman "compared him to [a] turkey-buzzard. . . . [T]hat proud man, who arose even above his bishop and the rest of the clergy has plunged into the filth, and feeds himself on it, and infects the world with his scandalous life." Coomes could have been a lesson to Catholic and non-Catholic alike: "behold, he is reduced to poverty to the point, after his sacreligious act, to work for 25 cents a day to gather up the grain of a neighbor."[33]

John Thayer

Father Badin was grateful to Bishop Carroll for sending new priests to assist with the fruitful but dauntingly vast field of Kentucky. Parishioners at White Sulphur were especially pleased to be welcoming a celebrity like Father John Thayer as their new pastor. Indeed, according to Badin, "public opinion was in his favor," and "Catholics and Protestants in the Counties of Washington and Nelson are anxious to see him." Father Thayer was a renowned figure. He had been a Congregationalist minister in Massachusetts until he visited Rome to prove to himself the falseness of popery and ended up converting to Catholicism. He was ordained in 1783. When he returned to the United States, Thayer's fanaticism born of conversion led him to begin attacking Protestantism. Once, he rashly told Benjamin Franklin and John and Abigail Adams over dinner that he planned to convert the entire country, beginning with Boston. Indeed, Franklin later told his friend Bishop Carroll that he thought the young man "sincere" but not "wise."[34]

Thayer proved to be great trouble in New England. He and a French priest, John Rousselet, struggled for control of the Boston parish, causing Carroll much difficulty, primarily due to the very public nature of their contest. It was unseemly for two Catholic priests to fight, not simply from their pulpits, but in the pages of Boston newspapers. Nothing, said Carroll, "can contribute more to vilify us in the eyes of our Protestant Brethren, or give more pleasure to the enemies of our religion." Thayer had started the press attacks on Rousselet and also began claiming that he alone had authority over all the Indians and Catholics of Massachusetts. Worse still, noted the exasperated bishop, Thayer had published in a newspaper a "sort of general challenge to all adversaries of the Catholic cause," telling them to "bring their objections" to his sermons. When a Protestant minister answered Thayer's challenge, the priest announced he would "stand his ground," and Carroll "gave him a good lecture for his rashness, & presumption in undertaking such a step without advising with, or being authorized by his Bishop."

For two years Carroll mediated between Thayer and Father Rousselet in Boston, trying to keep their "scandalous" affair from being front-page news. In March 1791 the bishop threatened Rousselet with publicizing certain unflattering information about the priest that had come from his former superior in France. Carroll assured Rousselet that giving up his pastoral claims immediately was the only way of "saving your reputation from the discredit into which it will fall, if the accts [*sic*] from France should be divulged." Later that summer, Carroll forced Thayer to sign an act of submission retracting an earlier public statement to the effect that "he would not obey the Bishop, but would place himself [only] under the Jurisdiction of the Pope." Carroll next sent Thayer to Maryland and then Virginia, but the priest's views on slavery caused him to be transferred again. By 1797 Carroll had need for him in Kentucky, but sent him there in 1799 with difficulty because Thayer objected to frontier postings and wanted to be "conspicuous" in a large city.[35]

Within weeks of his arrival in the western parish of White Sulphur, Kentucky, in February 1799, Thayer was causing a rumpus. He aggravated sectarian tensions and brought attention to his New England politics and views on slavery. Nevertheless, Badin, who was overjoyed at receiving help on the Kentucky frontier, initially reported, "The Protestant ministers look on him with an envious eye seeing their meeting deserted by numbers of their hearers" eager to attend Thayer's public appearances. Despite these early signs of promise, Badin began to notice the tactlessness, self-righteousness, and belligerence that had caused Carroll to exile Thayer from the east. The firebrand mocked local Protestants, even calling Methodists "fools" in his sermons, thinking his polemical style would ultimately win converts. Worse yet, reported Badin, he "enervates the authority of masters over the negroes" by speaking against the institution of slavery. Ironically, Thayer himself was benefiting from the labor of slaves attached to his parish's glebe lands, would later pin his grand hopes for founding a convent in Kentucky on the capital produced by his slaves, and within a year would be scandalizing even his slave-owning neighbors by his alleged ill treatment of his own slave, Henny. Badin claimed, in any case, that Thayer, "blindly & publicly devoted to their cause," was declaring slaves as "fully virtuous as the white people of his congregation." While insulting slave owners in the area by word and hypocritical behavior, the priest from Boston also criticized the political beliefs of his backcountry neighbors. He imprudently assailed the Democratic Republicans in a region long enamored of Jefferson and his party. His tenure in the Bluegrass state would be brief.[36]

Not only were Thayer's outspoken Federalist, antislavery, and anti-Protestant views tearing against the grain of his parishioners and neighbors, but just as he had been testing Bishop Carroll's patience and challenging his authority, once comfortable in Scott County he began to defy Badin's authority. Badin's first mistake was in telling Thayer upon his arrival in Kentucky that he wished Thayer to succeed him as Carroll's Vicar of the West. Perhaps the promise of higher office encouraged even worse behavior. In February 1801 Badin had the "painful task" of reporting to Carroll that the people of Scott County were united "in their regret that M. Thayer did ever come to Kky." Badin wished he had never encountered the man and his "overbearing dispositions" against any "who dare to oppose his conduct or his views." Thayer had the cheek to ask Badin, his superior, to appear before the Scott County congregation to declare that Thayer was his co-vicar-general in Kentucky. Thayer reportedly had been telling parishioners that he (not Badin) had authority over all priests in the state.[37]

Thayer's controversial western career was cut short in the end by scandal that could not be ignored. It began with shadowy accusations of what Bishop Carroll described as having "sollicited to base acts, or . . . had unbecoming writings, touches or words" in "the tribune of confession, or immediately before or after confession." In February 1801, only two years after his arrival in Kentucky, the priest stood accused of hugging, kissing, making indecent propositions to, and threatening several of his female parishioners. Mary Jameston, who had trained to become a nun in Maryland before leaving the religious life, was perhaps the most abused. According to Badin, she swore before the justice of the peace that Thayer had made "several infamous attempts in the Tribunal" (i.e., during confession) and committed "not adultery . . . but a sin by the eyes, which a chaste husband himself would not commit." Badin forwarded to Carroll the affidavit from Justice of the Peace Twyman, who wrote that Mrs. Jameston had testified that while in confession Thayer "asked & insisted on her to draw up her cloaths & shew him her private parts, and gave for reason that he wished to know what appearance that part of a woman bore." Upon her horrified refusal, Thayer then tried to swear his penitent to silence. Mary Jameston, her husband, and the parishioners who knew her secret must have been outraged. Months later, long after Thayer had left, Badin would give a lengthy and sympathetic account of Mary Jameston's long-standing virtue and piety, as well as her continuing mental anguish: "her sufferings have been inconceivable." And in the same letter to Carroll, several pages further, Badin remarked on his own efforts to allay suspicions about priests and women in close quarters. Not only was he keeping the "confession-door widely open," but he had advised Father Fournier not to hire a young housekeeper. Neither gambit prevented Badin and Fournier from being attacked—Badin by a protestant in Scott County; Fournier by a member of one of his own congregations.[38]

In the midst of the Thayer scandal, Badin had worked hard at damage control. While investigating complaints and subduing Thayer, the Vicar of the West also attempted to calm the parish and keep the news from spreading, particularly to non-Catholics. He issued six directives to the Scott County congregants: first, Thayer was still the "lawful Pastor" until the bishop said otherwise; second, the benefits of sacraments at Thayer's hands were still valid; third, like any other Catholic, Thayer could benefit from penance and absolution, and again become a worthy man and priest; fourth, the parishioners should visit Badin or Father Fournier for confession if necessary, and should remember that "they could receive absolution in danger of death from any Priest whatsoever"; fifth, Scott County Catholics were still required to attend Thayer's sermons, "as long as he does not Preach against faith or morality"; and sixth, to prevent any further complaints "let a confessionary or confession box be built" or "let the door of the confession-rooms be kept open." Badin's further request to the parish was that persons spreading the salacious details, "true or false," to members of other denominations should stop and ask forgiveness for their own sins. In the midst of the troubles gnawing at the heart of the congregation, Badin was worried about Protestant opinion. In addition, the vicar knew that word was spreading to Washington and Nelson counties and that the scandal "renders the situation of Priests in this state more disagreeable." Nor were Badin's fears about public perception of the sordid affairs exaggerated. If the accusations were true, then Thayer had violated his vows, the honor of the priesthood, the sanctity of the confessional, and the relationship of confessor to penitent. Such charges also had the potential of playing into the current anti-Catholic stereotypes of lecherous priests using the confessional to seduce young women. Apparently out of concern for themselves or their sisters in Scott County, the Catholic women of Pottinger's Creek and Bardstown took up a collection and raised a substantial sum to pay for the traveling expenses of a new priest.[39]

Bishop Carroll quickly ordered Badin to resolve the scandal. He empowered Badin and Father Fournier to investigate the charges, to cross-examine Thayer and other witnesses, to record the testimonies, and "then render judgement." The priests were to determine whether Thayer had "in the tribune of confession, or immediately before or after confession" of an unnamed person "by a pretext, word, deed or writing, or by any other means whatsoever . . . sollicited [sic] to base acts," or that Thayer " had unbecoming writings, touches or words." Carroll remarked that he believed the charges were true since he had heard similar rumors when Thayer was in Boston. In July Carroll wrote to Thayer and suggested he leave Kentucky quietly. Thayer retired to the east coast and later took a ship to England. He finished his career ministering to the poor of Ireland.[40]

Francis Fromm

One of the most complicated, drawn-out, and bizarre cases involving a renegade priest occurred in Westmoreland County, Pennsylvania, during the 1790s. The example of the Dutch priest, Father Francis Rogatus Fromm, is a fitting conclusion for this chapter because it illustrates so many of the difficulties before the church. Fromm was an unknown character, slow to learn English, most interested in securing property and an independent living for himself, inclined to incite factions in his congregation, unwilling to obey his bishop, and skillful in exploiting the delays of the mail and distorting the meanings of letters and written orders. Fromm's adventures also show how the exploits of a troublesome priest could be amplified and complicated by Catholic concern for Protestant opinion. Fromm caused controversy and recognized the advantage he gained from making it public. He was willing to ally with Protestants against his superiors and unafraid to challenge the church in court.

Fromm's arrival in the United States and appearance before Bishop Carroll in 1789 was inauspicious from the start. Carroll sent him to the mission at Conewago, Pennsylvania, where two German priests already resided, and wrote to Fromm's superior in Germany, indignant that the official had ignored Carroll's request for English-speaking clergy. To complicate matters, Fromm had spent Carroll's travel money on books and vestments instead of paying the ship captain for passage. In 1790 Carroll appointed Fromm to Lancaster as pastor, but soon after ordered him back to Germany, saying parishioners had complained that Fromm still could not speak sufficient English to preach or hear confessions, was unfriendly, had criticized the catechisms widely used in the parish, and rarely said Mass on weekdays. Carroll admonished the man: "whether it be from some weakness of your character or because of the prejudices of others it seems that your labors will bear no fruit for the spreading of faith here." Fromm retorted that he had been hearing confessions in English for seven months, that "the Germans who complained" were backsliders who persisted in their "manners by which they offend non-Catholics," and that the books he had condemned were non-Catholic. A few months later, Carroll ordered Fromm to stay in Lancaster while he sorted things out, yet the disobedient priest headed farther west, to the county of Westmoreland, in the vicinity of Pittsburgh.[41]

The parish of Sportsman's Hall, the Catholic center of Westmoreland County, would be Fromm's home for the next eight years as he tested Bishop Carroll's rule. Fromm arrived at Sportsman's Hall, the estate of the deceased priest Father Theodore Brouwers, in May 1791. This was the same parish that the German priest Father John Baptist Causse had attempted to commandeer the previous year. Accepted and elected by the local trustees, Fromm persuaded them to deny appointment of any other clergy while he went back east to secure the parish for himself. Bishop Carroll and his vicar-general in Pennsylvania, Father James Pellentz, began to suspect that the renegade Father Causse was encouraging Fromm's rebelliousness and that both were "purposely spreading the rumor among the Germans" that Carroll was not their lawful bishop. Carroll accused Fromm specifically of "trying to alienate the affections of my diocesans, especially the Germans for whom, you assert, I do not care." The controversy simmered for two years until Fromm boldly claimed he had a letter of commission, as a regular priest, from his archbishop in Mainz, Germany, that fully authorized his actions in establishing his own parish in western Pennsylvania. It would later prove to be a simple letter of *exeat* usually granted to priests leaving one diocese to travel to another. Still, Fromm demanded that Carroll and vicar-general Pellentz return the "priestly vestment and Church paraphenalia" that the previous priest had left at Sportsman's Hall. He concluded by intimating that Carroll had intercepted a "chalice of silver and gold plated which friends in Germany" had sent by way of Baltimore. Carroll was seething but could do little. As he put it, he and Fromm both knew Fromm was baldly disputing his rule: "though you deny being under my authority, I know that you exercised jurisdiction over those within my diocese. There you celebrate Mass, administer the Sacraments, and carry on other pastoral activities. I doubt whether you act in good faith and whether you are unaware that all duties performed by you were invalid." A thoroughly frustrated and disgusted Carroll revoked Fromm's faculties to serve as priest.[42]

Fromm faced a daunting situation but was in a strong position. Hundreds of miles from his bishop and on the other side of the state and its mountainous interior from his vicar-general, Fromm need not fear direct intrusion. Enough trustees of Westmoreland County sided with him, and he physically occupied the house and farmland at Sportsman's Hall that had been purchased and then left by his predecessor, the deceased Father Brouwers. Rather than replying to Carroll's letter revoking his powers as a priest, Fromm waited six months, then scribed an excuse for not leaving his parish. He even requested more religious items for his ministry. Between the lines, he was using the spiritual well-being of his flock as a point of negotiation. Fromm listed holy oils, missals, and catechisms partly to demonstrate how busy and needed he was on the frontier. The Dutchman knew the difficulty Carroll had in finding replacements. His gambit worked. Carroll offered to reinstate Fromm's faculties, appoint him to the parish, and supply him with cash if he retracted his public slanders and recognized "episcopal authority over seculars and regulars" alike. Fromm's reply in March 1794 was a long and careful analysis of the entire four-year scandal, concluding with his right to stay because he was fulfilling the terms set out in Brouwers's will. The bishop was baffled by Fromm's position in defiance of canon law. "How could anyone, with even the slightest acquaintance with the science of Theology, come to the conclusion" that Father Brouwers, who had headed a mission on the island of

Java, carried the same powers of appointment that Carroll did in the United States? "If a man of little learning had done this, there might be room for indulgence; but not so when you are the culprit."[43]

The next surprise was Carroll's. No sign of contrition appeared from Fromm. In summer 1795 the bishop suspended the disobedient priest "from every exercise of your (sacred) order even that of celebrating Mass and I hereby forbid you herewith to perform any function of your priesthood" until appearing in Baltimore to face charges. Simultaneously, Bishop Carroll notified the "Catholics of Westmoreland and the Neighboring Counties" that "Rev. Father Fromm was never commissioned to exercise pastoral functions" in their parish, that the wayward priest was suspended, and that all were warned not to attend his Masses. When Carroll sent a representative, Father Sylvester Phelan, to replace Fromm in October 1795, he soon learned that the renegade clergyman probably would be recognized as the legitimate pastor by the state and could rely on his predecessor's will, which made the priest's property (Sportsman's Hall) and the position of pastor the legal right of whatever priest agreed to care for the parishioners. Phelan did note a weakness, however, that should encourage the bishop to pursue a legal solution. Phelan observed that while Fromm on one hand claimed he legally owned Brouwers's old estate for having fulfilled the various stipulations of the will, on the other hand he had signed an additional contract with the parish trustees for use of the plantation in return for his services. In other words, if Fromm put so much stock in Brouwers's will, why had he signed a supplementary contract?[44]

A week later the intrigue thickened. Parishioners, executors of the will acting as de facto trustees, had gone to court to win back control of the Brouwers estate. They claimed that Fromm's supplemental contract for financial support in return for one year of his priestly service vitiated/nullified his prior claim to the Brouwers house and property. An astonished Father Phelan reported to Carroll that Fromm's play was to convince everyone that six of his enemies had conspired to shoot at him while he slept "about 10pm Sunday night." Conveniently, one of the alleged six was Phelan. More convenient for Fromm's court case, the rest of them were the "upstanding members of the congregation" or the "executors of Brouwer's will" who were trying to oust him. All were witnesses who could swear they had seen Fromm destroy "violently" the very "paper in which he obligated himself to serve the congregation" for a year in return for money and the use of the plantation. More suspicious still was Fromm's timing. He raised the alarm on election day for the sheriff when there would be the largest audience to hear his accusations. Phelan thought Fromm's attempt to discredit witnesses absurd and insufferable: "a most dreadfull man devoid of all religion and conscience and capable of any mischief." While Fromm thrashed about the county, Phelan and the majority of the congregation sought a way to eject him.[45]

The solution became a legal solution. Vicar-General Pelentz, the parishioners (particularly the executors of Father Brouwers's will), and the bishop united to use Pennsylvania state law to counter Fromm's physical presence and refusal to depart, his use of certain documents to bolster his claims, his handful of lay supporters, and a perceived sense of antagonism from some neighboring non-Catholics. Their legal strategy became twofold. First, they hoped for the state to provide an act of incorporation that would free them from the bonds of the old Brouwers's will and from Fromm. Second, Carroll had Phelan find a lawyer to counter the renegade with a legal suit. Their case was not solid, Phelan thought, because the congregation might be reluctant to pay the expense of becoming incorporated and because Fromm possessed a "paper signed by our rash, impudent and foolish blockheads" acknowledging Fromm's authority from the archbishop of Mainz, Germany, their satisfaction with the quality of his preaching, and their election of him to assume the pastor-for-life position of his predecessor, Father Brouwers.[46]

The context of Protestant-Catholic relations further complicated matters. Bishop Carroll's envoy, Father Phelan, worried that the region's Presbyterian population was waiting to capitalize on the brewing controversy. "It will be proclaimed throughout the country and made a dreadful story by the time it reached Baltimore and Philadelphia," said Phelan. "It may serve all in the country as a foil to presbyterians to deaden the scandal of one of their ministers being executed at Bedford for murder last Saturday." Phelan was referring to the case of a German minister named Spanzenberger who had stabbed a man to death. All was coming to a head that fall and would, hopefully, be resolved, Phelan thought, the following spring. In April, he crowed, "we will discover much and clearly show if the Calvinistic junto that glory in the ruin of rising Catholicity be able to give a bias to justice and uphold Fromm as they intend." It grew apparent in the winter of 1796 that Fromm was eager to find allies among local Protestants. Announcing that his life was in danger, he wrote a will naming three executors and signed by three witnesses—six men, most of whom were neighboring Protestants of prominence. One of Fromm's allies, according to Phelan, was "Mr. Campbell, a storekeeper in Greensburg, an apostate from Catholicity and a notorious libertine," who boasted that he would fight Carroll and his Jesuits. Campbell and another convinced Fromm to appeal directly to the parish, announce he would be confronting Carroll in Baltimore, and ask for their support. "This the people pray me to tell your Reverence," wrote Phelan, "they cannot think of" and would rather give up all public worship rather than submit to "such a reprobate."[47]

In April Fromm found a new way to aggravate his parishioners. He appealed to fellow Germans in the area, even Protestants, to attend his Easter sermon. Instead of being sympathetic, the German Catholics, said Phelan, were upset that Fromm, so much worse than the earlier renegade, the German priest Causse, still headed their parish after years of scandal. Later he was said to be preparing a community of non-Catholic Germans to receive him should he be ousted. Phelan described this new group as "German Calvinists who are at a variance with their poor tool for a minister" who "accordingly attend his [Fromm's] preaching every Sunday."[48]

The legal strategies had stalled over the long winter, and it was clear that the secular plans needed an injection of religious justification. First, parishioners were unwilling or unable to pay for an act of incorporation. Second, before a legal suit could be filed and heard, the church's non-Catholic lawyer, Mr. Young, had to learn the fundamentals of canon law, using materials supplied by Father Phelan, such as notes on the Council of Trent. In April, Phelan and Young agreed that the civil case should pivot on a religious point: "Fromm must be put out of the means of pleading himself a Catholic priest" by being excommunicated. Priest and lawyer recommended the bishop expel the errant clergyman from the fold and pen a clear and simple explanation of the Catholic canon laws in violation. Young, relayed Phelan, thought this "necessary on account of a court and country quite unaccustomed to" Catholic laws, for the locals were all "Presbyterians true blue."[49]

Carroll, however, decided not to excommunicate Fromm for three reasons. First, Fromm had already disqualified himself from sacerdotal functions by his behavior. Second, the excommunication process was too long, especially if Fromm resisted, and might not be completed in time for use in court by June. Third, Carroll predicted, Fromm's lawyer would use a decree of excommunication at this time and for this purpose to "conjure up the frightful tales of Popes, deposing, excommunicating, laying under interdict, etc." A preferable line of argument, Carroll thought, lay in making the following four points. First, Roman Catholic law prohibited a priest exercising care for a parish without its bishop's authorization. Second, the synod of the clergy in Baltimore in 1791 declared any priest attempting to do so could be suspended. Third, Fromm had admitted in letter to Carroll that he had never been appointed. And fourth, Fromm admitted in another letter that Carroll had officially revoked his faculties as priest.[50]

Tension persisted in Westmoreland County for years until the Court of Common Pleas of the Fifth District's verdict in December 1798. The lawyers on both sides had to establish a common understanding on a number of points of Catholic and Protestant tradition, dogma, and law. Their efforts were fascinating and reflect the complexity of contact points between religious groups, as well as the potential for mutual influence, dependence, and, especially, equality under the law. Fromm's lawyer made two key points. First, that the parish's first priest, Theodore Brouwers, who purchased the land and property at Sportsman's Hall for himself, wrote a will that would turn ownership over to the first priest who served the parish and said four Masses per year for Brouwers's soul. And that priest was Fromm. Second, the lawyer argued, the Catholic Church recognized that a priest remained a priest whether he was suspended or excommunicated. Even under mortal sin a priest could still say the Mass. For his Protestant audience, the lawyer made the following comparison, emphasizing the Calvinist aspects of a point of doctrine pertaining to the Catholic priest's situation: "[A] priest cannot Become a layman[.] [T]he laying on of hands Gives the holy Spirit which Cannot be Taken away[;] to suppose Otherwise would be inconsistent with the presumption on which the Ordination is founded, that he is in a state of Grace[,] [that] the perseverance of Saints is an Established Doctrine of the Calvinist Church, [that] the elect cannot fall away[,] [and] the Spirit of God cannot be taken away by the censure of the Church." Not to be outdone, Mr. Young, the opposing counsel, also borrowed a page from John Calvin. Applying the doctrine of proof, he argued that good, blameless, blessed people necessarily had the appearance of such. "I shall not Dispute whether the Defendent be in a state of Grace or not, all I say is, that, if he be[,] he has[,] by Contradicting the solemn obligation [of obedience] which he has taken Upon him[,] not shewn any markes of Grace." Where the defense portrayed Fromm as an individual before God and answerable only to God, Young emphasized Fromm's place within a system and obvious failure in upholding his vows.[51]

On behalf of the executors of Brouwers's will and Phelan and Carroll, Young appealed to any sense of shared heritage between the Protestant court and his Catholic clients. He drew on the U.S. Constitution and Pennsylvania state constitution first, followed by a plea to common sense and common danger, saying "all sects of Religion are Protected by Our laws; and if an intruder be Indulged in possession of Property belonging to the Roman Catholick Church, the same thing will happen in Every Church." This case, he declared, "must be Decided with a Due Regard to the Rules of the Church of which the Defendent is a member." Just because Fromm had permanent priestly skills and spirit, asked Young, did he have a right to exercise them anywhere? In case his listeners would distance themselves from the Catholic Church, again he drew them into a sense of common heritage, this time with biblical verse. If Fromm defied the rules of his own religion, then "he is not a pastor . . . he Cometh not in by the Door but Climbeth in at a window, and is not the True Shepherd, but a thief and a Robber." Young concluded with a nationalistic appeal that assumed his listeners shared a distaste for British arrogance, presumption, and tradition. Perhaps distracting them from the foreign qualities of Roman Catholicism, he called on a common American bias: "suppose a Complete scholar Bred at the University of Oxford instructed as a lawyer at the Inns of Court in Westminster hall advanced to the Degree of Sergeant or kings Counsel, arrives here, is he Intitled, without any Other formality to appear at the Bar of any Court in this Country?" Fromm should, said Young, "retire to his own Country and there Exercise" his "Gifts of learning and Grace" in the place "where the Exercise of them was first permitted." Refusing to submit to an American bishop's authority and claiming to rely instead on orders from the Archbishop of Mainz, said the lawyer, proved Fromm a renegade and a foreigner.[52]

In the end, the court ruled against Fromm. Old Father Brouwers, by dint of his written will, evidently wanted a good pastor for the congregation. Fromm might or might not be such a man. The court believed, however, that Fromm was "not Regularly admitted to Exercise the pastoral Functions in this Congregation." If this were not about Catholics but "an Independent Congregation acknowledging no superior Authority," then "the ascent of the Congregation might have been . . . sufficient." In other churches no minister can perform duties without approval of a superior, the court declared; "there are Grades of Jurisdiction, General and National Councils, General assemblys, Synods, and presbyteries, Pope, Patriarch, Metropolitan, suffragan Archbishop and bishop." The defendant had no right to defy Bishop Carroll, whom the court recognized as the head of the Catholic Church in the United States. Unabashed, unstoppable, Fromm appealed the case to a higher court. Waiting for the new case to be tried, he reportedly "harrangued against devotion to the Blessed Virgin, and against clerical celibacy," while making "frequent attempts at marriage." The church was spared further scandal when the man was taken by yellow fever during the plague year of 1799.[53]

Throughout Father Fromm's controversy, one of the church's principal concerns remained its reputation and the damage the rogue priest was doing to relations between Catholics and non-Catholics. Clamping down, Bishop Carroll responded by asserting orthodoxy and episcopal authority gradually over the space of several years. Subtle tactics and forgiveness solved nothing, however, and Fromm, like other renegade priests, made the most of any slack he found. Once other means were exhausted, Bishop Carroll shifted to a secular court to have Fromm removed. Carroll and his lawyer structured their case in a way that seemed to appeal to the clergy and lay members of Protestant denominations in western Pennsylvania. The bishop and his counsel ultimately asserted that the Catholic Church, like all other denominations, should be left free to organize and discipline its clergy. Catholic leaders, in other words, drew on similarities with Protestant authorities to make their own case for being free to be distinctively Catholic.

The problem of contumacious priests strengthened the traditional, authoritarian development of the American Catholic Church. A chronic shortage of clerical manpower, the desperate spiritual and social needs of far-flung congregations, the geographical distance between diocesan center and periphery, and early bishops' lack of alternatives left them more reliant on questionable priests than they would have liked. Such conditions, as well as the desire not to exacerbate scandal, and a willingness to allow congregations the chance to work out their own problems if possible, meant that episcopal authorities initially were moderate in reproaching or removing renegades.

By the late 1820s and early 1830s the church was better situated to crack down on dissent, ineptitude, and scandal. An infrastructure of church buildings, seminaries, schools, and convents supplied church leaders with the personnel necessary to monitor, discipline, and replace problematic clergy. Frequent experience with troublemaking priests from the 1780s in the East through the 1820s in the West made plain the need for immediate and strict church authority rather than gradual negotiation. After years of experience with controversy, Bishop Carroll and other church officials in the United States increasingly relied on guidance from Rome. As historian Thomas W. Spalding has noted, John Carroll's many encounters with problem priests were among the array of difficulties that caused him to adopt traditional European solutions. Continual headaches forced Carroll and the American hierarchy to turn to the Congregation for the Propagation of the Faith "more often than he probably wished and to become increasingly dependent on it for support," and to look to his extensive network of European friends and colleagues for advice.[54] The American Catholic Church in the 1830s, therefore, seemed tied more closely than ever to the Roman hierarchy, despite Carroll's efforts in the late eighteenth century to give it an American cast. Hoping to solve the problem of scandalous renegade priests, in part to defuse criticism from non-Catholic observers, Catholics in the United States set themselves even further apart from Protestant denominations.

Chapter 4

Making Sacred Place

Churches and Religious Goods

Just as priests proved to be conduits of custom and authority and focal points of Catholic-Protestant relations, so were the material manifestations of Catholicism a means of contact between Catholics and non-Catholics. Church buildings, their elements of decor, and the religious objects of Catholic ritual and devotion were representations of the lines of continuity anchoring the faithful in tradition and to the authority of the hierarchy in Europe. At the same time, they created unique spaces at which Catholic and non-Catholic could meet. As Catholics claimed western ground, sacralized the landscape with churches, and proliferated religious goods from statues to candles, they were re-creating a Catholic world within a Protestant context.

That these material expressions of Catholicism could be potent for Protestants as well as Catholics was made plain in the diary and letters of a twenty-year-old Presbyterian named John Brown. The young man departed on horseback from his home in Clarksville, Tennessee, in late September 1821 and headed for Kentucky, where he planned to study law in Louisville. Setting out on Monday the 24th, he was thrown from his horse, which he took as a bad portent. Friday the 28th brought "the most tremendous claps of thunder," a "dark gloomy valley," and "fogs arising." These again, he took as signs "ominous of bad consequences." Riding onward from

Bardstown on Saturday the 29th he heard the bell rung "for church in the Cathedral—the low hollow distant knell." Somber and foreboding, the aural effect "produced feeling" that he was unable to describe fully, yet which he thought echoed both the "quietness of the country," an ominous foreboding, and the grim seriousness of his youthful undertaking.[1] The Catholic church bell, a sign of the sacralization of the Kentucky landscape, had a powerful effect.

John Brown's response to the physical representation of Catholicism was more apparent, however, less than three weeks later, after he had settled into a routine of study in Louisville. Visiting a Catholic church for the first time, the young Protestant encountered an alarmingly different world. "When I entered the first thing that struck my eyes was an awful representation of the mangled body of Christ on the Cross," he said. "I was struck with astonishment and horror and still greater was my surprise when presently arose the priests to put on their ecclesiastical garb which was truly odd."[2] The law student was shocked by what he saw. Yet, like many of his contemporaries, Brown also was fascinated by the Catholic architectural space, its heavy and baroque decoration, and the exoticness of the European Catholic aesthetic.

Brown's careful delineation of the sights and sounds before him demonstrated the multiple ways in which Catholic liturgical proceedings and sacred interiors might affect the uninitiated. His senses were nearly overwhelmed, he wrote to a friend; the church "is executed with a degree of splendor entirely indescribable."[3] The image of a crucifix "struck" his eyes; he observed "kindled . . . fires upon the altar"; and he watched the "monkey capers the priests performed." His ears took in their "unintelligible words before the cross," their "muttering" in a "low tone of voice as not distinctly to be heard," the "ringing of a small bell" that caused people to kneel and to stand repeatedly. Brown claimed these Catholics were "deluded" and bewitched by a "Satanic spell" that dimmed their perception. He mocked the "variegated dresses and monkey shines of the priests before the altar." Still, he was mesmerized by the experience and impressed with the gilded grandeur on display.

The Catholic edifice itself was "one of the most splendid assemblages of ornament that can be imagined," he wrote. It was a large structure of brick "whose top appears to reach the clouds," its windows were "ornamental in the most beautiful manner," and the cross on its roof peak was "of the most brilliant gold." And that was not all. Inside there was more munificence: "the Bishops seats and his crozier are pure glittering gold," the various clergy were dressed in "the most rich apparel embossed with gold from head to foot," and upon the altar were "a vast number of golden and silver vessels, candlesticks, etc." Brown concluded his written description, he stated, only because he had run out of room on the sheet of paper; otherwise he would have given a fuller account.[4]

This Protestant law student struggling to define himself in his new vocation, in a new city, far from family and friends, would not have been alone in experiencing mixed reactions to such luxurious expressions of Catholicism. Few Americans outside the Catholic enclaves in Maryland, Pennsylvania, the urban East, north-central Kentucky, or near the old French settlements along the Mississippi River and Great Lakes, would have had close contact with the elaborate trappings of what John Brown would call "popery." Although this young man's rationalist distaste for superstition magnified his reaction, his description serves to remind us how startling Catholic ornamentation, architecture, ritual, and religious goods could be, set against a more austere Protestant American landscape. After making his way through forests, along winding tracks, anticipating the comforts of civilization, Brown found himself in a still-alien environment. His wide-eyed account suggests that when Catholics captured the attention of neighboring non-Catholics, the reactions could be highly charged.

Another Protestant westerner expressed surprise at the visual, aural, and olfactory opulence of a Catholic church on his first visit. John Wrenshall, a Methodist preacher and merchant from Pittsburgh, made a winter journey down the Ohio and Mississippi Rivers to do business in New Orleans. On March 3, 1797, Wrenshall attended Sunday Mass at a church he described as "an elligant edifice." When he entered the building he "was struck with the splendid decorations of the place," and although surprised and perhaps feeling out of place, Wrenshall "took a seat, and viewed myself for the present in a place erected for divine worship, and acted accordingly." His diary goes on to record the impressive style of the service, which began with a "number of Men and Boys, who sung well" and were "accompanied with the sweet and soft sound of a well played organ." Wrenshall was soon overstimulated by what he termed "a considerable share of veniaty [venality?]." Strange new sights, sounds, and other effects on the senses abounded, from "plenty of holy water sprinkled on the waiting assembly" to "a variety of prayers" and "movements backwards and forward before the alter." Wrenshall recalled "the curling smoak of perfumes, from Frankincense, which fill'd the church, almost to suffocation." This feeling, he said, "might arrise from the nature of my nerves, which, not being accustomed to perfumes of that kind, I was nearly overcome." This Methodist minister, nevertheless, was positively impressed by the rehearsed expertise of the three priests and their assistance in attendance, particularly the priest who spoke to the assembly "with a voice and all the graces of an orator."[5]

Direct Protestant contact with Catholic sacred space in America drew wonder and criticism, from the late eighteenth through the first half of the nineteenth century. John Brown's and John Wrenshall's sensorial experiences, and their reactions to them, were remarkably similar to those of John Adams on his first visit to a Catholic Mass. In Philadelphia in 1774, Adams, too, was overwhelmed with the visual and aural. The Catholics chanted, moved, and sang in odd ways, he thought; yet more startling was the church's decor. "The Dress of the Priest was rich with Lace—his Pulpit was Velvet and Gold. The Altar Piece was very rich—little Images and Crucifixes about—Wax Candles lighted up." Like John Brown fifty years later, Adams was most shocked by the images of Christ. "But how shall I describe," he wrote to his wife, "the Picture of our Saviour in a Frame of Marble over the Altar at full Length upon the Cross in the Agonies and Blood dripping and streaming from his Wounds." Despite the strangeness of it all, however, Adams, like Brown, was impressed. Organ music, a large choir, and even the chanting seemed to him to go on "most sweetly and exquisitely." In fact, here was the fundamental problem Brown, Wrenshall, and Adams had with what they witnessed inside Catholic churches. The appeal to the senses seemed to cloud the mind. As Adams explained, "here is every Thing which can lay hold of the Eye, Ear, and Imagination." In other words, Catholics depended on "Things," objects and activities that stimulated the senses, and "Every Thing . . . can charm and bewitch the simple and the ignorant." It was a wonder, thought Adams, that "Luther ever broke the spell."[6]

Historian Jenny Franchot has described such intense interest in Catholicism among middle-class Protestants as being part of a "new wave of sympathetic, and at times, voyeuristic, fascination," which was mixed with both an "imitative desire" and "extreme prejudice." American writers in particular tapped this Reformation and Catholic Reformation anti-Catholic discourse in extolling American, middle-class, and Protestant values while they, as Franchot phrases it, "indirectly voiced tensions and limitations of Protestant culture." Franchot made her case, however, for the antebellum period, though the origins of this sympathizing, voyeuristic fascination stretch to an earlier period, a time when Catholics started moving to the western edges of the United States in significant numbers between 1790 and 1820. It was a time when Bishop John Carroll's efforts in the East were producing new parishes, church construction, convents, seminaries, and other signs of successful Catholic transplantation from Europe. There were glimmerings of a Protestant sympathy and fascination at play in the early West, in those places where Protestants were in contact with Catholics and their chapels, churches, and assorted religious goods. Young John Brown's antipathy and awe seemed to be embedded in that encompassing discursive context. His reaction to what Franchot refers to as Catholicism's alternative spatial "interiority" and "temporality" in the lives of Louisville's Catholics foreshadows the broader, later cultural responses that Franchot has studied.[7]

Material expressions of the Catholic faith, from church buildings to religious objects, could be meaningful for non-Catholics as well as Catholics. What provoked and attracted John Adams, John Brown, and John Wrenshall, however, had entirely different meanings for Roman Catholics. For Catholics, the physical elements of faith—images, sounds, textures, smells, and even tastes—were avenues to spiritual experience and direct connections to the tradition, authority, and spiritual power of the European church. They were both an external point of contact with non-Catholics and internal, distinctively Catholic, links to piety and the Roman tradition. Buildings and objects functioned in part to enforce ecclesiastical authority and to connect Catholics in the American wilderness directly to continental sources of religious tradition and spiritual power.

Material expressions of faith were part of the transplantation of the institutional authority of the Catholic Church. From chapels to candles, statues to altar linens, the physical manifestations of Catholicism were a form of "institutional proliferation" common also to Protestant denominations in this post-Revolutionary period. Such items were clearly seen to be symbols particular to Catholicism. A traveler to Vincennes in 1804 took special note of the "Cathedral Church" there in which the Catholics had "their Cross" which they "worship"—an act that distinguished them, presumably, from other Christians. Likewise, the Methodist John Wrenshall noted the incessant "bowing to the crusifix" of the congregation he visited in New Orleans in 1797. Father Charles Nerinckx confirmed the distinctiveness of Catholic symbols in the trans-Appalachian West and hinted at their usefulness in claiming sacred space when in 1806 he wrote to his parents about the churches he would build in Kentucky: each would have its "bell and their Cross, until now, not known in this country." As historian Ann Taves suggests, the Catholic use of religious items, especially objects of devotion, strengthened the common identity of lay Catholics and increased the authority of clergy and the Catholic hierarchy. Church structures and religious goods, beyond their functions of serving the communal, liturgical, and spiritual needs of a congregation, also symbolized the growing authority of the Catholic hierarchy. This chapter emphasizes these internal and external functions of material Catholicism: the ways in which they united Catholics as an American subculture and as part of a European tradition and were a point of interaction with non-Catholics.[8]

Building Churches

Like officials in other denominations, Catholic leaders struggled to bring religion to growing and spreading settlements in the West. Although a great part of the effort lay in finding sufficient numbers of reliable priests, building enough churches was an important secondary concern. A lack of churches, like the shortage of priests, slowed the spread of Catholicism. In 1798 Father Stephen Badin thought Catholics were not moving quickly enough beyond the few central counties of Kentucky where they had settled. "Other religionists" did so, he wrote, because they were "unstopped by the motives that keep Catholics in reach of the chapels."[9] The church building was at the heart of the Catholic community. It was the focal point of religious activity and the link to spiritual power through the Mass, sacraments, and devotions performed there, as well as a visible sign of Catholic success in the West. Once a community secured a resident pastor, or at least regular visits from a priest, lay church members and clergy worked hard to build a house of worship.

Well into the early nineteenth century, priests in the trans-Appalachian region carried altar stones in their ministrations to dispersed Catholic settlements. Until a sacred space was constructed and a permanent altar was built, a priest carrying a portable altar stone was the moveable church, visiting distant communities of Catholics a few times each year. These stones were eight to ten inches square, contained the relics of saints, and could be inserted into the altar table.[10] They are intriguing, in part, because they were both a symbol of sacred space—a representation of chapel, church, or cathedral—and a moveable object or tool, such as a chalice, vestment, or catechism, carried by Catholic missionaries. Altar stones also represented the symbolic linkage between the individual priest, his scattered congregations, the spiritual power of the bishop (who could supply the stones), and the worldwide church stretching back to the pope.

As a temporary measure, when needed to establish a new congregation, Father Badin occasionally used altar stones, taking them with him on horseback. In 1798 Badin wrote to Bishop Carroll in Baltimore, more than six hundred miles away, about the awkwardness of this practice: "You have been so kind . . . as to send me several Altar-stones, but they are of such size, as renders them somewhat cumbersome to carry at a distance. I would be thankful for your procuring one or two more of smaller weight and size." Two years later, Badin again asked for a smaller altar stone, "one that may be easily carried in a saddle-bag." But portability created other problems. In 1801 Badin reported his altar stone "was broke into pieces in my saddle-bag because of its thinness and size." The stones were difficult to get, to carry, and to keep. One that had been inserted into an altar table waiting for installation at the Bardstown chapel was stolen from a parishioner's house that same year. Badin asked the bishop if he would "give me care to bless A. stones whenever as wanted." Carroll, ever cautious to maintain episcopal prerogatives, apparently never permitted the priest to bypass his authority in this manner, for in 1810 Badin again noted a need for altar stones. The trans-Appalachian region as of 1808 was part of the first western diocese, but the appointed bishop, Benedict Joseph Flaget, in 1810 still had not taken his seat at Bardstown, Kentucky. Since the "Clergy & Laity . . . feel the want of a residing Bishop" able to consecrate altars in the region, wrote Badin, he needed Archbishop Carroll to send an altar stone to Knoxville, Tennessee. The supply of stones Carroll had provided Badin during the latter's last visit back in Baltimore was "quite exhausted."[11]

Once a congregation incorporated enough willing Catholics, the whole community, a few selected lay trustees, or the lone priest would begin the process of gathering resources to build a house of worship. Often, money for construction was scarce, since currency was in short supply during the early republic, especially among westerners. Nor were American Catholics accustomed to supporting organized religion financially—particularly in providing salaries or support for the local pastor—but they generally could be counted on to help supply the capital, material, and labor for church construction. A show of effort to build a church, in fact, could be used to attract a priest by demonstrating a community's level of commitment. When petitioning the bishop of Baltimore for clerical assistance, Catholics in some trans-Appalachian settlements mentioned their willingness, or described their ability, to provide a church building. For example, Father Nerinckx in 1805 headed to Rolling Fork, Kentucky, to settle on a farm previously abandoned by another priest. The parishioners immediately announced they would help to finish clearing the land, and, more important, end their dispute about the location of the church and "put up, near the bend in the river, a frame building."[12]

Still, money was tight, and lay leaders and clergy spent months or years gathering support. It was typical to raise contributions through a subscription process in which individuals pledged money, land, building supplies, or labor. In a frontier community, individual donations were quite modest: "Father Nerinckx, when he built a church, made different persons subscribe one or two hewn logs of prescribed dimensions, and deliver them on the spot," said one former parishioner. This was necessary because, as Nerinckx noted, cash was scarce. A church structure raised in 1806 cost $400, he once noted, yet not even $50 in cash could be collected, so the remainder had to be "paid for in commodities." Known by his colleagues as a prolific church builder, Nerinckx understood the support and hard work required to complete a structure:

The people whom I serve are mostly poor, and not liberal enough to build a church of stone. Normally, the price of these churches is $500 to $600. Every church needs about $60 to $70 in money to procure the necessary materials for construction, such as iron, glass, etc.; items such as labor, can be paid in grain, meat, etc. This the congregation takes care of, but the priest must try to supply the money, otherwise he will seldom make progress. In addition, the priest has to be continually with the workers and apply himself to the task more than anyone, or else little will be accomplished.

In a busy community such as Bardstown and for a project such as the proposed cathedral, the offers of assistance were more extensive. Bishop Flaget gathered subscriptions "made either in cash (that is, in ready money) or in trade (that is, in work, provisions, materials, etc.) One individual has already offered the limestone, another the lumber; others will pledge so many days work as carpenter, joiner, mason, etc." Erecting the cathedral ultimately required $20,000.[13]

American clergy also relied on gifts from supporters in Europe. Bishop Carroll even turned to Napoleon Bonaparte in 1803 with a plea for assistance. Carroll commended the emperor's "beneficent views . . . in favor of Religion," and the way he had used his "power to raise its altars again" in the wake of the Revolution. American Catholics, wrote Carroll, could not raise a "public monument to their piety" by themselves and desperately needed French assistance to erect a cathedral in Baltimore. Badin, Nerinckx, and Flaget each made trips across the Atlantic to raise money for their trans-Appalachian church-building campaigns and collected funds from peasants, kings, and pontiffs. For example, Flaget was able to finish the cathedral in Cincinnati only after having traveled to Rome in 1823, where Pope Leo XII added twelve thousand Roman crowns to the sum acquired from the king of France and lay Catholics in France, Sardinia, Belgium, Spain, and Germany.[14]

Constructing Interfaith Community

American Catholics, however, were not limited to relying on themselves or on the funds from Europe. Priests accepted substantial assistance from non-Catholics to build the churches they needed.

It should be noted, however, that after the Bardstown diocese had been established, Catholics were not able to return the favor by helping Protestants. Indeed, Father Nerinckx in 1813 forwarded a long list of questions to the cardinals of the Congregation for the Propagation of the Faith, questions arising from the unusual situation of Catholics and Protestants living and laboring together in the American West. Nerinckx asked, "Is it permissible to build their churches?" Almost three years later, the cardinals responded in the negative. Those who assisted Protestants in building Protestant churches would be "taking part in their functions and instructions," and thereby impermissibly "to encourage their incredulity" and "to involve the danger of being seduced by their errors."[15] Helping to construct Protestant houses of worship was proximity too close and too dangerous.

Nonetheless, from the 1780s through the 1830s Catholics found their Protestant neighbors willing to help. Examples of non-Catholics providing support for Catholic church-building efforts are numerous. Gifts often included parcels of land on which to build and from which the resident pastor could extract a living from rents or the sale of agricultural produce. Assistance also came in the form of direct cash payments or subscriptions promising to help pay for a church's construction. In 1800 the governor of Tennessee offered Father Badin land for a church. In 1802 Badin noted another prominent non-Catholic's generosity in donating acreage in Springfield, the seat of Washington County, Kentucky. And Father Nerinckx was delighted in 1807 to find merchants in Bardstown, Lexington, Danville, and Louisville each contributing amounts between $50 and $400 for churches. The promises of land could be extravagant. According to Nerinckx, "In Hopkinsville, after a sermon which Father Badin preached in my presence, the non-catholic listeners called a meeting" at which they "circulated a subscription list for the building of a catholic church and a Loretto school." Surprisingly, in less than two days the non-Catholic community had pledged four thousand acres of land worth $20,000. Because the nuns at Loretto could not spare anyone to run a new school, however, the Catholics never collected the pledged acreage. Indeed, few of these offers of land resulted in churches since there were not enough priests.[16]

Sometimes clergy found such largess startling. When Badin attempted to procure a city lot for a church in Louisville, he first met resistance from one Colonel Johnson, a "Baptist zealot," as Badin put it, who argued that the Roman Catholics ought not have a piece of land to which all "129 Christian Sects" had a right. County officials ignored the colonel and offered a prime spot, "one quarter of acre in the public square," for a church. In 1810 Badin reported two of the trustees of this Louisville parish were Protestants and he claimed nine-tenths of the subscribers to the building fund were non-Catholics. Badin was astonished that it was the Protestant members of the building committee who argued for acquiring a lot large enough to accommodate the future resident priest of St. Louis Church. "If all the Catholics are not my friends," said the priest, "I am amply compensated by the friendship of many non-Catholics of respectability." Years later, when the construction of the Bardstown cathedral and the economic recession of 1819 left the diocese deep in debt, Flaget appealed to European Catholics for funds. Diocesan officials could pressure the Catholic and Protestant subscribers to the building fund, even "force them to sell their property" to make the final payments. But the only result would be "great inconveniences and distressing influence on the attitude of the Protestants."[17]

Another surprise for Catholic clergy was the kinds of non-Catholics who contributed on occasion to other church-building initiatives. At St. Anthony's congregation in Breckinridge County in 1810, Father Nerinckx learned that a Methodist preacher had offered two hundred acres, and another Protestant preacher's son donated $20. One-third of the capital raised for St. Hubert's Church in Lebanon, Kentucky, came from Protestants, claimed Nerinckx. The donors had turned down Presbyterians seeking funds for their own construction project in 1819, according to the priest, saying the Catholics "do not make much noise . . . but they do business bravely indeed." Two years later in Nashville, Tennessee, where only sixty Catholics resided, Bishop Flaget visited and was shocked to be offered a town lot by the local grand master of the Freemasons. Catholics and non-Catholics seemed to live peacefully together, thought Flaget, and the Protestants were congenial, especially the Presbyterian Reverend Campbell, who invited him and Father Robert Abell to tea. Only the Baptist minister who was visiting Nashville at the same time, the revivalist Reverend Vardiman, objected to the Catholic clergy's presence and their plans for church construction.[18]

Assistance from non-Catholics in church building raised numerous questions. What interest could Protestants and other non-Catholics have had in helping Catholics create sacred places? Why would leading Presbyterians, Baptists, Methodists, and even deists tie up their capital or prestige in Catholic church-building efforts? Some were simply being good neighbors. More important, however, it made good economic sense. Catholic leaders soon learned there was a demand in the young republic's western stretches for settlers and orderly settlement. "Indeed some protestants, with the hope of having their lands . . . between here and the Mississippi River . . . speedily settled," noted Father Carroll in 1785, "have been induced to give their bonds for the conveyance to a Catholic priest of very ample property." Twenty years later, Father Nerinckx found similar motivation on the part of Protestants in Tennessee. Their reason, according to the priest, was that "these people know that the catholics follow their priests, and that by those means they would gain settlers and have a chance of selling the public lands." Indeed, Badin reported to the bishop in the early part of 1800 that the Tennessee governor's plan to give him land for a priest and church fell through. The governor—perhaps becoming greedy, or having second thoughts—a few months later raised the price of land so much that "none of my Parishioners intend any more to settle on Oby's River where the governor's tracts lie." Land gifts for Catholic church buildings were one means of guaranteeing future land sales to Catholics.[19]

Protestant patrons also found useful what the Catholic church building and its resident pastor represented. In addition to satisfying an economic need by attracting many land-hungry Catholic settlers, church and priest could fulfill social needs of stability and order, values that large landholders, social elites, or other leading citizens in western communities held dear. From the viewpoint of Kentucky's upper echelons, the fast-paced growth of the West needed to be carefully controlled to prevent trouble from land squatters. A priest and the parishioners who would flock to him could ensure orderly settlement as well as civilized manners. Indeed, Catholics in some locations perpetuated civilization itself by providing schools for Catholic and non-Catholic children, often years before other schools appeared. As the non-Catholic citizens of Hopkinsville, Kentucky, demonstrated in 1807, they were willing to sell four thousand acres to pay for a Catholic church if it were accompanied by a nun-operated school. When Bishop Flaget sought support from the citizens of Bardstown to build St. Joseph's Cathedral, they complied on the condition he also establish a college for the young men of the region.[20]

Also important was the civic meaning of the venerable church building, wherever it might stand and whatever denomination it might house. Numerous and elaborate houses of worship were material symbols of a town's moral power, a barometer of respectability, culture, and virtue. And in growing frontier towns competing for investments, Protestant or other non-Catholics might support construction out of a sense of town boosterism—a mixture of local pride and entrepreneurship. In Bardstown, Father John Baptist David, an assistant to the diocese's new bishop, wrote in 1811 that a "full-sized church . . . of Gothic style" was practical because "the Protestants want it as much as the Catholics and . . . have said openly that if it were a question of a small church they would not contribute willingly." But, he continued, "if we wanted to build a 'good, large, substantial church' they would contribute generously." Similarly, when Bishop Flaget and Fathers David and Badin publicly contemplated establishing a new seminary or convent, the lay Catholics of Bardstown refused to support anything but a cathedral. Flaget reported to the archbishop, "all my arguments are of no weight when compared with the ornament which Bardstown is to derive from so magnificent a building."[21]

Nevertheless, the people of Bardstown and the Catholics nearby had been slow to reach this enthusiastic level of support for the proposed cathedral. Father David hinted that their change of heart might have been forced upon them by the desire of other towns to entice away the bishop. Upon arriving in the new seat of the diocese, Father David had been aggravated that "the people of Bardstown and the Catholics of the neighborhood ha[d] not bestirred themselves to establish their bishop in their midst." The existing "Cathedral" was a chapel of logs with "a sorry altar made of some pieces of board—all in a pitiable condition," and the "Episcopal Palace" was "a small house . . . almost falling to pieces." Newfound eagerness among the Bardstownians came as they began to notice "that the people of Danville, another small town at one end of Kentucky, intend to make very advantageous offers" to the bishop; "Doubtless Lexington and Frankfort will do the same," he added.[22] In this possibly unique case, Catholics and Protestants worked together to keep the bishop and the civic splendor of his diocesan organization in Bardstown, while similar coalitions hoped to attract the episcopacy to other towns.

Before construction started on the cathedral in the summer of 1816, Flaget counted nearly $10,000 subscribed by local Protestants—approximately half the total expected cost. "The protestants of Bardstown and its vicinity have so urged me to undertake the work that I should have considered myself guilty of sin had I not acceded to their solicitations." Father David also thought the planned cathedral was becoming a contact point between Catholics and non-Catholics. In October 1816 he explained to a colleague that Flaget "has gained the confidence not only of the Catholics, but of all the other religions, whose followers have contributed liberally to the building of the Cathedral." Many realized the patent truth: the more impressive the edifice, the better it might reflect on a provincial town.[23]

Church buildings, like the series of forts left along trans-Appalachian river valleys by the imperial powers of the previous century, were points of contact between peoples of differing cultural viewpoints. Like a military outpost, on the one hand, they represented an extension of institutional control and authority. On the other, they brought Catholics and non-Catholics together. Oftentimes church construction efforts required cooperation with non-Catholics, some of whom eagerly contributed their support for non-religious reasons. After a church was built, it became a space into which non-Catholics occasionally might be invited to observe and learn. Part of that interior experience was shaped by the material and visual richness of Catholic decor.

Religious Objects

Catholic clergy struggled to gather suitable objects of decoration and veneration with which to adorn the interiors of these new structures, as well as the material items central to Catholic ritual, devotion, and education. Like their efforts to construct houses of worship, the acquisition of religious goods connected Catholics to one another and to Europe and also provided points of interaction with non-Catholics.

These objects linked western settlements with the wellsprings of tradition, authority, and spiritual power in Baltimore and across the sea in Europe and, particularly, Rome. Historian Colleen Mc-Dannell has referred to a "spiritual economy of the sacred" connecting Catholics to the spiritual world and to each other. This existed in both an economic and a spiritual sense. First, the search for funds and appropriate religious goods took westerners back to Baltimore and overseas to European sources. Second, as we shall see, the hunt for suitable religious goods, or the attempt to manufacture meaningful replicas or replacements, was an effort, as McDannell suggests, to tap into an authoritative authenticity—to connect the faithful to the "sacred context, [of] a larger religious story" of Catholic faith, devotion, and spiritual life.[24] By trying to acquire objects to bind themselves to the sacred, American Catholics also kept alive a link to other centers of Catholic authority and power.

That these early exchanges and uses of religious goods were overseen by clergy further bolstered priestly and episcopal authority. As Colleen McDannell suggests, objects can become more powerful "by participating in the authority of institutional traditions and organizations." As she states, "Clergy sought certain material items and not others, assigned meaning to them (though this was never the final word), and, as the suppliers and arbiters of sacred goods, reinforced their institutional authority." Another historian, Ann Taves, has shown how the Catholic Church by the middle decades of the nineteenth century encouraged among the laity a heartfelt, devotional faith, much like the trend among evangelical Protestants, though involving religious objects. In part, this development was meant to reinforce the power of the church by reinserting priests into the laity's private devotional practices—accomplished by promoting particular, standardized devotions approved by the pope, which required some level of intervention from the local priest. Church leaders also strengthened authority by encouraging American Catholics at mid-century to define themselves increasingly as a distinctive subculture. This was achieved by the growing use of Catholic statues, ornaments, paintings, prints, wall coverings, chalices, vestments, medals, and crucifixes.[25]

Use of religious goods, therefore, was a key factor in cultivating a sense of community and mutual identity among Catholics on the western frontier. If the search for, importation of, and use of religious objects linked Catholics to Europe and to the sacred, these objects additionally acted to "bind people to each other," to help affirm the "symbols of community affiliation" of Catholicism. Religious objects could show who was a member of a group and who was an outsider. For example, a crucifix hanging on a wall at home indicated a family's Catholic faith. Beyond this inward focus, however, religious goods had an educational and symbolic role that extended to non-Catholics; according to McDannell, "they teach people how to think and act like Christians" and "are used to lure, encourage, and shock non-Christians into considering the truth of Christianity." Priests and bishops fully expected their churches to be richly decorated, and themselves and their laity well equipped with religious objects to make an impression on neighboring non-Catholics.[26]

Catholic clergy did not perceive their pursuit of sacred articles as extravagant, but as necessary and customary. Yet time and money spent getting these sundry materials—vestments, chalices, paintings, statues, oils, altar stones—were an added burden for priests and parishioners struggling to construct church buildings and provide remuneration for a resident pastor. Bishop John Carroll had to remind American Catholics in his first pastoral letter, in May 1792, of the central role such materials played in their religion. He was working to establish a tradition of support, especially for the "furnishment" of the churches. Carroll chastised the laity for failing to sustain the clergy and leaving their churches "without those sacred utensils, which its ordinances require, and which contribute to impress the mind with a becoming sense of majesty of religion, and conciliate respect for its august ceremonies." Furthermore, he admonished, Catholics should not settle for the "meanest materials" but ensure liturgical and other objects were "clean and entire," "suitable," "fit," and "decent." The bishop demanded more attention to "those things, without which the functions of religion seem to lose their dignity and authority." Catholics could not get by without these religious objects, and they would not flourish without religious goods of acceptable quality.[27]

Such items were expensive, often difficult to transport, and, in most instances, available only in Europe. Thus, they were a rarity in the trans-Appalachian region during the first decades of Catholic westward settlement. Religious items were brought with difficulty over the mountains and into the lands spread before the Mississippi River. Some materials were entrusted to lay Catholic travelers making the trip between eastern and western communities. Most were carried by individual priests traveling from Baltimore, to Pittsburgh, and down the Ohio or via overland routes. However the religious goods arrived, American Catholics relied on east coast and European sources.

Father Badin, pioneer missionary to Kentucky, asked for religious objects continually from the 1790s through the 1820s, long past the time of statehood and the establishment of the Bardstown diocese. Writing to Bishop Carroll in 1796, Badin remarked that he was drastically rationing his supply of holy oils, which the bishop had blessed and given him in 1793, and that he desperately required more supplies. Catechisms from two years before were now gone, and he still waited for Carroll's promise of additional books as well as instructional pictures. His last bit of cash went to a traveler returning east who promised to bring back a censer in which to burn incense. When an early colleague, Father Anthony Salmon, died while riding on mission, Badin brooded that his saddle bag had never been located, and thus were lost "Holy-Oils, a Paten, Missal book, ritual, breviary &c. which are a great loss for this country where such things cannot easily be had." Numerous times Badin repeated his pleas for fresh holy oils (which, by definition, had to be sanctified by a bishop), books, and other supplies, though in 1799 he and his colleagues were able to have catechisms printed in the West, and by 1811 they had their own bishop to bless oils and consecrate altar stones. Yet many years after Badin reached Kentucky, religious materials in general were still scarce, and certain items were still not produced in America.[28]

In 1815 Father Charles Nerinckx tried soliciting help from Catholics in the Netherlands, and told them of his decade of experience on the trans-Appalachian frontier. Americans were extremely grateful for material assistance, he assured his European audience; "even the Bishop and the priests stand in admiration when they saw the shipments of articles sent over" from benefactors in Europe. A few years later Father Edward Fenwick asked a friend in London to support the two churches he was building in Ohio. Land and parishioners he had, "zealous priests" he would find, but religious materials could only come from Europe. "I must not conceal from you," he wrote, "that we are in need of sacred vessels, vestments, missals, and everything required that the Divine Services may be conducted with due decorum and reverence." In 1821 Father Badin made an appeal to his colleagues in France. Any priests coming to the "infant missions" of America should "provide themselves with all the church books of the Roman rite, theological and biblical works in French, English, and Latin, also chalices, ciboriums, crucifixes, linens and church vestments, paintings for the altar, and in fine, everything that pertains to the divine service."[29]

One European priest who came to aid the American missions, specifically to assist Badin in the rough lands of Kentucky, was Father Nerinckx, who left Belgium in 1805. His correspondence over the years with Bishop Carroll in Baltimore, and with his own parents, colleagues, and lay supporters in Europe, demonstrate what he thought to be the crucial function of religious materials in bringing Catholicism to the frontier.

Nerinckx knew that trials awaited him in accepting appointment to the West. While in Georgetown, readying to depart for Pittsburgh and thence downstream to Bardstown, Nerinckx endeavored to assemble the religious supplies he expected to need in the backwoods missions. Nerinckx made a tentative list based on the advice of a group of Trappist monks with whom he was about to voyage to Kentucky. He had brought "nothing from the old country but a silver chalice," he told Bishop Carroll, and he had heard from his soon-to-be traveling companions, "that the region I am sent to is entirely destitute" of necessary things such as the priest's vestments and suitable wine for celebrating the Mass. Should he try transporting a barrel of wine? he asked. Could the bishop provide him with a book of rites and ceremonies and catechisms and other "pious" publications? Without these things, he felt he would be "going forth totally unarmed and unfit to fight the hard battles of the Lord."[30]

Nerinckx thought printed materials would be crucial to a successful mission. After his first year he became more certain. "Our holy religion suffers much here for lack of books, which could convince, instruct and move," he told his parents in Belgium. From a friend in Flanders he pleaded for "some good brochures" to share with frontier Catholics. "It would be very advantageous to have some good books on theology, cases of conscience, and interpretations of the Holy Scriptures," Nerinckx wrote, "in order to establish a library in this country"—meaning, Kentucky, southern Ohio and Indiana, and Tennessee—"where there is absolutely nothing except for the little that Father Badin and I brought with us." The same was true of the more visually didactic materials on which he and other priests relied. To a benefactor in Antwerp, Belgium, Nerinckx wrote, "I am enclosing to you a picture representing the jaws of hell with the damned." It seems the image might have been drawn by Nerinckx himself as an illustration to accompany his "very serious discourse" on the topic of perdition and salvation, a combination with which he "experienced the greatest effects" among his American parishioners. What he hoped for was a realistic printed image of sinners in the maw of hell, one that would instill true fear. Or, it would serve him even better, he added, if his friend could find "one like it on a block from which to print others," so the frontier priest might have a permanent supply to distribute. Nerinckx's backer eventually had five hundred copies printed for him.[31]

During his first summer on the frontier Nerinckx received $205 from Belgian donors to spend on himself and his missions, and his first thought was to make a grand gesture. He ordered three bells for three church steeples to be cast in Baltimore. Eventually he realized the expense for three would exceed his funds, so Nerinckx asked Bishop Carroll to change the order to just one church bell, with the remainder of the money to "be spent buying pious books, catechisms, prayer books, etc., of which people are in great need here." The ardent priest concluded, "I have thought it better to spend the money for what will tend most to the glory of God." For the time being, Nerinckx would stick to a few printed materials and small items, such as chalices, vestments, and statues. Still, catechisms and other "pious" publications, such as the "good brochures" and "cases of conscience" he had requested, were fundamental in his ministry, and they, like other religious goods, had to be imported for many years.

More decorative religious materials were hardly available in the West or from American sources. This was especially true for the items that would furnish churches, the religious goods useful for traditional ornamentation, liturgical rituals, the various sacraments, individual and group devotions, and the religious edification of the laity. Catholic clergy went to great lengths, as has been shown, to acquire religious goods from Europe. Lay Catholics reportedly appreciated seeing finely crafted religious goods and came to expect them in the Bardstown diocese. "The ornaments that I brought with me from the Low Country are greatly admired here. . . . It seems they are anxious to have objects of piety." Lay Catholics appreciated the items Nerinckx imported, and he redoubled his efforts to acquire them. Moreover, he looked for ways to reproduce appropriate religious goods in America. "Being constantly occupied in building churches and altars," wrote Nerinckx a year later, "I wish I could obtain books and pictures from Belgium, in order to give our workmen here some good models and sketches."[32]

After several more years, in 1815, St. Thomas Seminary outside Bardstown was slowly fashioning itself in the likeness of a church as understood by traditional European standards. Under the direction of Father David, the chapel's appearance was refined. A young French seminarian, Millet, made a tabernacle for the consecrated communion host, which David termed "a masterpiece." The altar was painted to look like marble, and Millet thought he was "equal to making an altar piece with four columns and baldachin," or ornamental canopy. An Italian seminarian fashioned a copy of the chest of drawers in the seminary, which had come from Europe, when the priests needed a storage place for the vestments in the chapel. David opined, "Our pillars are still rough, but they will not take long. . . . The gallery is still to be made. The ox-eye still has no light." Nevertheless, he wrote, "Little by little the bird builds its nest." David and his seminarians were building from an architectural and aesthetic tradition familiar to them but new to the region. Like Nerinckx in the previous decade, these priests relied on imported goods and styles.[33]

The cathedral in Bardstown became a focal point of construction and decorative attention. When St. Joseph's was consecrated in August 1819, the cost to the diocese already had soared to $20,000. Yet the cathedral had not yet been furnished. Most conspicuously missing was an organ, the absence of which Nerinckx, David, and Bishop Flaget each noted. Flaget spoke of adorning his church like the increasingly marvelous cathedral in Baltimore, which had received donations from bishops, cardinals, and aristocrats in France and Italy. He prized the paintings hanging there, because "nothing, it seems to me, [is] more holy than similar paintings since they have only God and his holy religion for ulterior end." Best of all would be an organ for the Kentucky cathedral, however. "Most fitting to me for the decency and the majesty of worship of my church would be an organ," Flaget told his archbishop. And since his requests to friends in Europe had not produced an instrument for Bardstown, Flaget proposed that his new cathedral should receive the old organ from Archbishop Maréchal's cathedral when a new one arrived. "If you put it up to sale," warned Flaget, "it is more than probable that it will only cause to be heard Methodist or Presbyterian sounds in temples consecrated to error," and this would be a "species of shame for the zealous Catholics of Baltimore." The organ and paintings in the Baltimore Cathedral were powerful means of glorifying God while in Catholic hands, as well as the envy of other denominations. Flaget and his clergy hoped to finish their cathedral in a manner that would make it the peer of Baltimore's. They expected to re-create an outpost of Catholic sacred space.[34]

To accomplish this translation of the sacred, Nerinckx, Badin, and their fellow American priests did not simply wait for materials and money to be sent to them; some made journeys back to Europe to drum up support. Trips for gathering resources continued for decades, and Badin and Nerinckx's early ventures focused as much on religious items for decoration, ritual use, and devotion as on financial support. According to Bishop Flaget, for example, on Nerinckx's two European tours made "in order to procure for his oratories and churches the more necessary objects for divine worship," the industrious priest gathered "precious objects" for Kentucky "estimated at more than fifteen thousand dollars." In 1815–1816 Nerinckx traveled to Rome and published a pamphlet directed at Catholics in the Netherlands. He asked them, as his bishop had phrased it, for help "to strengthen my diocese, where everything is missing and where everything has to be done." Nerinckx's charge from his superior was to persuade clergy and laity alike "to contribute to the decency of the divine worship" in western America by shipping to Kentucky "chalices, ciboriums, missals, paintings, images, rosaries, etc.,"—all the objects, said Bishop Flaget, that would be "extremely precious for my missions." In addition, the Bardstown bishop had asked Nerinckx to bring back prayer books, bibles, and "books on the fundamentals of the faith" as well as "sermon books for the young priests" for the "more than 15,000 Frenchmen" of the diocese "who live on the banks of the Mississippi, the Missouri, and the St. Lawrence."[35]

Five years later Nerinckx made his second trip to Europe to secure funds and materials for the Kentucky church. This time he was hunting for objects suited to the convent he had helped found for the Sisters of Loretto, situated just south of Bardstown. The trip was difficult, and Nerinckx was unsure whether his various shipments had or would make it across the ocean, over the mountains, and down the Ohio. Still, even if he returned to the United States and found nothing but "the old English books, with some new ones" already sent, his trip would have been "worth my pains." He appeared most excited about items destined for the convent and for other parish churches he had established: "I have ready half a dozen statues, or rather half ones, of our Lady, middling well done, and some more utensils for the church," and "some more things, and valuable ones" that were on their way.[36]

Obviously the link to Europe was economic, practical, and religious. Significant infusions of cash at critical times were gathered in fundraising efforts that could include letters from American clergy, pamphlets or articles published by American Catholics in Europe, and visits from American priests or bishops. And finding religious objects in Europe, which was awash in them after centuries of production and use there, was easier than in the United States, where the open practice of Catholicism was relatively new. In addition, there was an aesthetic preference among many of the European-born and European-trained priests who were predominant in the American church. Clergy had a predilection for the high quality, costly, traditional religious items available in Europe. In the fall of 1823, for example, Bishop Fenwick visited Rome and received many valuable gifts from the pope for his Ohio diocese, including gold vessels, vestments, books, and a tabernacle for the Cincinnati cathedral. Twenty-five years later it was still considered "unsurpassed by anything of the kind in the United States."[37]

Eventually books, religious clothing, candles, and other objects would be produced in America. But where other than Europe would clergy find the fine works of art such as paintings and statues of the saints, crucifixes, or crafted gold- and silverwork that was part of the Catholic institutional tradition? And above these mundane concerns about maintaining the economic and aesthetic connections between American Catholicism and Europe, however, was a sense that religious objects had the power to link the continents spiritually as well.

Europe ultimately was the source of religious objects that provided an immediate, transcending, time-and-space-defying link between an individual in the wilderness and the spiritual heart of the church in Europe. Until Americans had their own established holy places or their own traditions of miraculous events, the other side of the Atlantic would hold a monopoly on religious goods. Sacred objects such as certain statues, crucifixes, chalices, paintings, or altars that had once been a part of or used in a French bishop's chapel, or a Spanish cathedral, or the Holy Roman Emperor's court, or a sainted monk's abbey could carry with them the spiritual essence and heritage, to be transplanted to America. While on his second collecting trip to Europe in 1820, Father Nerinckx demonstrated the logic of this spiritual economy. He wrote to the Sisters of Loretto with the news of his successes in finding books, statues, and other objects. Nerinckx also shared the pope's recent announcement that "the body of St. Francis of Assisium . . . has been found with the sacred stigmata, whole and fresh." In describing the significance of the "great event which will turn to the benefit of the church," and "a great favor . . . bestowed upon the whole christendom," Nerinckx pointed out to the sisters that "our [own] Loretto chapel" housed a statue of St. Francis. He was implying they could expect special, direct spiritual benefits from the connection to the miraculous event involving St. Francis. As McDannell has noted, this kind of association was possible both through the direct "power of relationships" individuals could form with spiritual beings, mediated through religious objects, and through the individual and collective "power of memory" that material reminders of faith might trigger.[38]

Such imperatives suggest American Catholics would strive for authenticity, replication, and tradition rather than creating new styles, adapting uses, or fostering American innovation. Catholic clergy and laity worked hard either to transport from the east coast or to import from Europe the genuine religious article, or to make suitable replicas. This was especially true in ornamenting churches with the articles necessary for Catholic liturgical rituals, the various sacraments, individual and group devotions, and the religious edification of the laity. Catholic clergy went to great lengths, as has been shown, to acquire religious objects and ornamentation. Father Nerinckx once spent $160—fully one-third the total cost of constructing the church—for a carved and inlaid wooden altar—as he described it—"made after my own designs . . . inlaid with different kinds of wood, and . . . [with] a niche flanked with columns, in which . . . to place . . . [a] statue of the Blessed Virgin." For another church interior he spent $130 for an altar, raising the funds in part by encouraging the parish's children to contribute coins, corn, and spools of thread spun by their mothers.[39]

Churches and Their Furnishings as Contact Points

Church structures dramatically set on the trans-Appalachian landscape, lavishly fitted with fine objects of devotion, filled with the special sights and sounds of Catholic worship, were a means of reaching out to non-Catholics and inviting them to consider the Catholic faith. Visitors willing to enter a church and observe the celebration of the liturgy or other activities might grow in their understanding of and appreciation for Catholicism. The clergy welcomed this kind of attention and hoped that non-Catholic guests might someday consider conversion.

But interfaith exchanges could go too far. Bishop Carroll in 1801 denied a request from a Catholic layman who had asked permission to share the Catholic chapel in Natchez, Mississippi, with a local Protestant minister. Presumably the church was temporarily without a pastor and the Protestants were in need of a meeting place. "As far as civil toleration goes," wrote Carroll, "no one has a fuller persuasion than myself of its consonancy with the laws of God." Since there was only one true religion, however, and since Catholic "churches and implements" already were consecrated, it would be wrong to turn them over to Protestant ministers. "Would not those holy places be profaned, & the character of the sanctity acquired by their consecration be effaced, by their becoming the seminaries of error & false doctrines?"[40]

More common and more acceptable was the use of Catholic churches as gathering points on Sundays or special days in sparsely settled areas. In this way, churches brought non-Catholics into close proximity. Before and after a church service, social, political, and business or other community transactions might take place, as happened at Protestant churches. In 1808, for example, Father Badin ran into trouble when he chastised men of St. Joseph's parish, in

Bardstown, for conducting political affairs on church grounds during Sunday Mass. Disgruntled parishioners later petitioned against him, forcing Badin to defend his good name in a thirty-two-page letter to Bishop Carroll. In Badin's words, the affair started when he "observed after the sermon a multitude of people in the graveyard, who by their loud laughters and conversations are a distraction to those within doors." The angry priest rang the bell, which brought in some of the crowd, but still he saw "about 20 steps from the chapel a group of Protestant gentlemen . . . solicitous at that season to feel the pulse of the Catholics about the Election [for Congress]." Then, during the benediction, Badin made another sweep of the church grounds and found in the graveyard a group of fifteen to twenty men, at the center of whom was a Mr. Lancaster, a Catholic candidate for Congress. The politicos were caught by surprise; some were embarrassed, one faced the church and knelt, but most stood with Lancaster and looked defiant. Badin's response was to say, "Mr. Lancaster would rather electioneer than receive the benediction of the B[lessed] Sacrament." The priest's challenge was to impress visitors, as well as his own parishioners on occasion, with the gravity of worship.[41]

Even in the 1820s Father De Andreis, one of a group of several Italian clerics recruited in Europe by Bishop Louis DuBourg for his diocese of Louisiana, who were temporarily lodging at Flaget's St. Thomas Seminary while learning English, was impressed with the hard frontier life around him. De Andreis wrote to friends in France about the good American Catholics and their rough churches, noting that the buildings became gathering points on festival days for Catholics and Protestants within twenty miles.[42] Catholic churches were open to Protestants and other non-Catholics wishing to observe special events such as consecrations, novenas, and processions, but also to visit during regular services.

Return for a moment to the experience of the law student, John Brown, who "was struck with astonishment and horror" in the Louisville Catholic church when he looked upon the "awful representation of the mangled body of Christ on the Cross." What he saw "was truly odd."[43] Although he reacted with enmity, the munificence before him was mesmerizing. When the traditional sumptuousness of the Catholic church captured his eye and the liturgy aroused his curiosity, the clergy had momentary access to his heart and mind. And for an energetic, expanding, and optimistic American Catholic Church in the early nineteenth century, this was an opportunity to demarcate the boundaries of its religion, instill pride in local Catholics, and welcome non-Catholics who might be persuaded both to soften their prejudiced opinions and eventually to convert.

In 1818 Father Nerinckx gave the following traditional defense for Catholic ornamentation: "Let us believe that Christ, the King of Glory, is worthy of, and delights in, our tokens of the most profound veneration, in whatever place it may be." He added, however, another line of reasoning of special importance on the frontier of a Protestant nation: "Such things add to the splendor of the ceremonies of the church, and inspire the ignorant and lookers-on with a greater veneration of our religion; seeing, they admire; admiring, they inquire; inquiring, they finally desire the gift of faith, obtain it, and ever after love and practice the law of God."[44]

This rationale was repeated in 1827 when the Reverend B. Martial, a visiting priest, reported to officials in Rome that the Kentucky diocese should be a particular focus of the hierarchy's attention. The region was full of "heretics," and Catholics were a minority. After describing a recent procession of the Blessed Sacrament, the visitor concluded that public devotional displays, as well as "the ornaments and decorations of the church," still created a "majesty of worship" new to non-Catholic Americans. He added, "These contribute very effectively to attract Protestants. Such occasions as great feasts, like that of Christmas, draw the crowds so that the interior of the cathedral cannot accommodate all." As was the situation in earlier decades of church building and fundraising by Catholics, Martial noted, "These Protestants contribute generously to the calls for pecuniary assistance." Once drawn into the sacred space of a Catholic chapel, church, or cathedral, newcomers might be affected by the complete, resplendent visual package before them. "These two last years the brilliant tapestries have served in their magnificence to attract great crowds on Holy Thursday and Easter; of course, the liturgical ceremonies, these simple people, find entirely consistent with the decorations and with what we teach." Non-Catholic admirers of the "ornaments and decorations," such as the "brilliant tapestries" Martial described, were proof for the Catholic clergy that the public appeal of the church was increasing in the United States. It was evidence that Catholicism continued to attract curiosity.[45]

Advantages lay in the distinctive expression of Catholic orthodoxy, whether it was revealed in overt efforts to convert, public defenses of doctrine, traditional architecture, or the literal transmittal of European Catholic culture—in the form of devotional and decorative items—to Kentucky. Reliance on the tried and true strengthened the authority of church leaders struggling to meet demands of establishing churches in the trans-Appalachian West. It also ensured a unique identity—in the Catholic case, that of outsiders in a Protestant country—a solid foundation for church members buffeted by Protestant evangelical fervor or by rationalist, democratic republican skepticism. Finally, Catholic customs, orthodoxy, and particularities could intrigue, impress, and amaze non-Catholics. Some would feel threatened, as did John Brown: "Truly I was mistaken when I thought Popery had never set her idolotrous foot on Columbia's soil. She stalks abroad displaying her splendid trappings to lead the unwary pilgrim a victim to polluted shrine."[46] He was horrified, yet aware that such "trappings" might enchant non-Catholics. But church leaders remained optimistic. All things being equal, they believed the "splendid trappings" effectively communicated what they would term the Catholic majesty of worship. This ultimately might convince the non-Catholic mind and win the Protestant heart.

Chapter 5

The Promise and Risks of Proximity on the Frontier

In 1789 or 1790 a family living in the uplands near Harpers Ferry, Virginia, approximately seventy-five miles due west of Baltimore, took in a poor Irish traveler who had become severely ill. Although the Livingstons were Lutheran and the Irishman was Catholic, the family did not hesitate to open its home and nurse him through several days of sickness. Mr. Livingston, however, repeatedly refused the Irishman's request to send for a priest, and the Catholic died without the sacramental benefit of last rites. According to popular memory among Catholics in the area, for the next several years the Livingstons felt themselves plagued by malicious spirits that broke furniture and dishes, shredded clothing, burned down the barn, killed cattle and horses, moved furniture, and haunted them with strange voices. Mr. Livingston sent for Lutheran ministers and those of other Protestant denominations, as well as various conjurers and spiritualists, though all proved ineffectual.

After seven or eight years of torment, Mr. Livingston, prompted by his neighbors, finally asked a Catholic settler living in nearby Leetown to send for a priest. Father Dennis Cahill happened to be traveling through the area the next week and reluctantly agreed to investigate the community's claims of supernatural mischief. While sprinkling holy water about the house he witnessed enough strange activity to believe a demon inhabited the premises. Cahill later returned with Father Demetrius Gallitzin from a Catholic mission at Conewago, Pennsylvania, and the two priests together battled against horrifying noises and their own fears, finally succeeding in expelling the evil spirits. A trunk full of clothing that the demons supposedly had clipped to shreds, an item that Gallitzin carried back to Conewago for other priests to see, was considered proof that what became known as the "Cliptown" incident had actually occurred.

Besides local oral tradition, a lengthy written report by Gallitzin was the other record of the strange happenings. Gallitzin scribed the account after returning to the formerly afflicted backwoods community in September of 1797 and interviewing the families involved, as well as all of the neighbors. "No lawyer in a court of justice," the priest later wrote, "did ever examine and cross-examine witnesses [more] than I did all the witnesses I could procure." He investigated for many weeks and then spent several days writing his final document. According to Gallitzin, the story had not ended with an exorcism of evil spirits, but with the conversion of the entire Livingston family and a few of their neighbors to Catholicism. Once their home had been freed of demons, claimed the Livingstons, they were visited by kind voices and friendly apparitions who spoke consoling words to them and imparted the details of Catholic doctrine. Bishop Carroll and several clergy, including Fathers Brosius, Pellentz, and Cahill, all were said to be amazed by the quantity and accuracy of theological knowledge the family of converts eventually received from the benign spirits in their house.[1]

This peculiar episode helps to illustrate the fluidity of religious interaction between Catholics and non-Catholics in the backcountry of the early republic. From one perspective, despite persisting difficulties with troublesome priests and lingering concerns about the frontier's challenges, Catholic leaders could look west of the Appalachians with optimism, especially since it seemed to be a level field in which they could win over substantial numbers of non-Catholics who might become less bigoted, good friends, or even ready converts. Where Protestant ministers failed, Catholic priests thought they might succeed. The power of God invoked through Catholic ritual and prayer by two priests amazed an entire backcountry community of nonbelievers, ultimately resulting in a number of conversions.

On the other hand, the Cliptown incident reveals the serious obstacles to spreading Catholicism beyond the Atlantic coastline. Like itinerant Protestant ministers, Catholic priests confronted disorganization, uncertainty, and flux; they struggled to overcome long lines of communication and found it impossible to provide care to all of the settlers in their charge. In frontier settlements, away from civilizing influences in the East or across the Atlantic, morality, refinement, and religion seemed to dissipate. Or for individuals who wanted organized religion in their lives, access to clergy could be spotty, regular contact with coreligionists could be years away, and proselytizing efforts by ministers of other denominations might be frequent. Lay Catholics intermingling with the Protestant majority might lose their resolve to maintain and pass on their Catholic heritage. Moreover, each of these problems seemed to worsen the farther west one moved.

As *terra nova*, the trans-Appalachian frontier was both frightening and thrilling, a contested space of challenges and possibilities. It was new ground on which to encounter the non-Catholic, and clergy would employ a range of efforts to maintain the distinctiveness of their Catholic enclaves while encouraging interaction with non-Catholics. From conversion attempts and intermarriage, to baptizing Protestants, to adapting or making exceptions to religious practice, Catholic priests and bishops viewed the frontier optimistically when it came to conversion—despite very limited success. Clergy believed their efforts to reach individuals outside the faith would yield additional members and supporters of the Catholic Church. The clergy, however, did worry they might lose lay Catholics to Protestant proselytizing or antireligious indifference. Priests and bishops considered the frontier less optimistically when it came to interfaith or "mixed" marriages. Such arrangements might bring non-Catholics into the Roman Catholic faith, or, as most clergy believed was more likely, signaled declension and the eventual loss of a couple's descendants to laxity, indifference, or the allure of another denomination. Over time, Catholic hopes for winning the trans-Appalachian West through conversion waned, while concerns about intermarriage and other forms of interaction with non-Catholics lingered throughout the early republic. Clergy expected to make advances at the same time they worried about their ability to maintain the orthodox integrity and distinctiveness of their faith.

Peril in the Wilderness

One danger to Catholicism that clergy perceived in frontier regions was a persistent degenerative influence. Like most early nineteenth-century observers, priests and bishops considered the mobility of frontier life, in particular, to be conducive to a lowering of social status. Catholic clergy, as a result, saw themselves battling against a prevailing indigenous atmosphere of disorder, sloth, and immorality—though they found specific instances of such shortcomings not so frequently among people they knew but among distant groups of frontier settlers, particularly in fringe towns along the border between the Anglo-American backcountry and the more wild western territories. "Oh! What disorders in the congregation at Pottenger's Creek!" proclaimed Father Stephen Badin in 1796, during his third year in Kentucky. With their "ignorance, and indifference to instruction in the duties of a Christian life," the young people raised in the backwoods settlements were "almost strangers to faith and good morals." These were "the fruits of this boasted country" where all Catholics were in constant danger of forgetting "the principles and the exercise of Religion." In large part, as Andrew R. L. Cayton has noted, such complaints by clergy might have been a self-serving cant that helped justify and glorify their wilderness endeavors to themselves, their religious superiors in distant cities, and their fellow Catholics in Europe. Such a rhetoric of deprecation about disorder, incivility, and the decline of religion in frontier communities was more symptomatic of the lack of "sanctioned religious authority, not the desire for it" among Catholic settlers. Of course, the positive side of such threats was that the church had an opportunity to introduce Catholic institutions and practices to a region largely free of competing institutions and practices. Still, clergy worried about the effects of rustic living.[2]

Worse yet were towns along the Mississippi such as St. Louis or other river towns of the frontier, such as Vincennes, where iniquity and uncouthness thrived. The "moral character of the inhabitants, either Catholics or not, is with little exception very unchristian," reported Badin, and "there is a great mixture of Indians, mullattoes & white," while "Idleness, fishing & hunting and pleasures are mostly the calling of [the] many banditti there." Describing Vincennes in 1806, Father Charles Nerinckx depicted the inhabitants

as "sheep astray" and as "a very bad people." A Baptist minister passing through St. Louis in 1818 still noted the effects of frontier de-
generation on that town's inhabitants. Half of the population were
"infidels of a low and indecent grade," he wrote; they were vulgar,
profane, and "utterly worthless for any useful purposes of society." A
majority of those remaining were French Catholics who had grown
unresponsive to their own religion. Without frequent visits from
clergy, frontier settlements, it was believed, would deteriorate mor-
ally, socially, and of course religiously.[3]

Another challenge, one that came with the benefit of having a
fresh start and level playing field in the vastness of the Ohio Valley, was the closeness of non-Catholics and the interdependence
of settlers, regardless of religion. Such closeness, especially given
the preponderance in numbers of other denominations, meant lay
Catholics, in turn, might be influenced by Protestants. John Carroll, in spite of his enthusiastic optimism in 1785 about establishing the church from the east coast to the Mississippi River, worried
about Catholic declension. Carroll reported to Cardinal Antonelli
in Rome that "The abuses that have grown among Catholics are
chiefly those, which result with unavoidable intercourse with non-
Catholics, and the examples thense derived." The new superior of
the American mission was concerned that Catholic youth communicated with their non-Catholic counterparts too freely and without
supervision. These and other indiscretions were likely to be more
frequent in the sparsely settled frontier regions, such as southwestern Pennsylvania, which one priest described as "scattered [with
Catholics] in small number" and "settled with other persuasions." If
Catholics migrated too far too quickly, they would end up isolated
from the clergy, "exposed to live and die without the consolations
of Religion," wrote Badin. Their families "would go astray," and the
result would be the creation of "ignorant & vicious, or indifferent
and nominal Catholics who do much harm and bring disgrace on
the church in the eyes of Protestants."[4]

In addition to the threat of passive declension, Catholic clergy
believed lay Catholics could become subject to the active conversion efforts of Protestants in the West. Particularly worrisome was
the fact that priests were in short supply and communications with
church authorities could take months each way. Indeed, Father Gallitzin had moved to frontier Pennsylvania in the 1790s to found a

community of Catholics who might be free of undue influence by Protestantism, the many unsavory effects of which he thought he already had witnessed in the eastern part of the state and in Maryland. Gallitzin's goal from the beginning of his move westward, according to a colleague, was to create a community "in which no Protestant element could assert itself." When Father Badin reported on the great evangelical revival at Cane Ridge in 1801—which had attracted twenty thousand Baptists, Methodists, and Presbyterians—he told Bishop Carroll of enthused revivalists who had become "very troublesome among Catholics." Badin proclaimed he had "strictly forbid any communication in spirituality" because he was worried about the "Scandalous & nominal Catholics" among his own parishioners, even though none had yet left the church as a result of the Baptists' efforts.[5]

Clergy did have cause for concern because Protestants surely viewed Catholic settlers as potential converts. Evangelical ministers and a broadening infrastructure of missionary, Bible, and tract societies were reaching westward concurrently with Catholic efforts during the early republic. For example, between 1816 and 1820, the American Bible Society was created and distributed almost 100,000 Bibles. Between 1814 and 1823, the American Tract Society printed 770,000 tracts in addition to other publications with which to blanket the nation. In 1815, the Bible Society of Philadelphia gave $600 for copies of the New Testament in French to two representatives and sent 5,000 Bibles to Pittsburgh to be distributed to frontier Catholics living in the West and Southwest.[6]

The Promise of the West

But proximity to and close interaction with non-Catholics also could be beneficial. After all, the church had a long history of viewing the New World as an environment favorable for harvesting souls.[7] The presence of so many non-Christians—Indian and European—as well as Protestants scattered and potentially in a state of religious declension in the hinterlands, meant there were many possible contact points at which to attempt conversion. If the frontier was spacious, thinly settled, conducive to interdenominational mixing, sorely lacking trained clergy, and replete with Catholics of wavering faith, then it also held similar problems for Protestant groups. Catholic clergy perceived in this situation certain opportunities. Moreover, the spirit of religious revival cropping up from Cane Ridge, Kentucky, to Rochester, New York, inspired confidence that great advances were imminent in America for Christian religion. With a concerted effort and enough worthy priests, Catholic officials believed they could win over non-Catholics in trans-Appalachia.

Indeed, Catholic missionaries believed they had certain advantages over their Protestant rivals. In 1815 Father Charles Nerinckx sang the praises of intrepid Catholic priests who still traveled farther west than their Protestant counterparts in search of souls. "Still, it should be remarked," he said, "that the activity of the sectarians extends only to the already populated land, where the comforts of life can be enjoyed." Clinging to hearth and family, Protestant clergy also were uninterested, according to Nerinckx, in converting the Indian. "The preacher of the Reformation, surrounded by wife and children, and unwilling to abandon them after the example of St. Peter," he scoffed, "finds it easier to make Protestants out of Christians"—i.e., to steal away marginal Catholics—"than to bring the heathen and savages to Christianity." Converting Native Americans, or "bringing the gospel to the heathens," as he put it, was a higher calling and one "entrusted by the Lord to the Holy Roman Church exclusively." The missionary mind-set, especially when it came to converting souls to Catholicism, was laden with romanticized notions.[8]

If there existed a founding myth of Catholicism in the American West, tales of conversion would have been at its core, for convincing Protestants of their error was tightly interwoven with notions of success in frontier regions. Through these narratives Catholics convinced themselves and their European supporters of the Roman church's achievements on the American continent. It was said that Father Benedict Flaget's first journey to the interior of the continent in 1792 began with one such dramatic story. After his arrival from France, he had reached Pittsburgh by wagon and waited in the city six months for higher water on the Ohio River for his boat trip to Louisville and then Vincennes on the Wabash River. While waiting in Pittsburgh he made the acquaintance of General Anthony Wayne, who was in charge of the garrison there. Four deserters had been captured and sentenced to death, two of whom were Irish American Catholics, one a Protestant, and the last a French deist.

Offering spiritual succor to the four condemned men, Flaget supposedly was able to comfort the two Catholics and convert the Protestant, but was unable to convince the French liberal to repent and find faith. During the execution of the first three, Flaget swooned, and General Wayne ultimately spared the French prisoner, believing that Flaget had been deeply upset that a fellow Frenchman was so unprepared to die. Having seen the three Catholics off and saved a deist, Flaget continued his journey.[9]

Father Gallitzin's arrival on the frontier also began with a focus on conversion. In fact, he had two such stories, the first of which was the Cliptown incident in which spirits haunting a Lutheran family's house convinced fourteen people to become Catholics in 1797. Another predicament involving a Protestant interested in Catholicism was fundamental to Gallitzin's decision to dedicate his life to being a pastor in western Pennsylvania. In the summer of 1795, Gallitzin was called from Baltimore to western Pennsylvania to attend an ill Protestant, Mrs. John Burgoons, who had asked to see a Catholic priest. No Catholic clergy were present in the western half of the state, so one of Mrs. Burgoons's neighbors traveled 125 miles east to the Conewago mission for help, and from there word was sent to Bishop Carroll, farther south and east in Baltimore. Gallitzin made the arduous trip to the Clearfield/McGuire settlement, attended Mrs. Burgoons, and said Mass for the local inhabitants. This experience planted the idea in his mind of permanently settling at Clearfield, which he ultimately did in 1798, renaming his Catholic outpost the town of Loretto.[10]

Father Badin's formative experience with conversion was a vicarious one, though he felt its effects acutely. After being abandoned by a fellow priest within his first few months in the backcountry in 1793, he had worked alone in Kentucky for four years, continually calling on Bishop Carroll for help. Struggling to minister to the scattered Catholic families and settlements in Kentucky and penning increasingly desperate pleas for help to Bishop Carroll, Badin did not receive assistance—in the form of associate priests—until 1797. Thereafter he was finally able to write confidently about the progress he and his three compatriots were making, the churches they built, and the numbers of baptisms and other sacraments they were able to administer. But soon the foundations of their fellowship, the strength on which Badin's plans depended, began to shift and collapse. Within three years, one of his priests had died, another had been ejected in disgrace, and the third, Father Anthony Salmon, had been thrown by a horse and killed while riding to meet with a recent convert. The latter incident perhaps was made more painful for Badin because he and other Catholics believed Father Salmon had survived the initial fall in the woods, cried out for help, and sent a young boy for assistance, but had then been left to die because a Protestant farmer had refused the youth's entreaty on behalf of the fast-expiring priest.[11]

While not always optimistic themselves, conversion tales were at the heart of the frontier experience of western bishops and priests. These narratives expressed the high expectations that clergy placed on themselves, juxtaposed with the demands and promise of frontier missionary work. And at the beginning of the century, western prospects still looked good. In addition to romanticized conversion tales and sweeping pronouncements about opportunities for proselytizing in the West, clerical reports and correspondence in the period were replete with references to conversions hoped for, planned, or attempted.

In 1805 Father Badin described the consequences of the revival activity among Baptists, Methodists, and Presbyterians in Kentucky as an occasion for Catholics to make inroads into the Protestant hegemony. After three or four years of frenzied activity, here was a moment "when men seem to arise from a Lethargy, & express their amazement at the dying follies which have taken place for these three years past among various Religionists." It was clear to Badin that the evangelicals were exhausted and that some were ready for a more authentic religious experience. Protestant revivalism was an energized yet empty phenomenon, according to Badin. The camp meetings about which everyone was hearing so much were devoid of genuine religious meaning. Rather, they were places where men and women came together led by white and black ministers and female "Pythonesses of Apollo . . . in confusion, with wild glances, trembling violently, singing, exhorting, dancing, praying, clapping their hands . . . uttering without ceasing the name of God," making "either mornful or joyous cries . . . horrible shrieking," with some in the audience "stamp[ing] their feet, or skip[ing] towards one another for hours at a time" until "finally a number fall fainting." Badin generalized that evangelical Kentuckians were worn out by their revivalism, while "pretty near half" of those who remained "do not af-filiate with any religion but believe in general in a confused manner in revelation." These, he said, "die without having made choice of any sect." Given this muddled state of frontier Protestantism, Badin avowed, he and "Twelve Apostles" of the right temperament—men such as his new colleague, Father Nerinckx—could "make most of the Western Countries embrace the true faith."[12]

Some Protestants seemed willing to meet them part way, of-ten out of inquisitiveness. Just as their sumptuous and seemingly exotic church buildings and processions attracted attention, so did the presence of the first Catholic bishop in the trans-Appalachian West. Describing Bishop Flaget's first season in the Bardstown diocese, Father John Baptist David observed that not only were apostates coming "to throw themselves in his arms . . . everywhere he goes," but Protestants appeared "to have an extreme curios-ity to see him and even to speak to him." More than a show of good public relations, this attractiveness and accessibility, David believed, would mean "that in a short time he will make a great number of converts."[13]

Reporting to the pope on the condition of religion, this frontier bishop expressed the same optimism in 1815 with regard to con-verting Protestants in his vast trans-Appalachian diocese, particu-larly along its western edge. Most of the Protestants he met were "wholly ignorant of the doctrines proper to their sect," whereas many others simply claimed no religious identity at all but "live in complete indifference." For the latter, unfettered by civilizing influences and cast across the prairies and forests of the backcoun-try, "God is either Mammon or their belly." A depressing situation for Protestant clergy, perhaps, but, Flaget claimed, with enough priests, "many of these people could easily be brought back to the Catholic Church, especially in places where there is no min-ister of their own religion." By attending to their own flocks, set-ting a good example, and reaching out to non-Catholics whenever possible, clergy hoped to fulfill the growing religious needs among frontier settlers. There was also the question of Native Americans to consider. Flaget had identified uncommitted Protestants, liberal thinkers, and Indians as groups to target. "What shall I say about the numerous tribes of Indians who inhabit these vast regions . . . ?" he asked. "Here, Most Holy Father, is open a great and evident door for the propagation of the Gospel." Asking only for more missionaries, Flaget minimized the competitive threat from the "three principal sects"; he framed their presence as an opportunity for winning new converts.[14]

Two years later Father David continued the theme of proselytizing non-Catholics farther to the west. By 1817, six years after establishment of the expansive Bardstown diocese, David, Flaget, and other Kentucky clergy were looking toward the Mississippi River for potential converts. When a group of Italian missionaries stopped at Bardstown's seminary en route to St. Louis that year, Father David, himself a French immigrant, emphasized that this new cohort should learn English as quickly as possible. He gave them lessons himself, "with singular pleasure," he said, because he knew it would be crucial for them to communicate with American settlers along the Mississippi River. "Even the Protestants, who are already there in somewhat great number, not having any ministers of their sects," he added, "are favorably disposed to reenter the bosom of the Catholic Church."[15]

At the close of the decade, some in the church still looked westward with generally sanguine expectations. Archbishop Ambrose Maréchal, John Carroll's successor as superior of the American missions, reported to Rome that overall, good relations with Protestants across the United States prevailed, due in part to the "certain veneration" non-Catholics seemed to hold for American Catholic clergy. Referring to the American missions, Maréchal felt "there is no region which offers a wider or more fertile field for apostolic zeal," a quality that Protestant clergy, by Catholic definition, sorely lacked. In areas such as trans-Appalachia or, in particular, the "southern provinces," the archbishop argued that "a bishop can sow, foster and cultivate the seed of Catholic faith in this territory, before the Protestant ministers can disseminate their errors there." For the first twenty years of the nineteenth century, the clergy had grand ambitions about winning new souls to the church.[16]

Nevertheless, these conversion narratives and aspirations were vague in their own way, rarely accompanied by an actual name of the non-Catholic who had made the crossing or by a description of the ceremony or other circumstances involved. If details identified an individual, he was typically of prominent social status. One historian has calculated that priests would have effected no more—and probably even far less—than one to one and a half conversions each per year.[17]

It is therefore probable that true converts were relatively rare and that clergy were likely to trumpet their more celebrated successes. Father Badin, for example, referred to only a very few, illustrious, converts by name. In Scott County, Kentucky, he proudly announced Justice of the Peace James Twyman to be "one of our most zealous converts" of the 1790s. Near Brownsville, Pennsylvania, between 1803 and 1807, Badin cultivated for conversion Major Richard Noble "and his Lady, parents of a large and respectable family." A wealthy Episcopalian and "a man of great judgment, probity, and piety," Noble was, in Badin's opinion, likely to use his fortune to build a church on his own property. When Bishop Flaget wrote of conversion efforts, his comments were either vague or in regard to individuals who had not yet converted but who seemed to be potential candidates. In his diary in 1812, for example, he recorded that on February 5 he "Spoke to a young Protestant man who wants to become a Catholic"; on February 22 "Two young Protestant women" took the promising step of going to Catholic confession; on July 10 he "Baptized in the afternoon 3 children of a Protestant"; and on July 11 "Conversed with a deist, but without converting him I reduced him to silence." In 1818, while on a lengthy tour of his vast diocese, Flaget spoke of a strong desire to transform one Mr. Anderson, "a member of Congress, and a Presbyterian in Religion," who was pious and an excellent conversationalist. "I should be much surprised, if he and all his family do not become Catholics."[18]

Two years later, in 1820, Father Nerinckx surely overstated the success of Dominican priests at Somerset, Ohio, in winning converts to Catholicism. Nerinckx was writing for a European audience of Catholics, one that he was soliciting for contributions to help the parishes and missions in the American trans-Appalachian West. According to his account, the clergy at the mission of St. Joseph's in less than six months had "gained over to the true church" some "thirty families, mostly Methodists." Among the numerous converts was "a lawyer of great ability." There are reasons to doubt the veracity of this statement. Triumph on such a scale seems unlikely; no other clergy made claims of more than a few individual conversions at a time during this era. Moreover, the Cliptown incident, a remarkable occurrence by any account, only resulted in fourteen individual converts. In fact, at the heart of the Catholic presence in the West, in Bardstown—with its cathedral, Catholic schools, and episcopal see—a related claim of success in winning over Protestants involved only three families, not thirty. According to Bishop David, in the spring of 1822 there seemed to be "a movement in our town towards Catholicism." Three families, he reported, "already had their children baptized and seem disposed to follow their [i.e., the children's] example," although they had not yet done so. Still, if some eminent individuals had not converted or professed, they soon would: "a lawyer of great renown" said he would be baptized; "a doctor who had resided for many years at Bardstown has followed the Dominicans to Cincinnati for the purpose of embracing the Catholic Church and their Order"; and "an old magistrate, one of the richest and well-considered members of his congregation," had been baptized recently. In case there was any doubt that conversions had propaganda value, David told his correspondent that Bishop Flaget was collecting the details of conversion stories to send to Father Badin in France, who had asked "for such anecdotes to help him in the collection he is making for us." If Catholic clergy did not have sheer numbers to report, all the more reason to compensate by conversing about ideal candidates or claiming grand victories.[19]

Most significant was the perception that these conversions were taking place and that more were likely. It was necessary to convince themselves, their parishioners, and their non-Catholic neighbors that the church was providing sufficient spiritual services for its members, was retaining and invigorating nominal Catholics, and was even winning over significant individuals from among the Protestant denominations. This kind of celebrity focus would become more important in the 1820s as tensions increased between denominations and Catholic clergy grew less optimistic about conquering the West and more determined simply to hold their own among the Protestant majority.

Mixed Marriages

Maintaining their own—that is, ensuring that Catholics were not lost to frontier decline, the lure of Protestantism, or the influence of the non-Catholic world, was one of the most basic obligations for clergy. Conversions, however, could not be counted on to add significant numbers of new recruits to the church. They were more of a symbolic victory than a practical one. Even when clergy could point to specific cases of successful conversion, they usually involved a single individual. The more illustrious converts or potential converts on whom Catholic clergy seemed to focus typically were persons willing to cut themselves off from families and enter the church alone. A mixed marriage between a Catholic and a non-Catholic, however, was likely to sever from the church not just the Catholic spouse but all of the couple's future children. Where attempted, actual, or imagined conversions represented a gain for the Catholic Church, interfaith marriages generally were treated as a losing proposition for all involved and as a particularly harsh blow to the church, which stood to lose future generations of members.

Marriage across denominational lines was an unavoidable issue, particularly when Catholics began moving into new regions of the country. As Bishop John Carroll explained to a friend in England, "Here," in America, "Catholics are so mixed with Protestants in all the intercourse of civil Society, & business public and private," that problems such as intermarriage became all too common.[20] An overall scarcity of Catholic and non-Catholic clergy meant that Catholic and Protestant laity might drift in their beliefs and begin to rely on whichever member of the clergy happened to serve their community most frequently. Likewise, once Catholics moved away from predominantly Catholic towns or settlements for the less populated parts of frontier regions, they might be less likely to find Catholic spouses.

In Maryland, Catholic clergy had long discouraged the faithful from marrying outside their religion and instead had encouraged Catholics to wed Catholic relatives. By the end of the eighteenth century, intra-familial weddings were a common solution to the problem of maintaining the Catholic Church in a land dominated by Protestantism. Indeed, John Carroll, as priest and then as bishop, wrote to Rome many times requesting faculties to marry certain couples—Catholics and Protestants, blacks and whites—despite their close blood relationship. Presumably Carroll was under great pressure to permit these marriages since few other options were available. In 1785 Carroll received authority to marry up to forty couples who otherwise would have been prohibited because of the "line" (i.e., the type) or the "degree" (i.e., the closeness) of their blood relationship; that is, he received permission to grant dispensations for up to twenty first cousins and twenty in-laws. In 1794 the bishop was authorized to dispense the impediment of a baptized person marrying a non-baptized person. In 1802 Carroll received faculties to grant dispensations for another two hundred of each of the two kinds of consanguinity impediments, and his faculty to marry baptized with non-baptized was extended for three years. It was only in 1810 that Carroll was granted faculties to dispense with the impediment of mixed marriages, for prior to then interfaith marriages were discouraged but did not require a dispensation.[21]

Even with permission to grant such dispensations, Carroll was loath to encourage Catholics to join with non-Catholics, for as he once sermonized, mixed marriages were too often unhappy ones that exposed the children to danger: "The opposite religious opinions of the father and mother serve to perplex, and finally to make their children indifferent about the tenets or practices of christianity." As a result, said Carroll, the children of mixed marriages "fall an easy prey to the artificial sophistry of deists, and finally discard from their minds even the belief in God's moral government." The subject was as poignant for the bishop as anyone, perhaps even more so. His own relatives had married outside the church. In July 1800 the son of his wealthy cousin, Charles Carroll of Carrollton, was set to marry a Protestant. Bishop Carroll attended the wedding and was willing to officiate only because he knew if he refused "that the ministry of a Protestant would be resorted to," since the bride's family preferred this. Upon arriving, Carroll discovered he was scheduled to marry the couple in the morning; later that evening Bishop William White, the first Episcopal bishop consecrated in the United States, was to marry them again "in a more ceremonious style." Carroll refused this indignity, explaining that marriages were performed this way in England out of necessity, since Catholic weddings were not legally recognized. Not being the case in America, why agree to allow a Catholic ceremony an inferior status? Carroll was willing to compromise, nevertheless, and suggested the Protestant marriage ceremony be moved a few days later and that it consist of no more than the same level of fanfare and air of legitimacy as the Catholic.[22]

In 1791, when Carroll and his clergy gathered at Baltimore for the first diocesan synod, they took up the topic of mixed marriages and decreed the following: Priests were to "earnestly" dissuade Catholics from marrying outside the faith. Recognizing the minority position of American Catholics and that regular contact with non-Catholics meant intermarriages would continue, "especially in those places in which, as yet, there dwell but few Catholics," priests were to agree to them as a last resort and only after having explained the "great inconveniences" of marrying outside the faith. If the couple persisted, the priest should evaluate whether or not there was a "probable danger of perversion of the Catholic party." Then, if the priest felt obliged to proceed, he was to have the non-Catholic promise "before God and Witnesses" to permit all the children to be raised as Catholics. The synod also instructed priests to perform the marriage if otherwise "upon rejection" the couple appeared "to have recourse to a Minister not of the true Faith." Interfaith marriages, however, were not to receive the prescribed blessing for bride and bridegroom.[23]

Despite the synod's ruling, intermarriages increased, both because Catholics remained a small minority in the United States for several decades and because, as they moved to frontier areas, away from places such as Maryland where Catholic families were numerous, there were fewer potential Catholic spouses. As an exasperated Carroll stated in 1803, "the abuse of intermarriage is almost universal," and it "surpasses my ability to devise any effectual bar against it." If permitted only to marry within the faith, American Catholics would be reduced to "live in a state of celibacy" since "in sundry places," such as the young nation's expanding frontier areas, "there would be no choice for them of Catholic matches."[24] Confronted with a problem exacerbated by the frontier, Carroll and his clergy emphasized adherence to orthodoxy and tradition. Rather than ease the requirements for permitting marriage between Catholics and non-Catholics, the American clergy would acquiesce only if there seemed little other choice. Yet drawing too hard of a line might drive some young Catholics to seek a marriage with or without the pastor's approval, so the clergy were authorized to allow some intermarriages to occur. Where Carroll did exhibit flexibility was in seeking dispensations from the church's matrimonial laws on consanguinity for marriages between Catholic relatives who might otherwise have been too closely related.

Neither Carroll nor his priests in the West seemed concerned that a strict observance of marriage laws would adversely affect the church's relationship with non-Catholics. At issue was the fundamental problem of the church's survival in a country where Catholics were outnumbered and unlikely to live near a Catholic church or clergyman if they participated in the geographic and economic expansion of the nation. Carroll and the clergy in general took a hard line. Priests and prelate showed no signs of worry that Protestant observers might look on their rules regarding mixed marriages as a Catholic ploy to win new converts. It was a basic matter of survival.

Father Badin was particularly strict in applying the diocesan rules on mixed marriages. The Kentucky priest, who often found himself working alone or in the company of a few fellow clergy nearly overwhelmed with difficulties, tried hard to discourage interfaith marriages. In 1796 Badin asked Carroll about the validity of a mixed marriage involving a Catholic woman who had found a way to defy her parents and the church—by consenting to her own "seduction and rape"—so that she could marry a Protestant husband in a service performed by a Protestant minister. In 1798 he wondered whether he had mistakenly welcomed two Catholic women back into communion within the church after having successfully barred them for having married their own Protestant cousins. Badin had been able to force the women to make public penance and had separated the husbands temporarily "from their pretended wives," but then through his own "inconsiderateness" had given the impression eventually that the marriages were acceptable. He could hardly forgive himself for his negligence. It was better to be seen as too strict than to harm the faith by allowing laxity.[25]

Badin and other priests interpreted their own rigorous observance of marriage requirements as strengthening the church rather than weakening it by scaring off nominal Catholics. Explaining his application of the rule requiring the marriage banns to be posted in a betrothed couple's local church on three successive Sundays, Badin argued its effectiveness in sustaining the church. "Far from occasioning anybody to fall thro' weakness into schism"—that is, leaving the Catholic Church because of its many regulations regarding marriages—the banns were "rather a means of preventing this fatal transgression." "It is a link," he wrote, "that connects the parties already with the ministers of the Church," since "it is a public profession of their faith & attachment to its body & discipline." Badin felt an outward gesture of personal belief and public submission only strengthened a couple's religious resolve. "I have never seen any couple fly to heterodox ministers when that step had been taken," he stated; "on the contrary, I have seen several couples fall into schism for want of giving timely notice to Mr. Fournier of their engagement to marry." Father Nerinckx had a similar take on the subject. In 1807 he announced that couples to be married would have to "prepare themselves by a retreat," which, he pointed out, had the effect of drastically reducing the "number of those who attempt to marry persons of other denominations or of their own kindred." Those who defied the church's admonitions on marriage only jeopardized themselves and their progeny. According to Badin, a young woman named Nancy McFarling had ignored her priest's counsel and left her family for a divorced Protestant. After marrying themselves by swearing "on the Bible that they would remain faithful to each other," Badin reported, "the poor woman is in the greatest anxiety & even her health & brain has suffered much therefrom." This wayward Catholic's demise was to be expected.[26]

By 1810 it became apparent that strict enforcement of the church's rules on matrimony was pushing some of the laity to extreme measures and landing them outside the faith. Badin complained to Bishop Carroll, "The Marriages of Catholics with Protestants, Infidels or non-Catholics before Preachers continue to be frequent." At least within a mixed marriage sanctioned by the Catholic Church, the children had some hope of being raised Catholic. The situation Badin described suggested that mixed couples were giving up on Catholicism altogether. "Such an evil," said the priest, "which often is reproduced for some years past[,] demand[s] some efficacious remedy." It was clear to Badin and Nerinckx that a solution was necessary. It also was clear that they disagreed with Fathers Fenwick and Tuite, two Dominicans who seemed too lenient on mixed couples seeking marriages. One case involved Sam Abell, who asked Fenwick to marry him to his cousin, N. Abell, who was non-Catholic. Badin asserted that Fenwick encouraged Sam Abell in his folly by telling him he would perform the ceremony after the man had sought Nerinckx's or Badin's permission first. Since "no Priest could give a dispensation to a non-Catholic, and of course that no Priest could marry him validly to his cousin, unless she became Catholic," Badin refused to marry the Abells. Sam Abell's response to Badin suggested "he would not have carried on the courtship so far, if Mr. Fen.[wick] had not encouraged it." In the end the Abells had a Protestant minister join them in marriage, and Badin considered them and their descendants "lost to Religion."[27]

Badin recounted another case in which, he claimed, Father Fenwick had inappropriately encouraged a mixed marriage. John Stewart wished to be joined with Barbara Hunter, a woman with no religious upbringing, and Fenwick had agreed to baptize her and marry the couple. Since Stewart and Hunter both were members of Badin's congregation, Fenwick sent them to him for permission. Badin refused until Hunter had been baptized. "As she found some difficulty from her Parents to go to church, a place and a day after Easter were appointed, where I might meet her, to prepare her for Baptism," remembered Badin. But he discovered her to be "ignorant" of the most elementary Catholic prayers and points of doctrine, and had heard secondhand the woman's profession of "a partial disbelief of the Scriptures." Even though Badin gave her a "promise to baptize & marry her as soon as she was prepared," he learned, after he had gone to Vincennes for a time, that the woman and her fiancé were married by a Protestant minister.[28]

From the time of Badin's arrival in Kentucky until Bishop Flaget's early years as the first western bishop, interfaith marriages were a perennial problem. Flaget also tended to be strict in his response, typically imposing a public penance on Catholics marrying outside the church. He was severe in these cases. Improper marriages, he thought, were far too common and were the cause of "so much disorder on the earth." When Flaget was visiting the far northern reaches of his diocese in 1818, near the River Raisin in Michigan, he publicly excommunicated a man who had married outside the church. Flaget's toughness on the issue was also apparent in a question he posed, via Father Nerinckx, to the prefect of the Congregation for the Propagation of the Faith in 1816. The western bishop wanted Nerinckx to "Ask also whether I could not deprive of Christian burial one unfortunate, who, knowingly and very willingly, married an infidel or non-baptized person." The married Catholic man had "passed all his life in such concubinage," never bothering to persuade his wife to get baptized or to be converted. Nerinckx passed along the question, noting that "these cases are not rare" in western America.[29]

In 1813, Kentucky clergy sought guidance from Rome on the problem of mixed marriages, as well as an array of other conundrums involving Catholics and non-Catholics living together in the Ohio Valley. At Bishop Flaget's invitation, Father Nerinckx composed a long list of questions about how to properly interact with Protestants in trans-Appalachia. A major portion of these dealt with interfaith marriages or aspects of matrimony affected by the non-Catholic presence. Of Cardinal Michele de Pietro, prefect of the Congregation for the Propagation of the Faith, Nerinckx asked whether Tridentine law on marriage—probably meaning the portion of it dealing with mixed marriages—was binding "in this part of North America." How should clergy handle a conflict between civil law and the church if, for example, a civil law requiring the consent of the parents invalidates a marriage between Catholics? What about Catholics who "contract matrimony either before a civil magistrate or a non-Catholic minister"? How "should a pastor assist at marriages in which one of the parties is not a Catholic?" Was it required to publicize the prenuptial announcements or banns when two slaves were to be married? What were the penalties for Catholics who ignore their pastor and are married by a non-Catholic minister, and how could they be "reconciled with the Church if they come to their senses?" Because the state of Kentucky was requiring ministers of all denominations to take an oath, Nerinckx reported, he would be asked to promise "to observe peaceful social customs as long as I live in this part of the republic." Since he believed free exercise of religion was well protected in Kentucky, the priest agreed, though he still wanted to know what the cardinal prefect thought of the situation. Moreover, he added, "May one licitly take an oath on the Protestant Bible that is used?" Amidst change and growth, Father Nerinckx and Bishop Flaget were looking, like John Carroll, to Rome for guidance.[30]

After a delay of nearly three years, the cardinals of the Congregation for the Propagation of the Faith in Rome referred some of Nerinckx's questions to the pope and made decisions on others, forwarding these to the Kentucky priest and his bishop. With regard to marriages and Tridentine law, the cardinals confirmed its applicability in the United States, though they decided to consult with Archbishop Carroll of Baltimore about "whether it is expedient" to make the promulgation public. Marriages contracted before Protestant ministers or only by a civil magistrate were not to be considered valid in the eyes of the Catholic Church since, without the presence of the priest, such marriages were "not sacraments." Conversely, marriages contracted by a priest were "valid even if secular law declares otherwise." As for Catholic couples who left their pastor to be married by a non-Catholic minister, the cardinals of the Propaganda noted that under Tridentine law, "besides the penalty of excommunication" for the couple and any Catholics assisting them, "the marriage [itself] is invalid." In practice, however, the cardinals left the nature of the penalty up to the bishop. In mixed marriages, priests were not permitted to assist "unless the dispensation has been obtained with the usual conditions of endeavoring to convert the non-Catholic, and of educating the children in the Catholic religion." Regarding the oath that Nerinckx and other priests were required to take in order to conduct marriages in the state of Kentucky, the cardinals decided the oaths were permissible if they did not go "against the Catholic religion." And they permitted oaths upon Protestant Bibles, "as long as they are intact and in conformity with our Vulgate."

Proliferating Quandaries

Father Nerinckx and Bishop Carroll had had other important questions, which they raised in 1813, about interacting with non-Catholics, fitting into American society, and adapting to frontier conditions. Nerinckx's queries, approved by Bishop Flaget, were those of a European priest attempting to square orthodoxy with the unusual circumstances of frontier trans-Appalachia, where Catholics were in daily contact with non-Catholics and all settlers put up with certain privations not found in more urban and eastern environments. In the margin of his missive to the cardinal, in fact, Nerinckx asked pardon for the "not very neat letter" he was writing, a result of constant interruptions, much work, and long trips: "the circuit of the various congregations subject to my care is easily 600 miles."

Nerinckx was desperate for guidance. Should priests rebaptize people who had already been baptized by Protestant ministers? If Protestants brought their children forward to be baptized by a priest, should this be done, "even if there is little hope of their being educated as Catholics?" Nerinckx also wanted to know whether it was permissible for Catholics to charge interest like everyone else in America, if the "rate set by civil law is not exceeded." He indicated that he hoped Rome would concur, since currency was in scarce supply in the region and money lending was a necessary part of economic development. Bishops in England and Ireland already were permitting this practice. Likewise, living among non-Catholics in a diversifying economy in frontier Kentucky, Nerinckx wanted to know what to think of commerce in slaves, in particular "What is to be said of their sale to heretics or of their sale at public auctions?"

Nerinckx's other questions suggest he and his colleagues were dealing with what they considered frontier circumstances in a place that Nerinckx termed "this new region." Trained doctors could be as rare as clergy in the backcountry, and on occasion a priest might feel compelled to treat a patient after having been called many miles on horseback to provide spiritual assistance. Nerinckx therefore asked, "May a priest bleed people or practice other medical skills?" Furthermore, knowing how difficult it was to obtain an altar stone and how much they might be used by priests trekking from one Catholic settlement to another, Nerinckx wanted to know whether it was "allowed to offer Mass on a consecrated altar stone that is broken." He must have been thinking about a specific fractured stone because he went on to ask, "Is it allowed to offer it [i.e., the Mass] on a part of the stone that is sufficiently large to hold the host and chalice? Can it be offered only on the relics?" Furthermore, asked the priest, if the stone had not been consecrated, "is it permitted the priest to give it the common blessing," particularly "in missions far distant" from the bishop of the diocese?

Nerinckx next inquired about "the best way for providing for the livelihood of ministers in this new region." As has been previously noted, ensuring adequate sources of revenue for resident priests had been a perennial problem. Father Charles Whelan was taken to court by two of his parish trustees in Kentucky in 1788 after he complained about his salary. And Father Francis Fromm in western Pennsylvania in the early 1790s, as well as Fathers Anthony Salmon, M. Fournier, John Thayer, and Stephen Badin in Kentucky, from the late 1790s through 1805, grumbled repeatedly about their parishioners' stinginess. And Nerinckx himself, throughout the first decade of the new century, was vexed by lack of financial support from the laity. Bishop Carroll and his colleagues took up the matter at the first diocesan synod in 1791 and called on American Catholics to overcome their "backwardness" in contributing. Apparently, in 1813 Nerinckx and Bishop Flaget still had not found a solution. Nerinckx asked the cardinals of the Congregation for the Propagation of the Faith, "what obligation do the laity have of taking care of this?" More interestingly, he asked permission "to deny spiritual ministrations," such as "the baptism of their small children," to those parishioners who refused to contribute to their clergy's support. An alternative means of revenue, Nerinckx suggested, could be to demand a "tax of contribution" or "almsgiving" whenever the bishop granted a dispensation to a lay church member; for example, when allowing blood relatives to marry each other.[31]

The priest's final questions to his Roman superiors revealed the extent to which Catholics and Protestants relied on each other in this period in his corner of Kentucky. Was it permissible "to serve meat to heretics on the forbidden days if they are on a journey or are working among Catholics?" In other words, Nerinckx wanted to know whether or not Catholic rules applied to Protestants who, already under the stress of traveling, sought hospitality at a Catholic home. Or did it apply to those Protestants who either for pay or out of a sense of mutual support labored alongside of Catholics? Father Badin fifteen years earlier had explained to Bishop Carroll that backcountry exigencies pushed his Catholics to request indulgences during Lent to eat meat, since they claimed it was too much of a hardship to expect them to have on hand a "sufficient stock of vegetables." Now Nerinckx wanted to know whether and how to apply such strictures on meat eating to non-Catholic neighbors. Finally, Nerinckx inquired, "Is it permissible to build their churches?" How far should mutual assistance go? And if Catholics opened their activities to non-Catholics, was it acceptable in return for Catholics to "be present at their instructions, funeral services, funerals, and so forth?"[32]

Responding in 1816, the cardinals of the Propaganda adopted a moderate approach that emphasized orthodoxy while giving American clergy some leeway in dealing with the new circumstances of a backcountry area in a non-Catholic nation. The cardinals' decisions were likely to smooth interdenominational relations while fostering the growth and maintaining the distinctiveness of the church. On the issue of baptizing non-Catholics, they stated, "Those who have been baptized by heretics are not to be rebaptized." In other words, "as long as there were observed the formula" of water and words, Catholics should recognize and accept the baptism performed in other denominations if the "intention of the Catholic sacrament" were present. Children of Protestants brought before a Catholic priest for baptism—not an uncommon occurrence in backcountry settlements, where clerical visits of any kind were rare—must be baptized, declared the cardinal, "even if there is [only] slight hope of Catholic education and also [if] there be no godparents." Years later, American clergy in the West were still faced with numerous requests to baptize non-Catholics. In 1818, Father John Grassi reported how non-Catholic settlers still frequently called on priests to make sick calls, during which "it is often necessary to begin by giving conditional baptism to the sick, for they cannot tell whether they are baptized or not: the negligence of Protestants on this point is very great." In some instances, non-Catholics would ask to be baptized or have their children baptized because of a fear of imminent death, and the priest was left with "no time to Impart instruction." Father Grassi was describing conditions under which itinerant clergy continued to work into the 1820s in trans-Appalachia. Even as late as 1827, priests were baptizing non-Catholics. "Although we can count without difficulty the great numbers who are opposed to our doctrines," reported Father B. Martial in his survey of the Kentucky diocese, "still, it is amazing how many Protestants want Catholic priests to baptize their children."[33]

In regard to modern economic concerns clashing with traditional religious values, the cardinals gave scant guidance on the practice of charging interest on loans. The cardinals decreed interest should only be charged if both parties explicitly concurred, and if permitted by custom "introduced in the law" that assures "the facility of commerce." Interest charged, they added, had to be "moderate," not "excessive." Their answers were vague enough that Nerinckx would repeat this question eight years later in an attempt to get a clearer sense of their intention—one that would be simpler in practical application. As for selling slaves to "heretics" or at public auction, the cardinals took a hard line, replying bluntly, "It is not permitted."

Recognizing the difficulties of life in frontier regions, however, the cardinals bestowed some license on American clergy in trans-Appalachia. For example, the prefect responded in the affirmative to the query, "May a priest bleed people or practice other medical skills?" Yes, said the cardinal, but only "in case of necessity or in favor of the poor." These certainly were the circumstances under which clergy in Kentucky and elsewhere in the new West operated. Troubled by vast distances, shortages in religious supplies, and having to make do with resources at hand, these priests needed some flexibility. "Is it permitted to celebrate Mass on a broken stone that is consecrated?" Nerinckx had asked. "Affirmative as long as the part is capable of holding the chalice and the Host and the relics are present in the other parts." If the stone was not consecrated by a bishop or other church eminence, could a priest "give it the common blessing," especially in missions "far distant" from the bishop? "Affirmative," replied the cardinals, but only after obtaining in each case the permission of the pope. This latter concession could not have been much help. It saved the trouble of transporting ten to fifteen-pound rocks from Baltimore or Bardstown to far-flung missions, but necessitated sending a letter to Rome and waiting many months for a response.[34]

Nerinckx and Flaget's hints about forcing the laity to support the clergy financially elicited a firm answer from the cardinals. The laity's general parsimony had been inconveniencing American clergy, from western Pennsylvania to Kentucky, for twenty-five years, but the cardinals were not going to allow Nerinckx or others to use access to the sacraments as leverage in the struggle. To do so would be inherently wrong, and, furthermore, could cause the church public embarrassment. It would be a "scandalous thing" not to provide spiritual succor to individuals or the family members of individuals who had refused to contribute to the church. Instead, the western bishop would be permitted to establish a tax or tithe of one-tenth, and to urge the laity to demonstrate their faith and to remind them their "pious charities and generous offerings" were helpful to the church and its missions. The more severe measure of "deny[ing] spiritual help and, especially, the sacraments, to the laity," noted the cardinals, "is entirely disapproved." As for requesting a "tax," "contribution," or "almsgiving" whenever the bishop made a dispensation (i.e., an exemption from canon law), the cardinals replied in the negative. To link gifts for the church so closely with dispensations carried with it "the danger of becoming mercenaries and of becoming guilty of simony," that is, the sin of buying or selling ecclesiastical preferments or benefices.[35]

The last issues raised by the Kentucky clergymen were indicative of the pragmatic solutions to commonplace problems they sought, living as they did, side-by-side with non-Catholics. Serving meat to non-Catholics traveling or working among the faithful on "forbidden days," wrote the cardinals, "is no sin because already heretics do not acknowledge the obligations" to observe "this law" of abstinence. The hierarchy's decision would have been a relief for the Kentuckians, since, as Nerinckx had indicated earlier, strict abstention was extremely difficult at times. Vegetables were hard to come by during certain seasons, and travel and labor were exhausting endeavors in the West and required simple and nutritious sustenance. Drawing a sharper line, however, the cardinals ordered American Catholics to desist from helping to build Protestant churches or attending Protestant services of any kind. To do so was only "to encourage their incredulity" and "to involve the danger of being seduced by their errors." Catholics were to live close by non-Catholics, be good neighbors, invite non-Catholics into participating within Catholic services, institutions, and buildings, and yet maintain a level of vigilance toward the peril of that proximity.

In 1821, eight years after Father Nerinckx had made his initial set of inquiries and five years after the cardinals of the Congregation for the Propagation of the Faith had replied, Nerinckx and his bishop, Flaget, felt it necessary to resubmit some of their questions. The cardinals' responses had not been explicit in some cases, and, during the intervening years, Nerinckx and his colleagues had imagined or encountered new variants of the scenarios they had initially advanced. In other words, the situation of life in the West among a Protestant majority was growing more complicated. And Nerinckx worried he had not been descriptive enough in detailing the facets of that situation in his earlier correspondence with Rome. "There are in this new region of the world, as I indicated in my second and third letter to Rome, diverse practices and opinions." The "diversity," said Nerinckx, "begets many difficulties," and was exceptionally frustrating in a region where Catholics were working hard to make their religion "pleasing to all by the strength of its beauty." Rome and her servants had a "unique time" to set policy for the "principal practices" and for "controversial matters," said Nerinckx, because the U.S. government was "indulgent and cares hardly for religious matters," the spirit of the age was to remake all things new again, the bishops and priests were young and "docile," and the people were "new and uninstructed" and willing to listen.

Nerinckx's specific questions focused on several areas in which he and Bishop Flaget still desired guidance. Some were nuanced and problematical versions of what he had written in 1813. Nerinckx asked again this time about money lending, but in a more insistent manner and with a greater understanding of the issues involved in the region's economic maturation. Pressured by lay Catholics desperate to participate more freely in the region's economy, Nerinckx listed several arguments provided by locals in favor of the practice. Since the cardinals had responded ambiguously in the affirmative on this matter in 1816, Nerinckx may have been after a more enthusiastic endorsement of the practice. Also, he and Flaget may have been wishing for clarification since, as Nerinckx put it, they worked "in a region in which confessors do not always agree, and where the priests are not always of one mind." This priest, no doubt, preferred to hear a straightforward decree that it was "licit to charge interest provided that the legal rate is not exceeded." Kentucky Catholics would argue it should be so for a number of reasons. The interest rate was determined by the state; "Catholics in a non-Catholic country ought not be put at a disadvantage" by being forbidden "the lending of interest"; other westerners "freely and voluntarily pay interest and are, as they say, glad that they can get money in that way"; that "money is merchandise, and like merchandise, is subject to contractual agreement"; also that money is scarce and "there is difficulty in finding it in the new world"; finally, that it already was the "universal practice of bishops and devout priests in the region" to "admit the legitimacy of interest" and to "take part in such transactions."

A second area that Nerinckx probed again with an assortment of questions in his 1821 inquiry was marriage. Giving the issue a new twist, Nerinckx asked about couples who eloped and were married by non-Catholic ministers. What sins did they commit and censures did they incur? Should the couple or those "who welcome the returning couple into their home" be denied entrance into the church on Sunday? Should they be allowed "to assist at sacred functions" if they wanted to be reconciled with the church and while they are waiting to be reconciled? Taking a different tack, Nerinckx wanted to know, "What rite is the priest to use in matrimony when one of the parties is not a Catholic?" Eight years before, the cardinals had instructed the clergy not to assist unless such a couple had obtained a dispensation and had promised to raise the children to be Catholic. Now Nerinckx sought more precise direction. What was the officiating priest actually to say and do during such a marriage ceremony? "Is it licit to use the form, say the prayers, and bless the ring of the heretical spouse, etc.?"

Nerinckx also returned to questions involving slavery. He asked about slaves who married each other outside of the church, with or without their master's permission, by simply stating to each other, "I take you as my spouse." After they lived together as husband and wife and then presented themselves to a priest, what should the priest do? Must the master involved separate them? "If they are unwilling to be separated, ought some sacraments be denied them at the hour of death? 1) by reason of their illegitimate marriage? 2) by reason of the scandal that was given?" Obviously under pressure in a slave state to open up the matter of slave commerce, Nerinckx asked again about selling slaves to Protestants and other non-Catholics. The cardinals in 1816 had indicated it was not permissible, but now Nerinckx added extenuating circumstances: what if the slaves themselves were "infidels or heretics?" or, "What if the slaves are ill-tempered, unmanageable, and harmful to the family, etc.?"

Nerinckx again posed the matter of baptizing non-Catholics. Here he sought simple clarification, for the cardinals previously ruled it permissible to baptize the children of non-Catholics, even if there was little hope that the child would be educated as a Catholic. Nerinckx now asked, however, about cases in which the parents explicitly were "unwilling to have the child educated as a Catholic."

The last issue Nerinckx reopened was that of consuming meat during periods when Catholics were expected to abstain. This time, however, rather than asking how such strictures affected non-Catholics who happened to be visiting a Catholic home or working for a Catholic family, Nerinckx wanted to know whether or not Catholics must abstain. Specifically, if one was "In a non-Catholic region

where Catholics are very few in number, is flesh-meat entirely forbidden when making a journey in an area where fish and vegetables
are very rare?" The cardinals earlier had allowed Catholics to serve
meat to non-Catholics in such situations. And vice versa? Obviously
it was a hardship in the trans-Appalachian West to follow these rules
of abstinence for Catholics and non-Catholics alike, or Nerinckx
would not have had to raise the matter again. More interestingly,
Nerinckx hinted, these rules made Catholics stand out too much
among strangers in areas where Catholics were a rarity. Would a
Catholic be acting "prudently or badly" by not making the sign of
the cross before eating; that is, by giving "no other public signs of
religion" in these circumstances?[36]

A decade earlier, backcountry priests like Nerinckx had encouraged the display of Catholic identity in the midst of non-Catholics.
In 1807, for example, Nerinckx himself had written that a chief
characteristic possessed by all missionaries should be the ability to
lend an example to lay Catholics and get them to "own up to their
beliefs among infidels."[37] In his 1821 letter to Rome, however, the
priest voiced a different concern about non-Catholic opinion.

By the early 1820s Catholic clergy were less optimistic about winning the West through conversion and outward expressions of Catholic distinctiveness. Catholic priests and bishops had once imagined
the trans-Appalachian West to be an expansive region of promise
for the early church. Despite hardships and obstacles, shortages of
supplies and priests, and the predominance of Protestantism and
disbelief, Catholic clergy read the many points of contact with
non-Catholics as opportunities to prevail. Caught up in the general
Christian optimism of the age of revival and the young nation's faith
in itself, Catholic clergy in the early republic were confident they at
least could maintain the Catholic enclave and hopefully appropriate
friends and converts.

The idea of converting the heathen, infidel, and heretic was
a powerful motivation in the 1790s through the 1810s, when the
church was organized enough to begin focusing on the trans-
Appalachian frontier. Several of the key figures who helped spread
Catholicism westward carried their own mythic notions about conversions. Prospects in the frontier regions seemed good, since Catholics and non-Catholics lived side by side and, in many cases, were

mutually dependent. Priests and bishops were also heartened to see their Protestant counterparts struggling to keep up with westward settlement. During the 1820s, however, it became more obvious that conversions would be an infrequent and unreliable means of expanding the church. Even during the peak of the Jubilee excitement in 1826, for example, a time when each member of Bardstown's clergy was inspired and ready "to carry the fire with which he was filled," Bishop John Baptist David admitted the "fruits" of the Jubilee had been "little enough for the Protestants, none of whom, that I know of, was converted, except perhaps one or two women." Four years later David grimly reported that "Conversions are rare in Kentucky." Rhetoric about conversion efforts had been and would remain an important part of Catholic culture, but priests and bishops learned that to prevent the slippage among their own Catholic laity required almost their full attention.[38]

If the proximity of non-Catholics and Protestants presented an opportunity for conversion in frontier communities, then the door also could swing in the other direction. Close interaction might drain away members from the Catholic Church. In particular, intermarriages between a Catholic spouse and a Protestant or other non-Catholic threatened Catholic numbers. Clergy had discouraged mixed marriages during the colonial period, but frontier priests in the early republic were less and less able to prevent them when Catholics moved toward areas only thinly populated by other Catholics. Mixed marriages and aspects of matrimony affected by the presence of the non-Catholic majority were to be a continuing headache for Catholic clergy.

An imagined window of opportunity seemed to be closing. The "unique time" that Father Nerinckx described in his letter to Rome in 1821 was drifting away. Conversion efforts rarely met with success, though they remained powerfully symbolic. It became apparent that the church would not be adding significant numbers of converts in the region, and, in fact, should be more concerned about losing members to Protestant denominations, general laxity and disinterest, or through mixed marriages. And even if interfaith marriages became less of a demographic necessity, as Catholic settlement grew denser, questions about marriages between Catholics and non-Catholics, or involving Catholic couples and Protestant ministers, proliferated. In addition, a host of other concerns regarding day-to-day contact between Catholics and non-Catholics grew more complex as well. Clergy in the trans-Appalachian West continued to discourage interfaith marriages while simultaneously attempting to find ways to deal amenably with their non-Catholic neighbors. In the end, however, they turned to Rome for guidance.

Chapter 6

Emphatic Persuasion

Teaching, Processions, Preaching, and Polemics

Protestant opinion of Catholic public activities was an ever-present concern for Catholic leaders in the church's migration westward. Throughout the 1780s and 1790s, church officials worried about appearing too foreign in the American context or too cold toward the nation's principles of democracy, republicanism, and independence, particularly at the close of the century during the Federalist reaction against French influence. In the first two decades of the nineteenth century, however, Catholic optimism increased. Church leaders found they were able to maintain the hierarchical system of authority that was their inheritance, rein in the all too common renegade priests, and elaborate the church's physical presence in the trans-Appalachian West. As they did, it became apparent that the Catholic establishment in America would flourish. By the turn of the century, Catholic leaders, particularly as they looked westward, were decreasingly afraid of their religious activities appearing too distinctive. They began to worry less about upsetting non-Catholics and more about impressing, cultivating, educating, challenging, and, in some cases, converting them.

As church officials gained experience interacting with non-Catholics during the first two decades of the century, they began to express the distinctiveness of their faith and to seek engagement. In 1807 Father Stephen Theodore Badin was already celebrating the high level of visibility the Catholic Church would enjoy in Kentucky if a diocese were ever established there. He believed "the presence of a holy and learned Bishop" would provide "dignity, conspicuousness and firmness to the Catholic Church" in the region.[1] Other, more active outreach efforts escalated, and they were not simply one way or reactive. In addition to inviting outsiders to marvel at Catholic church architecture and ornamentation, clergy planned for non-Catholics to consider Catholic doctrine and to soak in the splendor of Catholic ritual and ceremony. Outreach efforts varied from instruction in schools to occasional, elaborate displays during ritual processions, and from opening regular spiritual services to non-Catholics to engaging Protestant antagonists in an open forum of debate. In these and other areas Catholics found contact points at which to interact with and influence their Protestant neighbors in the trans-Appalachian West. Over time, they also grew more confident about standing out and more willing to display their Catholic identity.

Educating Youth

Educating the children and young adults of Kentucky was both an early goal for Catholics and a significant point of interaction between them and non-Catholics. Regardless of religion, many frontier parents wanted schools. Indeed, Protestants and Catholics worked together as early as 1798 in the founding of Washington Academy, which included two prominent Catholics, John Lancaster and Robert Abell, on its board of trustees. Shortly before Transylvania University was formed in 1798 out of the merger of two other institutions, Father Badin had reported to his bishop that he was on friendly terms with the university's president, a Presbyterian minister. Badin also noted the university's impressive public library, to which he wished to supply "orthodox books." Catholic clergy, who arrived in the West with relatively advanced educations from seminaries and colleges in the East or in Europe, and typically in possession of small libraries or of connections to colleagues on the east coast or in Europe able to supply books, were well positioned to launch educational efforts. In some cases clergy assisted women who wanted to form religious orders, groups that tasked themselves with providing educational opportunities for children and young adults.

Present in all the initiatives to provide Catholic schools, academies, convents, and seminaries was consideration for what non-Catholics might think and an eagerness to welcome the participation of Protestant students.[2]

Father Badin, like his fellow clergy, the local parents, and lay Catholic leaders, wanted elementary schools for frontier youth, but Badin was cautious about proceeding too quickly in efforts to establish academies or colleges under the supervision of religious orders. In 1800 Badin resisted Father John Thayer's desire to found a nunnery. Despite the need for more teachers and the usefulness of other services that a convent might provide, Badin feared that "such an establishment in such a wild & corrupted country as this would (in Mr. Fournier's & mine opinion) give much room for calumny & ridicule." Badin and Father M. Fournier believed the region was not ready for nuns. "I think we must not go too fast; for churches ought to be founded first." A convent was not suitable for an area in the early stages of Catholic settlement because it would draw too much attention, especially disparaging criticism should problems arise. In 1805 Badin similarly resisted the establishment of an academy that the Dominicans hoped to build. Fathers Fenwick, Wilson, and Tuite eventually would build St. Thomas Aquinas College for men in 1808, but a few years earlier Badin raised serious reservations with Bishop John Carroll. First, he calculated that only a few Catholic parents would be able to afford the proposed board and tuition costs. Therefore, the school would be admitting students of all religious backgrounds, and the Dominicans' "labours . . . would be almost entirely applied to the benefit of other denominations." Second, the Dominican clergy would not be able to attend to their priestly duties for the many Catholics scattered across their mission.[3]

The years 1812 and 1813 were more propitious, and Fathers Charles Nerinckx and John Baptist David each helped to found an order of women religious in Kentucky that would be responsible for providing education. When Father David and Catherine Spalding established the Sisters of Charity of Nazareth in June 1813, the order's primary purpose was to provide education for young girls. In Nerinckx's case, he had attempted in 1805 to establish a new order, "The Lovers of Mary," that "would be intrusted with the instruction of poor children and slaves." His effort failed because he lacked the support of local Catholic families. Two years later, with support from Badin, Nerinckx began framing rules for the new sisterhood, drawing on European examples. The new society's primary purpose would be the spiritual advancement of the women who joined, but its second would be "to provide the community teachers for catholic schools." Nerinckx's opportunity arrived in the spring of 1812 when three young women asked his help in withdrawing from their worldly lives and starting a small school for girls. Nerinckx was quick to assist because he already had been planning to initiate such a society of women religious and because he saw the need for a new school where girls could learn in an environment free of boys. (Nerinckx found mixed schooling to be "promiscuous" and "subversive of morality.") The following year Nerinckx proudly wrote to the head of the Congregation for the Propagation of the Faith, in Rome, that he had been careful to establish the new Friends of Mary Sisters (later called the Sisters of Loretto) in "direct imitation" of nuns in Europe, but "with due consideration being given to the adaptations needed for this region." The "special purpose" of the group, he reported, was "the education and instruction of the weaker sex," a mission, he observed, that made the nuns particularly useful for spreading the Roman Catholic faith among non-Catholics. The girls' school was an immediate success and had begun to admit non-Catholics. Nerinckx explained how "various young ladies take advantage" of the school and "Consequently their prejudices are either destroyed or lost and they either become less hostile to the true religion or they actually favor it." His report continued: "From this it is clear that it was founded to easily and appropriately nourish our sacred religion among Catholics and to scatter and sow it among non-Catholics." From the start, according to Nerinckx, the sisters' academy for girls was meant to be a point of contact with, or even conversion of, non-Catholics.[4]

As Badin had argued in 1800, despite the widespread need for teachers, there were some difficulties in establishing these religious orders and convents in a frontier area. Catholic and non-Catholic families were happy to see schools opening to accommodate their children, but in some cases it was not easy to accept the nuns and their peculiar rules, appearance, and activities. Nerinckx, for example, attempted to adhere closely to the traditional, European model for the Sisters of Loretto. He offered to find nuns in Europe to instruct the Kentuckians, and when he ended up writing new rules for the sisters himself he later said he had done so in "strict imitation." On the other hand, Nerinckx realized the new sisterhood would arouse the curiosity of Catholics and Protestants in the neighborhood, so he took steps to prevent rumors and to prepare the community a few days before the first three Friends of Mary (i.e., Sisters of Loretto) took the veil. Nerinckx publicly and carefully announced what he was doing and tried to explain how the new religious order would benefit the community. Success led a few years later to greater friction. In 1815 three of the young female students in the sisters' school asked, with their parents' consent, to join the religious order. Local men had been joking earlier in the year that Nerinckx's community of nuns was really a home for all the area's women who were unfit for marriage. Now that young students had joined the order, some Kentuckians were said to be threatening him for shrinking the marriage pool. Others allegedly claimed the young nuns were wearing themselves out due to the austerity of Nerinckx's religious order.[5]

Father David faced his own public relations problem in constituting a branch of the Sisters of Charity in Kentucky in 1814. Unlike their mother order in Maryland, the western sisters simply could not have as their superior a woman bearing the title "Sister Servant." David reckoned such a title "would render her subservant in the eyes of the student boarders in a country where the name is synonymous with that of slave." Rather than risk other problems of translation from East to West, David, with Bishop Benedict Flaget's agreement, chose to keep his Kentucky sisters separate from the motherhouse in Maryland. Several months later the priest wrote to Archbishop Carroll on the matter, reiterating that nobody carried "the name of servant in this new and half savage country but slaves."[6] David, Flaget, and Carroll agreed to modify an important part of the religious order's culture to ensure that the order as a whole would be transplantable to the region.

Despite obstacles along the way, nuns proved ever more valuable to western communities primarily for their role in education. Catholic and non-Catholic parents alike wanted the schools that women religious provided. Moreover, Catholic leaders realized the nuns' schools could be a means both for improving relations with their non-Catholic neighbors and for winning converts. Father Nerinckx understood the potential educational appeal of his new religious order and repeatedly referenced it to promote the order and its school—to Kentuckians and to benefactors in Europe who might be willing to provide financial backing. In a self-printed circular entitled "To All Catholics or Others to Whom it May Belong," which was meant for distribution in Kentucky, Nerinckx defended his grand plans to build churches, convents, and schools across the state. The school at Loretto, he announced, was filling "fast of every denomination" and had the "approbation of parents and thinking judges of other denominations." As long as parents and student were "willing to submit to the rules of the school," Nerinckx emphasized, "no distinction is made of denominations."[7]

This was a point stressed over and over again by his colleagues and superiors. In 1818 Archbishop Ambrose Maréchal in Baltimore reported to Rome about the good relations with non-Catholics in America, citing how Protestants held the Catholic Church in a "certain veneration," which they exhibited by choosing to enroll their children in Catholic schools. Similarly, Bishop Flaget and his co-adjutator Father David described the School of Nazareth run by David's Sisters of Charity as successful, having a "great reputation," mainly because of its broad appeal to both Catholic and non-Catholic students. Boarders, the priests claimed, were taken in from as far away as Pittsburgh and New Orleans. While Catholic girls learned more about their own religion, non-Catholic girls became friends of the church: "The children who are non-Catholic, without being disturbed regarding their religion, see the Catholic religion practiced. . . . The principal effect of all this, is to make them lose any prejudices they may have had against the Catholic faith, and which they defend in their families, having known themselves the false imputations charged against Catholics." Flaget and David also asserted that education in the school was creating converts: "Several leave this school, Catholic at heart; others ask to become Catholic." Girls' academies were generating defenders of the Roman church both inside and outside of the faith.[8]

Kentucky's Catholic clergy made parallel claims about educational institutions for male students. In 1819 Bishop Flaget founded St. Joseph's College for the young men of Bardstown and its environs and then sent Father Guy Ignatius Chabrat to France in 1820 to raise money for the Bardstown diocese. Flaget provided Chabrat with a letter addressed to their "countrymen in France" in which he boasted of the new college, especially the fact that "Protestants as well as Catholics are admitted." Father Nerinckx made an even bolder claim about the new college: "The most influential protestants of the town send their children to it, although they have a public school under supervision of their own coreligionists; they allege they prefer to intrust their children to the care of two catholic Bishops."[9]

In an interesting exchange of letters, Father David in Bardstown and his friend in Maryland, Father Simon Bruté, who taught at St. Mary's seminary and St. Mary's College, discussed the best method of winning over Protestant students. Bruté, it appears, urged David and his western compatriots to press the teaching of the church more directly upon their non-Catholic pupils. David responded at length in 1822, 1827, and 1828 about the persistent but more subtle means that were effective in Kentucky. Bruté had implied that David, Flaget, and the others had given up their liberty to tell Protestant students "of the Catholic religion and to draw them to it." David answered, "But I well know that, if we do not give assurance to the parents that we will not take advantage of the influence we bear on the children to bring them towards the Catholic religion they would not send them to us." Instead, said David, he and the other clergy were using "an indirect manner" to more surely and "gently dispose them to become Catholics some day." Five years later David returned to the theme, repeating that "just as splendorous display will win converts, so will repeated, moderate contact and good example." We have not given up our "zeal of proselytizing," he wrote; "we are renouncing only the use of solicitation to engage our pupils to become Catholics." Why? First, because "The prejudices are much stronger here than in Maryland" and such solicitation would cause Protestant parents to stop sending their children. Second, David explained, the students were too young and "fickle" to remain converts once back with their families. It was better to use a method that "inspires them with respect for the [Catholic] religion and makes them forget their prejudices, and disposes them perhaps to become converts" later in life. That method included requiring all students to participate every day in Catholic prayers, attend Mass every Sunday and holy day and listen to the sermon, and "assist at the explanation of the Catholic catechism which is done by our Sisters, because it would look like proselytism if a priest did it; but which is none the less the reality." In addition, noted David, the students were using Catholic books and had access to copies of the newspaper *United States Catholic Miscellany*, which, he added, "is spread around them without affectation [and] certainly produces an effect."[10]

For two decades Catholic schools helped fill a western need for educational opportunities, and during these years the academies and other institutions, along with the nuns and priests operating them, met only minor opposition. On the contrary, well-to-do Protestant families enrolled their children in Catholic schools, while Catholic clergy celebrated their own success in establishing the schools, educating Catholic children, and reaching out to non-Catholic students and parents alike. By the 1830s, however, Protestant clergy and educators would interpret the increasing spread of Catholic schools, especially academies for girls, as a dire threat. Precisely their success in attracting Protestant students, especially the daughters of well-to-do Protestants to convent academies, would make Catholic schools a target of attack.[11]

Processions

Like distinctive church architecture and ornamentation, Catholic ceremonial processions served as markers of identity, difference, and pride. Parade routes and the number of people participating, as well as the elaborateness of the retinues, designated boundaries of influence and reflected a sense of success in bringing Catholicism westward. Catholics could take comfort in seeing symbols of their faith carried and displayed amid the rural setting of western Pennsylvania, Ohio, Maryland, and Kentucky. As with church buildings and other material expressions of religion, more profuse examples would appear in the 1820s.

Early attempts to orchestrate religious processions met significant obstacles, even though at a minimum a priest needed only a willing congregation ready to march. Lay Catholics, depending on their background, might have come to the western frontier without much experience in public displays of religiosity. Another challenge was the ubiquitous influence of Protestantism itself. Catholic parishioners, perhaps long used to being outnumbered or surrounded by Episcopalians, Baptists, Methodists, Presbyterians, or people of other religious persuasions, might forget or not even be familiar with their own traditions. Father Demetrius Gallitzin in the highlands of western Pennsylvania felt from the beginning of his mission in the 1790s that his parishioners were absorbing too many Protestant fashions. Running funeral processions in silence, accompanied only by the minister's voice at the grave, was a distinctly Protestant American tendency that he found to be commonplace in the Pennsylvania backcountry. Gallitzin advocated the traditional Catholic procession with music, bells, and singing. The German priest had gone west originally in good part "to begin something new" with a Catholic congregation free from Protestant influence. "Wherever something had already been undertaken," Gallitzin reasoned, it already "had been spoiled from the beginning because of the universal tendency to imitate the Protestants."[12] Ignorance of their own customs and the long shadow of Protestantism left Catholics impeded in expressing themselves.

Privations of backwoods life were another obstacle. In his early years of ministering to Catholics in Kentucky, Father Nerinckx also found his congregations hard pressed to stage a satisfying religious procession. In 1805 he described how he and his people paraded over a mile-long route from their Holy Cross Church to the Trappist monastery, where the Trappists joined in, adding to the spectacle because these monks were "clad in sacerdotal garments." The day's events he called "eminently successful," although he felt that the hardships and material scarcities of frontier life made it "impossible to do justice" to a proper procession—"it is as much above our strength as the sun is above our heads." Traditional accouterments were missing, for example, and too many adults were without basic religious instruction. "Scores of people of twenty years and over [had] never made their first communion." Moreover, all were worn out with "early rising, hard work, and late meals," and so could not invest the energy necessary to make a truly memorable cortege. In 1807 Father Badin, impressed with Nerinckx's headway, reported to Bishop Carroll that processions of the Blessed Sacrament would be expanded to three graveyards that year and would include a canopy and ostensoria, although they were still hoping for a censer someday. With or without all of the proper processional components, Badin felt "nothing revives more the activity & zeal of our Catholics." Moreover, these spectacles of "august ceremony," said the frontier priest, struck "the heretics and infidels themselves" with "awe."[13]

Resources gradually became available for embellishing processions. In the 1790s Badin planned one event to include four canopy bearers with the Blessed Sacrament, an officer leading twenty to thirty armed men, three boys on horseback following another carrying the cross, two men with the censer, two boys with candles, one boy with incense, and three men praying at the rear. Years later Father David described an immense procession "in which 600 persons marched two abreast in beautiful order . . . preceded by three men on horseback" with a large cross and pennant. After Bishop Flaget arrived in Kentucky in 1811, Badin again wrote a set of notes for a religious parade. This one was still larger and more elaborate. It began with two men on horseback accompanying a third with the cross, a large number of men on the left "in Indian file" separated by four feet from a similar line of women, followed by three men and three women praying, three boys with bells, a group of singers, a group of girls strewing flowers, several clergymen, then four canopy bearers with the Blessed Sacrament, four swordsmen in uniform guarding it, several horsemen in a line abreast, and everyone else following while "devoutly saying their beads." From year to year, Catholic processions became more intricate, distinctive, and impressive.[14]

In 1826, when Father B. Martial visited the Bardstown diocese to survey the progress of religion there, he witnessed an even more remarkable parade of the faithful. Eighty young girls dressed in white and "wearing crowns of flowers" followed a banner at the head of the train. Forty women religious clothed in black followed them, then the boys from the Catholic college. Next came the rest of the diocese's children, then the choir, the members of the clergy, the coadjutator bishop, and the bishop carrying the Blessed Sacrament. Martial claimed that one participant had traveled three hundred miles for the affair and that the crowd watching was "prodigious." The visitor from afar might have been the same man to whom Father David referred in a letter about the same procession. "A gentleman from Pittsburgh" who had read an account about Kentucky processions in a magazine had "thought it was an exaggeration" and came only "to assure himself with his own eyes of the truth or falsity" of the published report. According to Father David, the man "declared that he found this ceremony beyond his expectation." Catholic displays of pride and piety in the West had matured into truly impressive events.[15]

While processions grew in size and grandeur, so did the clergy's perception that they were under scrutiny by non-Catholics, that their ceremonial displays were measured moments of interaction. In the years after Flaget's arrival as first bishop of the West in 1811, particularly at the end of the decade and into the 1820s, religious processions became key points of contact and gauges of sectarian relations. Father Badin's notes for a procession in 1811, for instance, stressed that as the Blessed Sacrament passed by, Catholics would be asked to kneel down and then join the end of the train. Non-Catholic bystanders, he wrote, would be expected to "at least take off their hats & observe silence." Badin's hopes for success among Protestants and his high expectations of non-Catholic neighbors were apparent here, for the issue of ritual deference toward the church had been a significant point of contention between Catholics and Protestants since the Reformation. Indeed, by refusing to doff their hats before sacramental processions, Lutheran princes and clergy had shown their defiance at Augsburg in 1530. For a backcountry priest in Kentucky, a Catholic procession, among other things, was a point of contact at which to impress his non-Catholic neighbors and to estimate their regard for Catholicism and Catholic people.[16]

Badin's associates also looked on processions as crucial moments of interfaith activity. In June 1816, Father David described to a colleague in Baltimore a long procession held in the woods prior to the next month's intricate ceremony for blessing the cornerstone of a new cathedral. Bishop Flaget presided over the blessing, which began with a small but impressive cortege of the seminarians from St. Thomas, four miles outside Bardstown. Pausing a quarter-mile away from the cathedral site, the Catholic clergy reassembled and proceeded into town, where "a great crowd of people gathered . . . from the town and the surrounding parts," among whom were "several ministers." One of these, a Presbyterian, whom David thought full of malice and envy, reportedly "showed great signs of amazement" upon seeing the "line of our seminarians arrive" in priestly garb. "Leaning his head on his hand," claimed David, the Presbyterian "remained in this position a few minutes in profound silence."[17]

Recounting the same day's events, Bishop Flaget rejoiced to

his comrades in Baltimore about the grand impression made by his "eighteen ecclesiastics in surplice" preceding the cross carried forward to the building site. Before a large mixed crowd, Father David "mounted a platform, elevated for the occasion, to explain the ceremonies about to take place." It was a grand assembly, a performance, and an informative exercise for the gathered throng. David's personal objective was to reach the non-Catholics in the audience. Flaget described the priest's manner as unusually "clear and in a style and tone so touching that the spirits and minds even of the most prejudiced listened to him with greatest attention while retracting their prejudices." The bishop may have been more wishful than accurate in painting the non-Catholics so pious and unaffected by anti-Catholic biases. In any case, he found the crowd unusually quiet and attentive throughout what even he felt was a protracted event. Among the "more Protestant than Catholic" multitude, wrote Flaget, "the deepest silence reigned throughout the courtyard during the long ceremony." Moreover, he claimed, non-Catholics who had come solely "to ridicule the proceedings" were heard to have said things such as, "I never experienced such feelings in my life," or "What an awe-inspiring ceremony!" One woman told Flaget that she had been on the verge of being baptized by a Baptist minister, but that sight of him in his "pontifical dress attended by so many clergymen" brought her to tears and the decision not to join the Baptists.[18] Bishop Flaget and his clergy trusted that processions and attendant ceremonies could grab the attention of non-Catholics, set a stage for their listening to a sermon or other religious instruction, and induce them to look favorably on Catholicism.

Processions also symbolized a growing certainty within the church of Catholicism's place in America by confirming that the laity and clergy possessed both the freedom and resources to make public displays. In 1816 Father Nerinckx returned home to Belgium to raise money, collect religious supplies, and recruit priests, afterward publishing an account of his trip. The Catholic Church was under attack in Europe, and soon might be in America, he declared, but for the moment "our holy religion is nowhere less interfered with than here." Leading his list of examples—"we have public processions and celebrations; we wear religious regalia and ornament [the] streets." What could represent freedom of worship more than this outward lavish display? "Who can wish for greater liberty?"

asked Nerinckx. A few years later another priest speaking to a European audience used a similar example of religious freedom and progress in America. Again, the license to exhibit religious beliefs publicly headed a list of other signs of Catholic success: "We go in procession around our cemeteries, and we erect crosses in them," wrote Father Badin. "We preach in the town halls, and even in the Protestant meeting-houses where we have no chapels, and all sorts of sectaries come in crowds to hear us." Parading before Protestants was irresistible, using their meeting places was satisfying, and getting them to listen to Catholic preaching was a final prize.[19]

Preaching

Some non-Catholics on the frontier, Catholic clergy believed, were eager to hear the word of God delivered in the Roman Catholic fashion. This was due in part to difficulty in finding clergy of any denomination in many of the settlements sprinkled across this vast region. The Protestant appetite for Catholic preaching was also possibly due to the insufficiencies of Protestant ministers and their preaching. Priests and bishops increasingly felt they had the advantage—with regard to the Protestant clergy—in training and the ability to instruct and inspire the laity.

Catholic clergy repeatedly criticized what they perceived as ignorance on the part of Protestant ministers and their congregations. It seemed to them that members of other denominations worried little about adhering to specific, clear doctrine or about inculcating religious understanding. For example, when Father Badin was still new to Kentucky, and the evangelical spirit of revival was beginning along the Green River Valley, eventually erupting most famously at Cane Ridge in 1801, Badin observed what he believed were glaring instances of Protestant incompetence. The priest grumbled in one of his many lonely letters from the frontier that the Presbyterians were racing to imitate the "absurd" revival techniques, or "tricks," of the Baptists, who, he said, "themselves were indoctrinating individuals . . . wholly unaware of the meaning of baptism or the doctrines particular to that denomination." In 1805 Badin recounted for his superiors in Rome how Protestant clergymen permitted anarchy and immorality at their camp meetings. Most deplorable, according to Badin, were the preachers who "utter their jargon consisting of Sacred texts gathered without order" and "phrases drawn from Scripture, without the trouble of trying to make them reasonable." It was this lack of rationality that most mortified Badin. He criticized them for "striking the senses and imaginations [and] renewing superstition." These ministers, he continued, "are for the most part persons without education, who lack learning" and who "boast of their ignorance, which, they say, makes them preach like the Apostles." Although evangelical clergy might have felt divinely inspired, Badin avowed that their "hearers for the most part do not understand what the orators say."[20]

Likewise, the Protestant minister's problem, from the priest's point of view, was not a lack of enthusiasm or piety, but profound ignorance, disorder, and lack of reason. In 1815, for example, Father Charles Nerinckx mocked his Protestant competitors for these same shortcomings but extolled the fervor with which evangelical clergy approached their work in western America. Addressing a European audience, he wrote, "I must confess to our shame that much more zeal and sacrifice is shown by our erring brethren in order to spread their false doctrines." The Protestant failing lay elsewhere. It seemed as though blind preachers were leading blind followers. In a letter to a fellow priest in 1807, Father Badin ridiculed Methodists in particular by referring to them as "Philistines" who "play their pranks about Washington, Ky." under the guidance of a "so-called Bishop." Bishop Flaget of Bardstown in 1815 informed the pope about the sectarian situation in Kentucky and criticized Protestant denominations for continuing to propagate religious ignorance and misunderstanding: "The majority of those who belong to these sects," he said, "are wholly ignorant of the doctrines proper to their sect." This alleged lack of religious knowledge of the otherwise zealous Protestant ministers was seen as an immediate danger, particularly for nominal Catholics who might be persuaded by the enthusiasm of the evangelicals.[21]

Such a situation, however, was interpreted as a long-term opportunity for Catholicism. Obstacles to Protestant expansion, inept ministers for example, could aid the Catholic drive to convert non-Catholics. As Father Phelan had described the situation in western Pennsylvania, "I am still more and more convinced that there is a great deal of good work for a priest in these counties where the ministers are the very dregs of the pretended reformation." If the frontier was spacious and conducive to interdenominational mixing, and if other denominations failed in their ministries, or if itinerant Protestant preachers were few and far between, non-Catholics might accept attention from a trained and educated Catholic clergy. And this seemed to be the case. Throughout their travels across the vast dioceses covering western Pennsylvania, Ohio, Kentucky, Tennessee, Michigan, and Indiana, clergy regularly welcomed non-Catholics to their services. Priests and bishops throughout the years of the early republic recorded significant numbers of Protestants coming out to meet them and hear their preaching, from curiosity as well as genuine spiritual hunger. In the summer of 1812 Father David recounted for an eastern colleague the kind of interest that Catholic activities generated among Protestants. Many of them "come to our services; several even remain for my catechism, which follows Mass," he wrote. "Some young ladies of other religions, or rather of no religion, take their places without fuss on the benches among our Catholic girls," and "some already have surrendered." As late as 1817, primitive conditions continued to exist that drew together Catholics and non-Catholics in search of community and religious fulfillment. Father De Andreis, one of a group of several priests and other Italian clerics recruited by Bishop DuBourg for his St. Louis diocese, made special note of what seemed to his European eyes the hard frontier life of clergy and laity in Kentucky. He was struck by the roughness of the churches, but more importantly, that they became gathering points on festival days for Catholics as well as Protestants within a twenty-mile radius.[22]

When presented with an opportunity of preaching to Protestants, Catholic clergy shaped their message accordingly. Even Trappist monks established in Casey County, Kentucky, who were not expected to hold Masses for the community of settlers around them, were pressed into service because of the distances the laity otherwise would have had to travel. Catholics as well as "some Protestants were present on Sundays and feast days," according to Father M. J. Dunand, when special processions or other activities might take place. These parades were an additional opportunity for Catholic-Protestant dialogue and instruction, as it was not uncommon for the officiating priest to explain the meaning inherent in the symbols and accompanying rituals to non-Catholic observers. Father Badin, for example, used the Feast of St. Patrick in 1811 to make a "short but sol-

emn address showing the meaning and purpose of the celebration"—
a needed reminder for his parishioners, no doubt, and useful for
others present. Accordingly, the "citizens of Bardstown were so impressed that some non-Catholics present solicited" him to repeat
the service later that day. Badin took the opportunity, summarized
his St. Patrick's day sermon, and proceeded to elaborate on "certain
doctrines of the Catholic Church."[23]

A year and a half later, Badin, Bishop Flaget, and a Father Chabrat, en route from Bardstown to Baltimore, found other groups of
Protestants eager to hear them preach. Near the town of Shelby
they stayed with a Mr. Horrell, who guided them on their journey
and shared his house. On Sunday they said Mass in his home, where
"the congregation was considerable,—the most being Protestants."
Flaget noted their patience in listening to "the advice I gave them,
and to two sermons from Mr. Chabrat—one on the good use of
time, and the other on the necessity of baptism." Farther down the
road, two days later, the three clerics ministered to "a score of persons assembled—part Catholic and part Protestant." The priests
heard several confessions, but found only one Catholic ready for
communion. "If I do not provide for this congregation," wrote
Flaget, "soon the faith will be lost." Two weeks afterward, while
staying at a Catholic family's house, Flaget said Mass "in a fairly
large room filled with Protestants." The bishop sermonized with
the non-Catholic audience in mind, speaking "to them on the Sacrifice of the Mass in a manner to make some little impression." Father
Badin, perhaps notorious for his preaching style, "was requested by
the men of the town to give a sermon in the court house, which he
did, to the delight of the Catholics, and the very great displeasure of
some of the Protestants." Badin's topic was baptism, which, Flaget
claimed, inspired a local crypto-Catholic to step forward, declare his
faith, and have his five children baptized.[24]

Beyond the repeated preaching to Protestants and conversations with them regarding religion described in the journal for this
trip, Flaget's later writings indicated his and his priests' concern for
reaching non-Catholic audiences throughout his administration of
the western diocese. In the spring of 1819, for instance, the bishop
made his way to the northern stretches of his diocese to inspect,
inspire, and instruct the Catholics scattered in pockets between
Bardstown and Detroit. Visiting settlements along the River Rai-

sin, he held public lectures during Lent to edify the faithful and the curious. On several consecutive Sundays Flaget attracted what he described as being a mostly Protestant audience, which listened respectfully. With disappointment, however, he felt their attention in the end would bear "little fruit." Father Badin sought Protestant audiences in a similar manner, but cast his attempts in a more favorable light when writing for a Catholic readership in Europe. In his 1821 booklet "Origin and Progress of the Mission of Kentucky," the priest explained he and his colleagues traveled about and preached "in town halls, even in the Protestant churches (meeting houses) lacking chapels" themselves. Members of disparate denominations attended these free sermons "in crowds." Even during Mass they "behave in a decent and respectful manner," Badin recounted, and bringing them within earshot of Catholic clergy at work could have other far-reaching effects. "Some of them even bring their children to us for baptism, and they entrust the education of their daughters to our Religious," reported Badin, though, most surprising of all, he concluded, was "to find non-Catholics sometimes taking up the defense of the dogmas of our belief."[25]

Bishop Flaget's success in bringing Catholic and Protestant together at moments of celebration and edification continued. On occasion he considered his own triumphs overwhelming. In 1830 Flaget presided over a ceremony to consecrate the foundation of Father Robert A. Abell's new church in Louisville, an event at which he was accompanied by Bishops Henry Conwell, Francis Patrick Kenrick, and John England, as well as five priests. Although there was "a great crowd under a very hot sun," noted one of those priests, Father David, the clergy were able to maintain the "greatest order." Much of the crowd was non-Catholic. After the ceremony, remembered Flaget, he, the priests, and the visiting prelates "went to the meeting house of the Presbyterians." Bishop England rose before the smaller crowd inside "and during one hour and a half held his audience spellbound" while preaching "from the large Protestant bible" before him and making the characteristic Catholic sign of the cross. "What a sight for a Catholic, whose very name was a reproach only 20 years ago to find himself in a meeting house of Calvinists," said Flaget, "when a Roman Catholic was preaching the words of truth in the presence of three other bishops, 5 or 6 ministers of different sects and an audience of which two-thirds were Protestants."

After years of processions in front of non-Catholics in his diocese and reaching out to them through sermons and lectures, Flaget was astonished that a fellow priest was preaching to Protestants within their own sacred space, using their own version of the Bible, standing in a Protestant pulpit, and, with a show of clerical strength, being accompanied by three bishops! "Who could believe that I should live long enough to be a witness to such a triumph?"[26]

Polemics

Bishop Flaget's triumph was noteworthy because it had not been an easy accomplishment during his two decades at the head of the diocese. Bishop and priests were the targets of provocations by Protestant ministers, and bishop and priests handed out challenges as well to defend the church. These public confrontations ranged from formalized public debates, to printed apologetics, to commentary within Sunday sermons on non-Catholic beliefs and activities. Prior to the formation of the diocese in Bardstown, when Father Badin and his handful of associates had not yet established a robust religious infrastructure, polemical activities were minimal, typically defensive, and construed as informative rather than aggressive. After Bishop Flaget arrived in 1811 and had a few years to settle in, outreach activities and polemics occurred more frequently and acquired an edge. It was after 1815, and especially in the 1820s, that Catholic clergy formalized contentious activities such as debates and written apologetics.[27]

Through various formats, Catholic priests and bishops tried to answer challenges with learned arguments that ultimately might edify their listeners, Catholic and Protestant alike. Sectarian and adversarial by definition, public debates provided a chance to correct misperceptions that stood in the way of community or even conversion. Catholic clergy hoped their own arguments turned on logic, erudition, and convincing the audience, and less on showing up their opponents, though certain priests certainly were delighted by the occasional flamboyant victory. In general, however, Catholic clergy decried their Protestant opponents' flashy style, fancy oratory, specious reasoning, and appeal to emotion. Just as priests hoped to instruct onlookers by explaining the rituals and objects involved in processions, and as they strove to preach in a manner that would inform their Protestant listeners, Catholic clergy worked to convince their non-Catholic audiences with reason during polemical exchanges.

Father Badin claimed to be reluctant to engage in controversy—his frontier missionary life already being suffused with other hindrances—although he believed answering "the letters of heretic ministers" was one of his regular backwoods obligations during his early years in Kentucky. The priest was challenged in early 1798 to a public debate by the Methodist minister Barnabas McHenry. Badin felt he had done quite well in the confrontation. This was confirmed by McHenry's second challenge, which was directed not at Badin but at his colleague, Father Fournier, who was known still to be having a difficult time expressing himself in English. Fournier wisely responded to the Methodist by saying he would not "interfere" until the minister had finished with Badin. At their second encounter, Badin believed he had soundly defeated McHenry, which was obvious to him by the fact that rumblings from other Protestant ministers in the area quieted and never again turned into open invitation to debate. McHenry's motivation was a curious one, more complex than the outright fervor of a rabid anti-Catholic mind, for later the same year he joined two Catholics, John Lancaster and Robert Abell, and eleven other trustees in founding Washington Academy. McHenry may have wanted to debate Badin and Fournier to prove Catholic doctrine flawed, but at some level he was willing to work with leading Catholic laymen in organizing an institution that would be shaping the minds and character of the region's young men.[28]

Although Badin was not again overtly dared to defend his beliefs in public, continuing tensions led him to consider another means of answering his Protestant opponents. In March 1798 he wrote to Bishop Carroll that he had "been engaged of late in several controversies" and that his colleagues, Fathers Fournier and de Rohan, "think with me it is necessary to have some papers now in my hand printed" so that the "Church will gain by her doctrine being better known in this State, freed from the gross misrepresentations of heretics." A year later, however, Badin changed his mind, realizing there was little to be gained by upsetting the generally good relations between Catholic and Protestant in Kentucky. The "controversial engagements are over," he reported, and "we live in peace with the Methodists [etc.]" Badin added that he was resisting the pressure to publish rebuttals, primarily because of his "desire of not renewing the spirit of religious discussion," and because his opponents, so far, had refrained from carrying the debate into print. Badin's reluctance at this juncture helped explain his sharp reaction in February 1800 to Father John Thayer's jabs at the local Protestants. Thayer, the militant convert, was sent west by Bishop Carroll partly because of his too fervent attempts to defend Catholicism by repeatedly, publicly, and assiduously attacking Protestantism in New England. Soon after Thayer's arrival in Kentucky he had started referring to local Methodists as "fools" in his sermons. Badin at first had valued the envy that Thayer's popularity and oratorical skills aroused among Protestant leaders, but the convert's confrontational style threatened the general sectarian rapprochement.[29]

Despite his initial hesitation to publicize further his difference with non-Catholics, Father Badin eventually felt compelled to explain Catholic dogma if the church ever was to make progress in trans-Appalachia. In 1805 his book, *The Real Principles of Roman Catholics, in Reference to God and Country*, became the first Catholic work ever published in the West. It was an effort to clarify misconceptions, to explain Catholic doctrine, not adapt or modify it for American life. Badin and others who wrote apologetical materials wanted to make a clear statement to defend the church against false impressions, inform non-church members, and draw in marginal Catholics. Badin's confrontations in 1798 with the Methodist Reverend Barnabas McHenry and with other Protestant preachers, he claimed, were answers to their attacks. Badin hesitated for a few years before publishing his apologetical book, because he initially worried about fanning the flames of sectarian disagreement. This kind of quiet defense, put forth in hopes of winning friends and converts, was exhibited by Badin's neighbors, the reclusive Trappist monks who had established a large plantation, mill, and clock workshop in Adair County (now Casey County). In 1808, the monks requested the bishop of Quebec to send copies of a particular apologetical publication, which they planned to distribute to Protestants who might visit the monastery's workshop to have their watches repaired.[30]

Lay Catholics also participated in publicly defending the faith and challenging non-Catholics. As historian Mary Ramona Mattingly has recounted, one James Elder, an early Catholic immigrant to the Bardstown region, "was in the habit of attending Protestant services held in the neighborhood of his home, for the purpose of contradicting any statement made by the minister which was derogatory to Catholic belief." This self-appointed lay champion of Catholicism said on his deathbed "that he was resigned to die but regretted that he had no son to take his place 'in keeping the Presbyterians down.'" Catholic clergy, in contrast, approached debate with the more ambitious objective of moving beyond simply silencing the Protestant message. And they encouraged a less disputatious approach by the laity. In a pamphlet published in France, Father Badin boasted that his Kentucky parishioners were perusing books about sectarian controversy and Catholic doctrine. "In every congregation," he wrote, "one finds . . . some who study and are able to sustain a discussion with the Protestants." The result, he added, was that "they contribute, from time to time, to the procuring of conversions to the true faith." It was defense of the faith accompanied by conversion of the Protestant, after all, that Catholic priests sought.[31]

Direct confrontations in public and print became increasingly common as Catholic communities grew stronger. Where clergy initially trod lightly, by the middle of the second decade of the nineteenth century, the Catholic response was aggressive. Without continual guidance, nominal Catholics appeared to be in danger of losing their faith and being lured away by deistic or Protestant arguments. Without continual refutation, such attacks would do irreparable damage. And without continual elucidation of Catholic beliefs, non-Catholics could not be converted.

In 1814 Father Gallitzin in the mountains of western Pennsylvania made a more combative defense of the faith. He struck back at his attackers in newsprint. The provocation for this exchange was the nation's declining fortunes during the War of 1812 and the resulting accusations against Catholicism made by certain Protestant ministers. Gallitzin hoped to correct their misrepresentations, educate his American audience, and win converts in the process. Whether or not he was successful in the latter effort, he claimed he had been. During the war, as the British marched on Washington, D.C., President James Madison called for a national day of fasting and prayer. In Huntingdon, Pennsylvania, a Protestant minister was said to have defamed Catholicism during the course of his fast day sermon, calling Catholics the worst danger the nation faced. Gallitzin rejoined in the pages of the Huntingdon *Gazette* and eventually published *A Defence of Catholic Principles* (1816), which went through four editions during his lifetime. The same minister who had begun the fight answered with *A Vindication of the Reformation* (1818), which impelled Gallitzin to respond with an aggressive *An Appeal to the Protestant Public* (1819), and then another treatise, *A Letter to a Protestant Friend on the Holy Scriptures, Being a Continuation of the Defence of Catholic Principles* (1820). In the forward of this book, Gallitzin claimed the polemics were netting conversions to Catholicism. The more the minister wrote, the more people could distinguish which was the true faith. With bravado, Gallitzin stated, "If I had any favor to ask of the Protestant minister, it would be that he would please continue to write against the Catholic Church, and to vindicate the doctrines of the Reformation." Gallitzin exuded optimism and confidence in his own intellectual abilities to counter what he, as a well-educated priest, saw as the ineffectual arguments of Protestant clergy.[32]

Bishop Flaget, Father Badin's successor as the religious superior of western Catholics, initially sought peace between the faithful and their neighbors, though he occasionally could not avoid open arguments. In 1816 he felt forced to confront a Protestant preacher named Tapscott, who had been heard to preach "that the Catholics sprang from hell, and into hell they must fall." Flaget traveled south to meet Tapscott in Taylor County and debated him in the open air before a crowd too large for any of the local buildings. Tapscott began the exchange and closely questioned Flaget for most of the time. According to popular Catholic memory of the event, the pugnacious minister only relinquished the floor when the bishop proved his superiority by more accurately quoting Scripture. Regardless of who had scored the most forensic points or been most persuasive, the primarily Protestant audience was said to have sympathized with Flaget simply because Tapscott refused to take his turn at answering the bishop's questions and because he wouldn't shake the Catholic's hand.[33]

A few years later, Bishop Flaget again found himself involved in a public quarrel, which he seemed surprised to have provoked. Heading west and then south from Bardstown, Flaget met Father Abell in Breckenridge County and the two traveled to Nashville, Tennessee, to establish a congregation. Unlike Kentucky, where Catholics and Protestants had settled almost simultaneously, Tennessee for two decades had been an evangelical stronghold and remained only lightly populated with Catholics. Flaget estimated sixty lived in Nashville itself and a mere thirty resided in the rest of the state. Perhaps because Catholicism was so meagerly represented and nonthreatening, and because a new church meant more development and more inhabitants for the growing town, the leading citizens of Nashville turned out to receive the Kentucky bishop and priest. Flaget found the Nashvilleans polite and willing to support his mission. Protestants and Catholics alike gave donations, made subscriptions, and came to hear Father Abell's evening sermons at the courthouse. A Presbyterian minister named Campbell welcomed the pair to his home for tea. Two other Tennessee preachers, however, read the Catholic visit as a dire threat. The Reverend Vardiman, a Baptist revivalist who happened to be in Nashville at the same time, attempted to end Father Abell's sermons by claiming he would use the courthouse on an evening that the Catholics already had scheduled. Open conflict was avoided, however, because Vardiman's supporters persuaded him to refrain. Later, when Abell began preaching in Columbia, he was attacked verbally by the Reverend McConico. Abell's response to the sectarian outburst was said to have been so impressive that a group of non-Catholic lawyers and other witnesses gave him $200 and a new set of clothes for having "dressed" down his opponent so well. Abell played the controversialist, and Flaget was free to make grand gestures of goodwill toward Tennessee Protestants.[34]

As Catholicism expanded amid the blossoming of evangelical revivalism in the Ohio River valley, Bishop Flaget himself avoided public controversy by relying on a few of his subordinates to answer sectarian aggression. Like Abell in Tennessee, other priests, closer at hand, acted as Flaget's champions in the vicinity of Bardstown. That these men were vitally important became clear when the bishop was asked to relinquish one of them for service back East. In 1816, Flaget was supposed to send Father Chabrat, the first priest he had ordained in the Bardstown Diocese, to a new assignment. Chabrat, however, had become crucial in the West. According to Flaget's feisty assistant, Father David, Chabrat was "doing tremendous work" and had "become the scourge of the heretics, particularly the Baptists." He had delivered sermons to Catholics and Protestants alike, and was skilled in defeating attacks by evangelical ministers. Chabrat preached on the sacrament of Baptism at a Baptist revival in the woods, "to a large crowd who gather for this kind of controversy." Father David explained to his eastern colleagues that Chabrat had made "an unbelievable impression." A number of people who had shared their conversion experiences and were about to have themselves baptized changed their minds, while some asked Chabrat to baptize their children. Another time, the priest was planning to preach about infant Baptism, and a minister requested an opportunity to challenge his sermon. Chabrat agreed, though he investigated until he discovered what questions the Baptist preacher was planning to ask. The priest, therefore, himself raised and answered each issue during the course of his sermon, which left the Baptist and his supporters with nothing to say. Father David applauded Chabrat's cleverness and his service to the diocese. Thanks to Chabrat, he claimed, "These heretics who make such a loud noise around us and have what they call a revival are now beginning to change their opinions."[35]

David himself, as Flaget's coadjutator (assistant bishop) after 1819, also played a strong part in countering perceived Protestant attacks. Things grew hot in the spring of 1821. Bishop David felt "plunged up to my neck in controversy," and understood the cause to be the year-and-a-half-old Bardstown cathedral, which he thought "a heartache to our Presbyterian and Baptist ministers."[36] Said to be incensed by this symbol of Catholic ascendancy, a Presbyterian minister in Springfield, Kentucky, the Reverend Nathan Hall, began speaking out against Catholicism in the surrounding communities. David claimed he tried to ignore the calumny, but eventually sent a priest and a seminarian skilled in theology to sit in on Reverend Hall's next sermon and to announce that there would be a public refutation of the Presbyterian's misstatements. Bishop David then answered Reverend Hall with a series of long public sermons every other week on the Eucharist and other points raised by the minister. Bishop Flaget, who spent these weeks at his various far-flung stations across Kentucky, also took on controversial subjects. He spoke out publicly in communities where Reverend Hall had already been preaching.

Eventually Bishop David decided to challenge Hall to a personal debate. David had hoped to avoid facing Hall, but felt compelled

because of the minister's continuing attacks against himself and
Flaget, because the town leaders had invited him to counter Hall
in the courthouse, and because Flaget had asked him to defend the
faith. While David prepared for the encounter, Bishop Flaget ordered public prayers in Bardstown's St. Joseph's Cathedral, both for
victory and to compensate for any blasphemies that the Protestant
preacher might use. Despite Hall's "fiery and furious eloquence,"
claimed David, he had answered the Presbyterian's assault on "the
Catholic doctrine on the veneration of images and especially of the
cross, the cult of saints, and their relics." Apparently Hall had chosen obvious targets, the visual symbols of Catholic distinctiveness
and tradition. David spoke to these but avoided various other topics. After five hours of debate, he did not want "to drag the thing
out too much." There remained much for each orator to address,
so Bishop David decided to finish his thoughts in pamphlet form. A
few months later he had a ninety-page pamphlet printed in Louisville with the help of lay Catholics there who paid for and kept half
of the one thousand copies.[37]

Throughout the summer of 1821 Reverend Hall continued his
sorties. At first these did real harm to the Catholic cause, wrote David, though eventually the "violent sermons" backfired and began
producing more conversions to Catholicism. David and his priests
answered the minister "at St. Roses, at Bardstown, at Lebanon, at St.
Marie," and the Catholics and Protestants alike "can see his errors
. . . [and] are disgusted with his declamations." Several conversions
were linked directly to Hall's diatribes. The most renowned was that
of a doctor from the minister's own denomination who converted
on his deathbed. As he lay dying, Dr. Brown allegedly asked that his
friend, Bishop Flaget, be summoned to attend his bedside. Flaget,
as was typical, was away traveling to a distant parish. The doctor's
own family refused to send for Flaget, so his Catholic neighbors
sent for Father Byrnes. Afterward, when Reverend Hall showed
up, Dr. Brown took his hand and announced he had just converted
to Catholicism. By February 1822, Hall and David's battle had become clearly personal. "Hall is now in fury; everywhere he preaches
against me and my book." David relished the contest, thought Hall
was pushing even his most sectarian followers toward the Catholic camp, and believed the Presbyterian minister was working on a
pamphlet to answer his own.[38]

Conflict between Catholic and Protestant clergy increased in 1822 and 1823. In Kentucky, priests squared off against Presbyterians and Baptists. With regard to Methodists David said, "I do not bother about their errors," because the other two denominations were numerous and "we have enough to take care of these." Father Nicholas Dominic Young, in the company of his uncle, the newly consecrated bishop of Ohio and Michigan, Edward Dominic Fenwick, toured the diocese in the summer and fall of 1822, stopping to debate a Protestant in Truceville, Ohio. During the next year, Father David prepared a second apologetical publication to counter Reverend Hall's. The bishop's hard work—"I am taking advantage of every free moment to answer Minister Hall"—received the attention and approval of Archbishop Maréchal in Baltimore. Bishop Flaget promised to keep the archbishop informed, particularly about the Protestant minister's response: "I am persuaded that the whole College of Presbyterian Elders could not answer" David's pamphlet, "except by foolishness and impertinencies." In addition, Flaget hinted how with financial assistance he and David could quickly publish four or five more pamphlets "of very great force," or send the manuscripts to the archbishop to be printed out East, if sufficient copies might be sent for use in the Bardstown Diocese.[39]

Bishop Flaget in effect institutionalized public debate as a form of sectarian outreach by sending a pair of priests around the diocese to conduct mock debates or panel discussions before mixed Catholic and Protestant audiences. These forums were in part a response to challenges from non-Catholic clergy, a strategic response to growing anti-Catholicism, as well as a show of force or a display of learnedness, confidence, and structure. Besides foreshadowing the arrival of organized "missions" (what Protestants would term "revival meetings") within Catholic parishes in the 1830s, these carefully choreographed forensic exercises echoed the formal intra- and interdenominational debates popular among Protestants in the antebellum period. The 1820s would prove to be a fractious decade.[40]

Jubilee

During the next few years, contention between Catholic and Protestant clergy in the trans-Appalachian West grew intense and more organized. In fact, polemical exchanges proliferated across the country in response to several factors. The struggle over Catholic Emancipation in the British Isles during the 1820s produced literature and arguments heard both sides of the Atlantic. In addition, evangelical Protestant presses and communication networks grew as the revivalists perfected their message and means of conveyance. European immigrants, especially Irish Catholics, arrived in large numbers during the postwar depression of the 1810s and were pivotal in Jacksonian politics by the 1820s. National attention focused throughout the decade on the schism in the Catholic Church of Philadelphia led by Father William Hogan. The result was renewed criticism of Catholics.[41] In the midst of these events came even greater attention on Catholicism when Pope Leo XII promulgated his Holy Year of Jubilee to the United States in 1826–1827. Efforts by Catholic officials in the trans-Appalachian West to engage non-Catholic audiences grew more vigorous in response to the jubilee as well as the heated climate of sectarian relations.

Pope Leo XII announced the jubilee—a time for renewal of faith, pilgrimage, special observances, and plenary indulgence—from the Holy See in December 1824, and extended it to the rest of the world on Christmas Day 1825. The Jubilee of 1825–1827 commemorated Pope Leo's election to head the church, while in America it both strengthened the clergy and laity's connection to Rome and provided an opportunity to answer the spirit of Protestant revivalism of the Second Great Awakening. A retreat for the clergy followed by a celebration in the Bardstown cathedral in September 1826 marked the beginning of the jubilee in the Kentucky diocese. In December the jubilee was promulgated in Cincinnati. Thereafter a series of church services, retreats for clergy, and other more public events took place sequentially around both dioceses. Bishops Flaget and David in Kentucky and Bishop Fenwick in Ohio, accompanied by their clergy, toured from county to county, from congregation to distant settlement, to reach and to reinspire Catholics. They also attempted to stir non-Catholics and gain converts where possible.[42]

Bishop Fenwick's biographer describes that prelate's sermons as "doctrinal, calm and sober. All were designed to make the people realize the value of the soul, the importance of salvation, the purpose of the jubilee." As a result, continued the biographer, Fenwick and company "were invited to preach in court-houses, sectarian churches, or public places . . . wherever an audience could be gathered." Near the town of Wooster, one of the priests was invited to preach before a mostly Presbyterian audience in the local courthouse. Roaming from settlement to settlement, the missioners readily answered questions and objections, paying particular attention to Protestant listeners. Fenwick's jubilee exertions across Ohio and into Indiana and Michigan were said to have netted approximately four hundred converts.[43]

In Kentucky, the jubilee reached Louisville in late September, and Bishops Flaget and David made a special effort to share the religious fervor of the moment with non-Catholics. At the Church of St. Louis the Kentucky bishop and his coadjutator delivered a sermon in the morning, while at the Louisville courthouse that evening, where there was room for a larger crowd, the clergy put on a conference. It was a new development in the American West, an inventive method of instruction involving a panel discussion between two Catholic clergy on doctrine and moral topics. One interlocutor would ask questions, the other answered, taking time to expound on theological, doctrinal, and moral issues. A particular priest who took seriously his performance as interrogator was said to have approached his role "with the gravity of a *Methodist.*"[44]

It was a form of educational entertainment for Catholic and non-Catholic alike. In describing their effectiveness, Bishop David wrote that "These conferences brought a great deal of fruit." At the very least they drew attention. "We have followed the conference method which has more interest than sermons, which, however are not lacking," said David. Still, "the Protestants at first ridiculed them, saying it was a plot among the priests." Bishop David explained how these critics believed a pair of priests would not chance "proposing the strongest objections" to each other's statements in public, and that a Protestant preacher should be given the opportunity to ask questions and provide a different point of view. Catholic clergy responded that "there would be no plot on the part of the Catholic priests"; that "their only aim was to teach and to make known the truth"; and that involving a Protestant minister "would not fulfill that aim because the conference would degenerate soon into arguments where many would become angry," and this would "become rather the cause of scandal than a cause of edification." Not wanting to be accused of being either unfair or fearful about responding to difficult questions, Father Francis Patrick Kenrick of-

fered to accept objections and comments in writing left on the seats
in the courthouse. Indeed, the Kentucky clergy were sensitive to the
public perception of these conferences, the major purpose of which
was to make a good impression.[45]

Father Kenrick soon proved to be the most adept of the conference speakers, and Flaget selected him to travel the diocese during
the jubilee year of 1827 to perform the principal role of respon-
dent. "Our great conference master is Fr. Kenrick, who excels in
this," wrote Bishop David. "His profound knowledge of theology,
his excellent memory along with exquisite judgment . . . have made
him the joy of the Catholic and the terror of the heretics." Perhaps
after having settled on this useful format and having found a reliable
champion, the Catholics were confident enough to begin answering points raised by non-Catholics during the conference. Rather
than having written questions left behind on seats to be answered
at a later date, Kenrick invited all his listeners to "prepare their difficulties in writing" for his interlocutor to read aloud. "Up to now,"
claimed David, such objections "have been resolved with such force
and clearness that [Kenrick's] adversaries had nothing to answer."
One Presbyterian minister, however, decided to challenge Kenrick
openly: "After a beginning, which was very calm and very sincere,
he vomited forth all the venom that the enemies of the Catholic
Church have in their heart." According to David, the supremely
confident Kenrick, "who did not seem to pay much attention," answered each argument and "played" with the preacher "like a big cat
playing with a rat which he holds in his claws—and the defeat was
so complete that one person exclaimed: 'I would not have received
such a whipping for 500 dollars!'" Another listener was said to have
responded that he would not do so for a thousand, to which a Presbyterian added, "I would give a hundred dollars had the preacher
held his peace."[46]

Kenrick topped his career in Kentucky by publishing a book
that left him with a national reputation as a Catholic apologist. *Letters of Omega and Omicron on Transubstantiation* was a collection of
letters he, "Omicron," had exchanged with the Reverend Dr. Black-
burn, "Omega," the president of the Presbyterian College in Danville, Kentucky.[47] In 1830 Kenrick was transferred to Philadelphia to
become coadjutator bishop. He gained national attention by quickly
settling the trusteeism controversy and schismatic efforts of Father

Hogan. Kenrick's efforts, however, earned him the opprobrium of Protestant critics across the country who had long interpreted the Catholic hierarchy's actions in the Hogan controversy as anathema to democratic republican principles.

During the first forty years of the Catholic Church's movement westward, cautious optimism gave way to a more assured sense of progress and freedom to be distinctively Catholic. From John Carroll's appointment to lead the church in the mid-1780s, to the celebration of the Catholic Holy Year of Jubilee in 1826–1827, the hierarchy looked on the Ohio River valley as an area of repeated successes in establishing Catholic institutions and traditions, tapping wells of non-Catholic sympathy, and countering polemical challenges to the faith. Despite early hindrances, nuns and priests built schools, academies, and colleges that attracted even Protestant students and provided a body of tolerance and support among non-Catholics. Religious processions grew more elaborate and reflected the confidence of Catholic priests and parishes in displaying their cultural identity. More intricate and developed parades and greater use of traditional religious objects and accouterments were accepted as signs of progress.

Trans-Appalachian communities had proved to be especially open to public exhibits of Catholic religious belief. Priests and bishops imagined not only that Protestants and other non-Catholics were curious about Catholicism, but that Protestant clergy were doing a poor job of providing religious guidance among their own. Protestant preaching was fundamentally erroneous anyway, Catholics believed, and in the early West the problem was compounded by the misplaced zeal of ignorant and poorly trained ministers who played to emotion while missing substance. This presented an opportunity for the Catholic Church. Clergy eagerly took advantage of occasions to speak to Protestant and other non-Catholic audiences. Perhaps the culmination of this trend of openness and sanguinity was Bishop Flaget's experience at the consecration of Father Robert A. Abell's new church in Louisville in 1830. Local Protestants took part in the ceremonies, and Louisville Presbyterians permitted the clergy and visiting bishops to use their meeting house and Protestant Bible. Indeed, Flaget could hardly believe he had been "witness to such a triumph."

The ground was shifting, however, and Catholic clergy by the early 1820s were devoting greater attention to challenging Protestant ministers in print and speech. Overt attacks were not common prior to 1820, and Catholic clergy claimed to be reluctant to answer them. There were a few exceptions, yet, in general, priests would not respond to the calumny with vigor until several years after the establishment of the episcopal see in Bardstown in 1811. With the arrival of more priests and a bishop, individual clergy had more time to engage in polemical exchanges. They also had additional support from the growing Catholic communities and were less dependent on a mix of Catholic and non-Catholic supporters. Moreover, after Bishop Flaget's arrival, he and his priests had several years to institutionalize the defense of the faith. Certain members of the clergy, such as Father Abell, Father Chabrat, Bishop David, and Father Kenrick, demonstrated keen ability as debaters; others, such as Father Badin, as well as David and Kenrick, scribed apologetical tracts that garnered widespread attention. Bishop Flaget could go on the attack or choose to stand aloof as the gracious and accommodating yet strong prelate. Created during the Jubilee Year of 1826, the formal and didactic debates systematized by Flaget and his clergy, the public "conferences," signaled an important departure. These developments readied western Catholics to respond to the surge of anti-Catholic animosity welling up by the 1830s. Now Catholicism was firmly ensconced in the trans-Appalachian West, and the clergy had the means, and the need, to formally display, explain, and defend it.

Conclusion

For forty years, Catholics in the trans-Appalachian West got along well with neighboring Protestants and other non-Catholics. Through many points of contact, and in dynamic and dialectical ways, Catholics interacted with those around them. Sometimes they invited, occasionally they opposed, and always they considered their non-Catholic neighbors while establishing a religious presence from the eastern seaboard to the far western edges of the country. Catholic growth and success in frontier areas was more interconnected with Protestant denominations and the presence of non-Catholics than historians have recognized.

The region was one of high aspirations for church leaders; and Catholic clergy, like their Protestant evangelical counterparts, had exuberant visions of success. Priests and bishops planned to overcome hindrances involving manpower, money, and distance to establish congregations, build churches, start schools and seminaries, reinforce ecclesiastical authority, and win acceptance for Catholicism among a Protestant people. They also hoped to win friends and converts. The West was full of obstacles and opportunities that made clergy focus their energy and optimism outward, in a way that convention has associated with Protestant evangelicals on the frontier. In western Pennsylvania and Maryland, Ohio, Kentucky, Tennessee, and Indiana, Catholic clergy saw themselves apart from, even superior to, Protestant preachers but engaged in a similar endeavor. Priests ended up in backcountry settlements to minister to Catholics scattered far and near and in the company of non-Catholic neighbors. A myriad of new problems faced the missionaries: the population was transient, Catholic settlers could be extremely parsimonious in their support of the church and their priest, the priest was expected to travel constantly, and he had to do without many of the religious supplies he was accustomed to using. On the other hand, frontier life increased the authority of the lone priest. He could migrate farther west, leaving his people without access to the sacraments. In addition, the individual clergyman often assumed economic, social, and moral leadership in backcountry communities.

Priests saw themselves as being central to the larger project of bringing the Roman Catholic faith to the American West. In too many cases, however, the church hierarchy watched as corrupt or otherwise unworthy priests damaged local Catholic communities and the church's reputation. Renegade clergy were extremely difficult to control in a nation where the Catholic Church was still in a fragmentary and embryonic state, and where frontier opportunities and freedom seemed to beg the attention of European and American scoundrels. Over time, Bishop John Carroll and other members of the hierarchy cracked down on troublesome priests, always being mindful of how their words and deeds might be interpreted by non-Catholics. In the West, problem priests were more easily controlled after Bardstown became the seat of a diocese and home to Bishop Benedict Joseph Flaget in 1811. Using civil courts, a variety of threats, careful documentation, coordination among bishops, and appeals to Rome, the American Catholic hierarchy enforced its authority and its connection to that of the pope.

Efforts to build churches, decorate them, and provide the materials necessary for Catholic religious life also preoccupied the clergy and reinforced ties to Rome. Not only were religious items, such as statues, bells, vestments, candles, and holy oil, seen as necessary for the proper performance of the Catholic liturgy, the sacraments, and other rituals, but such objects were representative of all that distinguished Catholic from Protestant. Through their use and display, western Catholics demonstrated their distinctiveness, pride, and sense of superiority, all of which they hoped might draw the positive attention of non-Catholics. Church leaders, however, had ended the eighteenth century continually worrying about provoking Protestant Americans by appearing too distinctive or too foreign. By the beginning of the nineteenth century and through the 1820s, Catholic clergy were willing to exhibit the traditional, European material expressions of Catholic faith and devotion in an increasingly triumphant manner. Not only was the church more secure in the United States, but the clergy wanted to use the distinguishing features of material Catholicism to impress, overwhelm, win over, and even convert non-Catholics in the West.

Feeding the general sense of optimism among Catholic clergy regarding trans-Appalachia was the idea that it was new ground on which to interact with non-Catholics. Protestants there seemed to be less bigoted—and less well organized. More important, they appeared to be good targets for conversion attempts, and this notion fueled the Catholic imagination and hopes for success. On the other hand, living in proximity to non-Catholics in frontier regions presented difficulties in maintaining the Catholic enclave. Non-Catholics might be candidates for conversion to the Roman faith, but wayward Catholics or those who intermarried with Protestants might fall away from the church. Through the 1810s and 1820s, Catholic efforts to produce conversions waned, while questions about intermarriages only grew more complex. In addition, Catholic clergy continued to face difficult decisions in regulating interaction between their parishioners and non-Catholics: was it licit to rebaptize Protestant children, help Protestants build their churches, permit Catholics to be married by Protestant ministers, swear loyalty to the state government, serve meat to non-Catholics on days when it was forbidden for Catholics, or perform rituals with damaged religious objects that were difficult to replace? The early years of the century's third decade marked a high point of expectations, a "unique time," as Father Charles Nerinckx phrased it, when the church had many advantages in the American West and waited only for clear policies from Rome with regard to such "controversial matters" that arose because of the presence of Protestants.[1]

Despite the mounting complexities of living side by side with non-Catholics in the trans-Appalachian West, Catholic clergy continued to reach outward, to try to educate, impress, and otherwise enlighten their neighbors. Constituting orders of women religious allowed the church to offer schooling for the children of Catholic pioneers, as well as sound educations for non-Catholic students. Clergy and nuns overcame a variety of obstacles to found sisterhoods and build institutions of learning that would become the choice even of Protestant families. Religious processions, a symbolic form of expressing confidence and cultural identity, like elaborately decorated church buildings, invited attention from non-Catholics. As the Bardstown diocese built its own institutions, added nuns and priests, and strengthened connections to Baltimore and to Rome, processions grew more elaborate. So also did the clergy's efforts to reach Protestant audiences. Priests and bishops looked for occasions and venues at which to preach to non-Catholics, whom they believed were either too distant from religion altogether or being served only by less-than-competent Protestant ministers. Throughout the 1820s, however, interreligious tensions grew because of such proselytizing and because Protestant denominations were fighting less among themselves and were ready to challenge Catholicism. Catholic clergy turned their attention from outreach and proselytization to defense and polemics.

By 1830 Protestant evangelical denominations were ready for the upsurge of anti-Catholic animosity that spread across the country. As historian Ray Allen Billington has suggested, Catholicism in the United States during the 1820s "was showing new life" and drew national attention for the first time. Catholic immigration from Europe, a robust national network of evangelical Protestant associations, anti-Catholic propaganda from Europe, and conflict between Americans and Catholic immigrants over jobs and politics paved the way for years of controversy. While immigration became a national debate, simultaneously Catholics were drawing notice to themselves as never before. The national scandal made by Father William Hogan and his lay trustees, who defied the bishop and led a schism in Philadelphia, resulted in much sympathy for the defiant priest and parishioners. Then the Papal Jubilee promulgated in America in 1826–1827, followed by the first Provincial Council of Catholicity in Baltimore in 1829, confirmed that the Roman church was a significant force in American religion.[2]

Catholic leaders were well versed in the arguments their enemies would make against them. From the 1780s onward, Catholic Church leaders, such as Bishop John Carroll, had been checking themselves against their own standards as well as those by which they believed Protestants judged them. Priests and bishops felt their efforts were under the scrutiny of America's Protestants and non-Catholics, who only waited for an excuse to return to the prejudiced and restrictive customs toward Catholics that had characterized the eighteenth century. As a result, Catholic clergy were particularly sensitive about public opinion and strove to fit into American society without either compromising their religious principles or permitting scandal. Bishop and priest also recognized the challenging opportunities of the American economy, political system, and liberal democratic culture, particularly in the backcountry, where the sparseness of population made the Catholic presence more influential. Robust strains of anti-Catholicism lingered in these years, but sectarian relations temporarily improved, adding to the optimism with which Catholic leaders viewed the church's place in America and its future to the West.

In spite of this close contact and relative harmony, and sometimes because of it, Catholics continued to rely on standard techniques of establishing the authority, institutions, and activities of their faith. Some adaptations to the American situation and to frontier conditions were attempted, though the church by the 1830s was conservative, strongly supportive of the pope's authority, and traditional. Good feelings between Protestants and Catholics from the 1780s to the 1830s were ephemeral and did little to change either group.

Nor did the geographical frontier democratize or "Americanize" the Catholic Church. The very openness of the frontier, and the immense scope of both its problems and its possibilities, caused Catholic bishops and their clergy to invoke standard techniques of establishing authority, supplying access to the sacraments, inspiring devotion, seeking conversions, settling questions over mixed marriages, and establishing communities of women religious. So much seemed to be at stake in the early West. Challenges of too much distance, too few clergymen, resistance to episcopal authority, and short supplies of ritual and devotional materials, as well as the prospect of attrition of the faithful and too much aping of Protestant manners by Catholic laypersons in things religious, were daunting obstacles. On the other hand, much could be gained. Catholics saw opportunities to establish parishes and dioceses, schools and convents from Baltimore to Vincennes. Land seemed plentiful for creating Catholic communities or mixing with Protestants in mutually profitable ways. And chances to convert neighbors abounded. In other words, frontier conditions might call for innovation as Catholics and Protestants were thrown together in new ways, but traditional responses eventually worked better in maintaining authority, preserving the faithful, winning converts, and elaborating the institutional presence of the church.

Not only did the trans-Appalachian West do little to Americanize Catholicism, but the frontier experience reinforced and invigorated the distinctiveness of the Roman confession. American religious toleration and the expanse of western lands created a spirit of optimism, which Catholics saw as an opportunity to fully and assertively express Catholic identity and tradition. Moreover, Catholic leaders sought to minimize the influence of Protestantism on their charges. In 1785 Carroll, as the new prefect apostolic of the American missions, reported to Rome that besides a lack of good priests, his main challenge lay in countering "the abuses that have grown . . . with unavoidable intercourse with non-Catholics."[3] Isolating Catholics from their neighbors and minimizing contact were impractical, however, and a more effective response was bold, outward religious expression and the exercise of orthodoxy and authority. This included training and stationing zealous clergy, educating lay Catholics, and reaching potential converts. Particularly American problems—caused by vast geography, a dearth of religious resources both human and material, the proximity of so many aggressive and innovating Protestant denominations, and the intensity with which these challenges were felt because of rapid western flow of America's borders—necessitated traditional European solutions. This rigidity may have limited the number of conversions and general acceptance among non-Catholics for the short term, but it laid the foundations for steady, rapid, predictable growth later as immigrant European Catholics arrived in the settled West in need of stability and the familiar.

The Return to Conflict

Ultimately, the dispatch with which Catholicism spread, its rapid success in exploiting the potential and solving the problems of westward settlement, would alarm Protestant critics. By the end of the second decade of the nineteenth century Catholic bishops and institutions, priests and women religious, laity and apologists, were well poised for even greater growth. As immigrant Catholics poured across the Atlantic, a whole set of further frontiers in the trans-Mississippi West, to the Protestant eye, seemed ripe for conquest. At the same time, the early success, quick settlement, and re-creation of European Catholicism in America aggravated latent nativistic bigotry and anti-Catholic prejudice. As Father Nerinckx explained in 1824, the extent of Catholic achievements in Kentucky aggravated sectarian relations. "Bardstown used to be a pleasure garden of Presbyterians and Anabaptists," he wrote. "Hence it is a great mortification for these sects to see that Old Church which they so cordially hated and persecuted for the last three hundred years, looming up triumphantly in their midst." Protestant enemies of the church, likewise, took notice of signs indicating that Catholicism was succeeding. Some discounted what they saw, or hoped the signs of Catholicism's rapid expansion were an indication of impending collapse—as simply the "lofty pretentions of the Pope" that "stood upon nothing" and were soon destined to fall. "It will not be many years," wrote a Presbyterian publisher, a former pastor of Bardstown, "till the 'Beast and false Prophet and Satan' will all go into perdition and these fine Cathedrals will be cleansed of their idols and be converted into evangelical sanctuaries." Catholic and Protestant clergy alike, for the moment, saw Catholicism rising triumphant.[4]

The more visibly organized, hierarchical, and institutional the Catholic Church became in the United States, with its growing numbers of clergy, women religious, cathedrals, convents, seminaries, academies, and newspapers, the more it seemed to fit the anti-Catholic fears and stereotypes. Nativist suspicions and criticisms of Mormons, Masons, and Catholics hinged on common themes, and these typically portrayed Catholicism, like Freemasonry and Mormonism, as a tightly controlled pyramidal structure. Individual members were not necessarily evil; rather, they were duped and blinded by immoral leaders who oversaw a vast and complicated "machine-like organization."[5] Proliferation of Catholic edifices, religious orders, and other examples of the Vatican's influence in American life only fed nativist fears of subversion.

Protestant leaders began recognizing the marks of Catholic success in the Midwest, and would begin responding with focused energy in the 1830s as the number of immigrants increased and Catholic institutions for them multiplied. Protestants in the East came to see this region as a battleground for the soul of the nation. In August 1830 the head office of the American Home Missionary Society issued a document outlining the nature of the test before Protestant Americans. "Look at that single section of our country called the 'valley of the Mississippi.' In twenty years if it should continue to increase as it has done in population, it will contain a majority in the halls of Congress." Now is the time, argued the missionary society, to bring the region "under the influence of religion." Catholics and other enemies of Christianity had a head start. "Already the infidel is there—the *Socinian*, the *Universalist*, the *Roman Catholic* is there. *Now or never*—is the watchword of all the benevolent Societies in reference to that region. Every Agent that goes there to explore—every Missionary, every intelligent Christian layman—writes back—*What you do for this Country, do Soon*." A series of letters to the *New York Observer* by Samuel F. B. Morse, inventor of the telegraph, warned of an international antidemocratic conspiracy headed by the pope, cardinals, bishops, and Jesuits that was using Catholic immigration to dominate America. Temperance reformer and Presbyterian revivalist preacher Lyman Beecher highlighted the geographical dimension of the problem and what he agreed was the intrigue behind it. While touring the East to raise funds, he delivered three anti-Catholic sermons in three Boston churches, thundering against Rome and the reach of its tentacles to the United States. Immediately afterward, on August 11, 1834, a mob burned the Ursuline Convent school in nearby Charleston, bringing national attention to the Catholic/anti-Catholic struggle.[6]

Later that year Beecher published his *Plea for the West*, in which he elaborated Morse's thesis, adding that the battle for the soul of America was taking place in its western reaches: "if we gain the West, all is safe; if we lose it, all is lost." Not only were Catholics quickly gaining an advantage in the Mississippi Valley, but others were readying themselves to cross the Atlantic, "like the locusts of Egypt . . . rising from the hills and plains of Europe . . . preparing for flight in an endless succession." As in 1774 when King George III's Quebec Act sanctioned the French Catholic presence south of the St. Lawrence all the way to the Ohio River, anti-Catholic minds reeled at the thought of papal minions dominating the West.[7]

Protestant observers, like Catholic officials in earlier decades, recognized the momentous significance of churching the western edges of the nation. In establishing new parishes and dioceses; in bringing traditional items of religious expression, such as European statues, paintings, and liturgical materials; in founding religious orders and offering schools that would enroll non-Catholic students; in vigorously interacting with non-Catholic neighbors; and in so successfully transplanting European Catholicism to the United States, Catholics in the early republic helped set the stage for this Protestant backlash by the late 1830s.

A few years into this era of nativism, Bishop Flaget mused about the vitality of the church in the West and its promising future. Writing to Bishop Joseph Rosati of St. Louis in 1834, Flaget wondered about the impressive majesty that a consecration ceremony for a new archbishop of the West in St. Louis would present to non-Catholics. "We could wish for nothing better than that all the prelates of the West be numbered among those officiating," he said. "They would assemble in the capital of the valley of the Mississippi for all these august and splendid" ceremonies, and "Such a spectacle would assuredly be very new for the country, very imposing for all those who would be witnesses of them." The spectacle should have a dramatic effect, but no longer were Catholic displays of splendor expected to change Protestants hearts or minds. The visual power of rich ornamentation in Catholic churches, Father Nerinckx had reasoned, would "inspire the ignorant and lookers-on with a greater veneration of our religion." As he put it in 1818, "seeing, they admire; admiring, they inquire; inquiring, they finally desire the gift of faith." A decade later Father B. Martial could still suggest that "ornaments and decorations" and the Catholic "majesty of worship" in Bardstown were attractive to Protestants, many of whom saw the consistency of truth that connected the "liturgical ceremonies," decorations, and "what we teach." Looking ahead to the archbishop's consecration ceremony in St. Louis, however, Bishop Flaget could only joke that the display would be "capable of giving the Asiatic *cholera* to all the unbelievers and heretics." The cautious optimism of Bishop John Carroll at the turn of the century, and Flaget's own confidence in outreach efforts through the 1810s and 1820s, had been replaced by defensiveness and resignation. Catholic and Protestant would live side by side but draw no closer.[8]

Notes

Introduction

1. John Carroll to Joseph Edenshink, April–June 1785, in *The John Carroll Papers, 1755–1815*, ed. Thomas O'Brien Hanley (3 vols., Notre Dame, 1976), I, 186.

2. The Sacred Congregation, now called the Congregation for the Evangelization of Peoples, is the international agency within the Roman Catholic Church that since the seventeenth century has been in charge of spreading Catholicism and regulating ecclesiastical matters in non-Catholic countries. Regarding Carol's concern about foreign interference, see Joseph Agonito, *The Building of an American Catholic Church: The Episcopacy of John Carroll* (New York, 1988), 16–29.

3. Much of the older scholarship on Catholicism in the early republic has been institutional—"steeples and peoples" studies. Part of a long tradition of religious denominations carefully recording places and names in their past, Catholic histories of the trans-Appalachian West generally have been celebratory descriptions of leading personages and institutional growth. Although thoroughly researched, most tend to treat Catholic communities in isolation, as though they had been insulated from the influence and opinion of non-Catholics. An exception is Sister Mary Ramona Mattingly's *The Catholic Church on the Kentucky Frontier, 1785–1812* (Washington, D.C., 1936), which connects the development of Catholicism in the Bluegrass state with that of Protestant denominations. Other early institutional histories include Martin John Spalding, *Sketches of the Early Catholic Missions of Kentucky* (Louisville, 1844), and *Sketches of the Life, Times, and Character of the Rt. Rev. Benedict Joseph Flaget* (Louisville, 1852); John Gilmary Shea, *History of the Catholic Church in the United States, 1763–1815* (Akron, 1888); Benedict Webb, *The Centenary of Catholicity in Kentucky* (Louisville, 1884); Joseph William Ruane, *The Beginnings of the Society of St. Sulpice in the United States, 1791–1829* (Washington, D.C.,

1935); and Leo F. Ruskowski, *French Émigré Priests in the United States, 1791–1815* (Washington, D.C., 1940). For a more recent study of Kentucky Catholicism, see Clyde F. Crews, *An American Holy Land: A History of the Archdiocese of Louisville* (Wilmington, 1987).

4. Ray Allen Billington's and Jenny Franchot's works are the definitive studies of early American anti-Catholicism. Billington's *The Protestant Crusade, 1800–1860: A Study of the Origins of American Nativism* (New York, 1938) focuses on anti-Catholicism's roots in colonial America and its rematerialization among nativists in the 1830s. Franchot's more recent exploration of anti-Catholic discourse as a crucial point of contact between Catholic and Protestant cultures is concerned with the antebellum period, long after the initial years of religious interaction between Protestants and Catholics in the trans-Appalachian West. See her *Roads to Rome: The Antebellum Protestant Encounter with Catholicism* (Berkeley, 1994). The degree to which trans-Appalachian Catholics and Protestants held each other in fascinated disgust or admiration has been understated. Whereas Franchot explores the Protestant observation of Catholics, the present study emphasizes the reverse. In addition, it outlines the mutual observation and self-comparison in the decades before the 1830s, when Franchot's work begins. It should be noted that it was Sydney E. Ahlstrom's suggestion that the origins of this American Protestant sympathizing fascination with Old World Catholicism lie in an earlier period of romanticization, when Catholics began moving to the western edges of the United States in 1785–1830. See Ahlstrom, *A Religious History of the American People* (New Haven, 1972), 548. A work that does give close attention to the early republican period and which argues that anti-Catholicism continued unabated, though it was accompanied by new, more positive opportunities for Protestant-Catholic interaction, is Ira M. Leonard and Robert D. Parmet's *American Nativism, 1830–1860* (New York, 1971). Although he has little to say about religion or the frontier, Paul Foik shows that anti-Catholicism had an important role in late eighteenth- and early nineteenth-century politics. See Foik, "Anti-Catholic Parties in American Politics, 1776–1860," *Records of the American Catholic Historical Society of Philadelphia* 36 (March 1925): 41–69.

5. In general, Catholics have been left out of the recent pivotal treatments of frontier religion and of religion in the early republic, which focus on Protestant evangelicalism. Nathan O. Hatch's and Jon Butler's immensely influential books on late eighteenth- and early nineteenth-century religion do not cover the spread of Catholicism nor the vibrant interaction of Catholics and Protestants in this period. See Hatch, *The Democratization of American Christianity* (New Haven, 1989), and Butler, *Awash in a Sea of Faith: Christianizing the American People* (Cambridge, Mass., 1990). The dichotomy of democratization versus entrenchment of

authority over which Hatch and Butler disagree, however, is at the core of the struggle to establish Catholicism in the trans-Appalachian region. Roman Catholic development during the early republic includes instances of democratization at work, especially in the perennial battles between lay trustees, priests, and bishops, but the ultimate victory of the Catholic hierarchy supports Butler's thesis. Christine Leigh Heyrman's *Southern Cross: The Beginnings of the Bible Belt* (New York, 1997) describes a process of acculturation through which evangelical Protestantism came to reflect the values of the South, losing its radical edge and establishing the authority of church leaders. Like Butler and Heyrman, the present work finds a religious denomination, in this case Catholicism, experiencing a gradual process of church cohesion, increasing authority, and conservatism. Roger Finke and Rodney Stark explain the hierarchical and well-ordered strategy of the Catholic Church in spreading westward, but they do not weigh the effects of sectarian relations. Instead, Finke and Stark portray Catholics in a quiet isolation, establishing their missions and parishes while awaiting a later juncture of contact with non-Catholic America. See Finke and Stark, *The Churching of America, 1776–1900: Winners and Losers in Our Religious Economy* (New Brunswick, N.J., 1992).

6. Andrew R. L. Cayton and Fredrika J. Teute, eds., *Contact Points: American Frontiers from the Mohawk Valley to the Mississippi, 1750–1830* (Chapel Hill, 1998), 1–5. For a nuanced discussion of differing points of view between cultures in a frontier setting, see Elliott West, *The Contested Plains: Indians, Goldseekers, and the Rush to Colorado* (Lawrence, Kan., 1998). See also John Mack Faragher, "'More Motley than Mackinaw': From Ethnic Mixing to Ethnic Cleansing on the Frontier of the Lower Missouri, 1783–1833," in Cayton and Teute, eds., *Contact Points*, 304–26; Stephen Aron, *How the West Was Lost: The Transformation of Kentucky from Daniel Boone to Henry Clay* (Baltimore, 1996), 2–3; and Gregory H. Nobles, *American Frontiers: Cultural Encounters and Continental Conquest* (New York, 1997), xii, 11–13, and "Breaking into the Backcountry: New Approaches to the Early American Frontier, 1750–1800," *William and Mary Quarterly* 46 (1989): 641–70.

7. Leonard Thompson and Howard Lamar, eds., *The Frontier in History: North America and Southern Africa Compared* (New Haven, 1981), 7–8, and Nobles, *American Frontiers*, 15–16. For the frontier period ending with statehood, see, for example, Stephen Aron, "The Significance of the Kentucky Frontier," *Register of the Kentucky Historical Society* 91 (1993): 302–3, and *How the West Was Lost*.

8. Colleen McDannell has pointed out that "While the American environment certainly made an indelible mark on Catholics living in the United States, we need not overlook the continuing presence of Europe in

shaping American Catholicism." McDannell, *Material Christianity: Religion and Popular Culture in America* (New Haven, 1995), 162. Likewise, Joseph Agonito has stated, "Of all the major American churches that of the Catholic was perhaps the least influenced by the American 'frontier.'" Agonito, *The Building of an American Catholic Church*, 285. A large group of scholars, however, has portrayed the frontier as the most important transforming and Americanizing influence on Catholicism in the United States. Echoing Frederick Jackson Turner's frontier thesis, Thomas McAvoy suggested in the 1940s that the "American" nature of the U.S. Catholic Church lay in its frontier experience, not in the urban, immigrant eastern seaboard studied by earlier church historians like Peter Guilday. See McAvoy, "Americanism and Frontier Catholicism," *Review of Politics* (July 1943): 275–301, and "The Formation of the Catholic Minority in the United States, 1820–1860," *Review of Politics* (January 1948): 13–30. McAvoy also claimed that the acculturation of Catholic immigrants happened most quickly on the Midwestern frontier, where the settlers' struggle to tame the wilderness inhibited the spread of anti-Catholicism. He cautioned, however, that American heterodoxy was never as severe as conservative European theologians imagined, and that doctrine in the American Catholic Church remained fully consonant with Rome. At most, McAvoy claimed, "frontier privations" caused lapses in liturgical and devotional practices, and preoccupation with frontier exigencies resulted "in a less intensive understanding" of doctrines and a "greater emphasis on its practices and external conduct." Catholic pioneers were socially and culturally changed by the trans-Appalachian West, but not significantly with regard to their beliefs and practice. Thomas W. Spalding, Leslie Woodcock Tentler, and Clyde F. Crews are more recent and more fervent Turnerians. Spalding urges historians to take up McAvoy's challenge to test Turner's thesis and agrees that the frontier made Catholicism individualistic, active, nonsectarian, and tolerant, and free of the defensive ghetto mentality of their immigrant brethren in eastern cities. See Thomas Spalding, "Frontier Catholicism," *Catholic Historical Review* 77 (July 1991): 470–84, and "The Catholic Frontiers," *U.S. Catholic Historian* 12 (Fall 1994): 1–15. Tentler concludes that frontier conditions made frontier Catholicism "discernibly American," yielding quasi-democratic parishes, an ordered and tolerant mixing of ethnic groups, close relationships between laity and priest, and localized parishes not focused on episcopacy. See Tentler, "'How I would save them all': Priests on the Michigan Frontier," *U.S. Catholic Historian* 12 (Fall 1994): 17–35. Crews, in *An American Holy Land*, 28–29, suggests that the growth of Catholicism in Kentucky was due to the crucible-like effect of the frontier as it created stronger individuals and institutions through adversity.

9. Much has been written on the assimilation and Americanization of

Catholicism. In such studies, Catholic development in the early republic is a story of improving sectarian relations and adaptations to "American" conditions. These "Americanizations" include absorption of democratic and republican ideology, generally with the temporary outcomes of greater toleration toward non-Catholics, liberalized theological and ecclesiastical attitudes, and other changes that brought Roman Catholics closer to mainstream Protestant values and institutions. A liberalized, more tolerant American Catholic Church was "temporary" in that it was replaced after Archbishop James Whitefield's First Provincial Council of Baltimore (1829) by an episcopally dominated, anti-trustee, pro-Roman Catholicism. More centralized and seemingly more European, the Catholic Church for the rest of the nineteenth century helped produce a "violent nativism." My thanks to A. G. Roeber for pointing this out. See Patrick W. Carey, *The Roman Catholics* (Westport, 1993), 30–31, and Dale Light, *Rome and the New Republic: Conflict and Community in Philadelphia Catholicism between the Revolution and the Civil War* (Notre Dame, 1996). Jay Dolan and Patrick W. Carey have stressed the effectiveness of republicanism and American democratic values in influencing Catholics to create a more decentralized, nationalistic church, and in building better relations between Catholics and Protestants. Carey's work, although focused on eastern urban settings, is useful for understanding trans-Appalachian Catholic communities. He reveals the internal and external conflicts of the Catholic Church caused by trusteeism (i.e., control of the congregation, particularly its finances, by lay trustees) and revolutionary republicanism. Both had important influences on frontier Catholicism, but markedly less than in eastern cities. Jay Dolan has termed 1783–1830 an "irenic period" or the "republican interlude" in Catholic history. The most recent major surveys of American Catholicism provide sparse coverage of Catholic/non-Catholic relations in the early republic and conclude simply that life was easier for Catholics than it had been before the Revolution. Taken at face value, these works make it difficult to explain the violent outbreak of sectarian hostilities of the mid-nineteenth century. Jay P. Dolan attributes the improved sectarian relations to an "infectious spirit of tolerance"; James Hennesey ambiguously states that "the turbulent decade worked substantial change in the American psyche. It was not that toleration . . . became universal. . . . But the general picture was favorable." See Jay P. Dolan, *The American Catholic Experience: A History from Colonial Times to the Present* (Garden City, 1985), and James Hennesey, *American Catholics: A History of the Roman Catholic Community in the United States* (New York, 1981). More recently Dolan has claimed the improved relations were in large part due to a new Catholic outlook. American Catholics, he states, grew to accept Protestants because they knew they were a minority in America and because there existed a "new theology of church," which developed out of the Revolution and the Enlightenment. See Dolan, "Catholic Attitudes toward Protestants," in Robert N. Bellah and Frederick E. Greenspahn, eds., *Uncivil Religion: Interreligious Hostility in America* (New York, 1987), 72–85. Two other historians have argued that post-independence sectarian relations were amicable, but again, neither incorporates the history of the church on the western frontier or in other nonurban areas of the early republic. See Joseph A. Agonito, "Ecumenical Stirrings: Catholic-Protestant Relations during the Episcopacy of John Carroll," *Church History* 45 (September 1976): 358–73, and Joseph P. Chinnici, "American Catholics and Religious Pluralism 1775–1820," *Journal of Ecumenical Studies* 16 (Fall 1977): 727–46. Although relations with non-Catholics did improve, and some attempts at Americanizing the church occurred, Catholic economic, cultural, and spiritual connections to Europe remained crucial, and strong traditions of anti-Catholicism continued. Dolan, however, has helped counter earlier works that overstressed the Americanization of the church in the early republic. He notes that Archbishop John Carroll planned to shape the Catholic Church to the American situation—with the use of the vernacular in liturgy, the creation of a level of autonomy for local congregations, the use of the trustee system for controlling church property and founding new parishes, and the election of bishops (rather than their appointment by Rome)—but ultimately helped to bring about a "shift from [his own] republican blueprint of the 1780s to a more traditional model of Roman Catholicism." See Dolan, *The American Catholic Experience*, 124, and Thomas W. Spalding, *The Premier See: A History of the Archdiocese of Baltimore 1789–1989* (Baltimore, 1989), 44–45. Thomas W. Spalding, like Dolan, has highlighted the Americanized nature of the church in the 1780s through the 1830s. The "Maryland tradition" of Bishop John Carroll and his immediate successors yielded eventually to what has been called the "immigrant tradition." The Maryland tradition of the early republic was open, engaged with American society and culture, imbued with patriotic, republican, and democratic ideas from the Revolution, supportive of the autonomy of the local church with regard to Rome, and reliant on state and church separation. The later immigrant church would be exclusive instead of inclusive, European, and focused on a defensive strategy of "ghetto building," or carving out Catholic and ethnic organizations, institutions, and identities. Spalding's history of the Baltimore diocese is framed by this polarity. He admits that "there would always be a tendency to replicate European prototypes and patterns," that "the more difficulties he encountered, the more the first bishop fell back on traditional forms and time-honored procedures in the church." Yet Spalding's and others' demarcation of an early church versus a later church, a republican Maryland tradition versus an immigrant European tradition, implies a greater, if temporary, absorption of American ideals than the present study finds in the trans-Appalachian region. Even though the Baltimore bishop's and then archbishop's authority spread as far west as the Mississippi, Spalding's story is primarily centered in the densely settled and urban East. Indeed, Spalding and Dolan clearly show that any plans Bishop John Carroll may have had to Americanize the church were fleeting, lost in the swirl of exigencies he faced from 1784 to 1815. "Whatever inclinations he may have had to tread new paths and reshape the local church to harmonize with the American scene . . . he found greater safety and stability in European patterns." See Spalding, *The Premier See*, 17–19, 45–46, 123–25. The pages that follow take up this theme of traditionalism and stress its continuing presence in the early West.

10. Cayton and Teute, *Contact Points*.

1. The View to the West

1. See John Carroll to Giuseppe Doria-Pamphili, 26 November 1784, in *The John Carroll Papers, 1755–1815*, ed. Thomas O'Brien Hanley (3 vols., Notre Dame, 1976), I, 153. Sermon quoted in Joseph Agonito, *The Building of an American Catholic Church: The Episcopacy of John Carroll* (New York, 1988), 178.

2. John Carroll to Cardinal Leonardo Antonelli, 20 September 1793 and 15 October 1794, in *John Carroll Papers*, ed. Hanley, II, 102, 130. Agonito, *The Building of an American Catholic Church*, 276.

3. John Carroll to Cardinal Hyacinth Gerdil, December 1795, in *John Carroll Papers*, ed. Hanley, II, 160.

4. For calculations of Catholic population, see Gerald Shaughnessy, *Has the Immigrant Kept the Faith? A Study of Immigration and Catholic Growth in the United States, 1790–1920* (New York, 1925), 37–38, 43–51. The population of the United States in 1790 was 3,929,000. See U.S. Bureau of the Census, *Historical Statistics of the United States, Colonial Times to 1957* (Washington, D.C., 1960), 7.

5. Gallitzin to Carroll, 9 February 1800, quoted in Sarah Brownson, *Life of Demetrius Augustine Gallitzin, Prince and Priest* (New York, 1873), 122. It is estimated that Gallitzin spent $150,000 of his own money on developing the small community that he eventually named Loretto in 1803. Andrew Arnold Lambing claims that Rev. J. A. Stillenger, Gallitzin's neighbor and friend for ten years, showed him the papers for this amount of land. Lambing cites Rev. Thomas Heyden, another colleague of Gallitzin's, for the dollar amount spent. See Lambing, *A History of the Catholic Church in the Dioceses of Pittsburg and Allegheny from Its Establishment to the Present Time* (New York, 1880), 295–96, 311.

6. The Presbyterians/Congregationalists had built 43 churches before the Catholics had their Sportsman's Hall church in 1790; by 1800 there were 81 Presbyterian/Congregational churches. The Baptists had 10 by 1790 and 38 by 1800; the Lutheran and German Reformed had 17 by 1790 and 26 by 1800; the Methodists had 18 by 1790 and 24 by 1800; and the Episcopalians had 2 by 1790 and 5 by 1800. See Gaius Jackson Slosser, "A Chapter from the Religious History of Western Pennsylvania," *Journal of the Department of History of the Presbyterian Church in the U.S.A.* 16 (September 1934): 107–16, 102. Lambing, *A History of the Catholic Church in the Dioceses of Pittsburg and Allegheny*, 20–21, 44. John F. Schermerhorn and Samuel J. Mills, sent by a Presbyterian missionary society to reconnoiter the West in 1814–15, found southwest Pennsylvania still to be a Presbyterian stronghold. There were fewer non-Presbyterian Protestants, they remarked, "than in any other part of the western country. The public, and men of information and influence, are decidedly in favor of Presbyterianism." See their report, "A Correct View of That Part of the United States Which Lies West of the Allegany Mountains, With Respect to Religion and Morals," in Edwin S. Gaustad, ed., *To Win the West: Missionary Viewpoints 1814–1815* (New York, 1972), 5.

7. Father Stephen Theodore Badin, "Origin and Progress of the Mission of Kentucky, United States of America" (1821), in Phillip Gleason, ed., *Documentary Reports on Early American Catholicism* (New York, 1978), 830. See also Lawrence J. Kenney, "The Gallipolis Colony," *Catholic Historical Review* 4 (October 1918): 415–51. Victor Francis O'Daniel, *The Right Rev. Edward Dominic Fenwick, Founder of the Dominicans in the United States* (Washington, D.C., 1921), 191–92. Badin to Carroll, 7 January 1808, Letters to Archbishop Carroll, 1786–1815, Records of the Administration of John Carroll, Baltimore Cathedral Archives, Baltimore, Md. (microfilm, University of Notre Dame Archives).

8. O'Daniel, *The Right Rev. Edward Dominic Fenwick*, 199, 211.

9. Ibid., 215, 219–22. Ohio's total population in 1820 was 581,434 according to the U.S. Bureau of the Census, *Historical Statistics of the United States, Colonial Times to 1957* (Washington, D.C., 1960), 13.

10. Badin to Carroll, 14 March 1807, Box 1-H, Letters to Archbishop Carroll, Records of the Administration of John Carroll. Badin to Carroll, 4 August 1800, Letters to Archbishop Carroll, Records of the Administration of John Carroll. See also Martin John Spalding, *Sketches of the Early Catholic Missions of Kentucky from their Commencement in 1787, to the Jubilee of 1826–1827* (Baltimore, 1844). Badin to Father Charles Nerinckx, as recorded in letter of Nerinckx to unknown recipient, 28 October 1807, Bollandist Library, Brussels, Belgium, as quoted in Camillus P. Maes, *The Life of Rev. Charles Nerinckx* (Cincinnati, 1880), 153–54.

11. The estimates for 1815 are based on those used by Bishop Flaget and Fathers Badin and Nerinckx. See Martin John Spalding, *Life, Times, and Character of the Right Reverend Benedict Joseph Flaget* (1852; New York, 1969), 98; Mary Ramona Mattingly, *The Catholic Church on the Kentucky Frontier, 1785–1812* (Washington, D.C., 1936), 103, 113; "Reverend Charles Nerinckx's Pamphlet, 'A Look at the Present State of the Roman Catholic Religion in North America,'" ed. Joseph A. Agonito and Magdeleine Wellner, *Records of the American Catholic Historical Society of Philadelphia* 83 (March 1972): 14–15; and Maes, *The Life of Rev. Charles Nerinckx*, 125. For the remarkable imprint that early Catholics left in Kentucky, see Clyde Crews, "Holy Valleys and Holy Lands: Selected Historic Catholic Sites along the Lower Ohio and Middle Mississippi Rivers," *U.S. Catholic Historian* 18 (Fall 2000): 55–63. Figures on Flaget's arrival are from Spalding, *Life, Times, and Character of the Right Reverend Benedict Joseph Flaget*, 98. Numbers for 1818 are from Maes, *The Life of Rev. Charles Nerinckx*, 363–70. Nerinckx's 1815 quote is from "Reverend Charles Nerinckx's Pamphlet," ed. Agonito and Wellner, 14.

12. Badin, "Origin and Progress," in Gleason, ed., *Documentary Reports on Early American Catholicism*, 833. The actual total population of the diocese—including all of or parts of what were or would become Ohio, Indiana, Illinois, Michigan, Kentucky, and Tennessee—was 1,779,859, according to the U.S. Bureau of the Census, *Historical Statistics*, 13. Regarding St. Thomas Aquinas College, see John B. Boles, *Religion in Antebellum Kentucky* (Lexington, 1976), 63. On schools for girls, see Flaget to Bishop England, 8 December 1824, as quoted in Spalding, *Sketches of the Early Catholic Missions of Kentucky*, 204; and Mary J. Oates, "Catholic Female Academies on the Nineteenth-Century Frontier," *U.S. Catholic Historian* 12 (Fall 1994): 122.

13. Robert Davidson, *History of the Presbyterian Church in the State of Kentucky* (New York, 1847), 85. Robert Bishop, *An Outline of the History of the Church in the State of Kentucky during a Period of Forty Years: Containing the Memoirs of Rev. David Rice, and Sketches* (Lexington, 1824), 306–7. Lutherans, for comparison, got off to a slow start in the trans-Appalachian West. Of the forty Lutheran ministers in the United States in 1787, very few made it away from the eastern seaboard. Between 1782 and 1806, only one to three covered the territory of western Pennsylvania and eastern Ohio at any one time. Roy H. Johnson, "The Lutheran Church and the Western Frontier, 1789 to 1830," *Lutheran Church Quarterly* (July 1930): 229.

14. John Adams to Abigail Adams, 9 October 1774, in L. H. Butterfield, ed., *The Adams Family Correspondence* (4 vols., Cambridge, Mass., 1963–1973), I, 166–67.

15. Mattingly, *The Catholic Church on the Kentucky Frontier,* 150. Regarding the convention, see Spalding, *Sketches of the Early Catholic Missions of Kentucky,* 26. Badin to cardinal prefect of the Propaganda Fide, 7 June 1805, typescript trans. (Sisters of Charity Archival Center, Nazareth, Ky.). Letters of 1807, Bollandist Library, Brussels, Belgium, as quoted in Maes, *The Life of Rev. Charles Nerinckx,* 148. Petition to Bishop John Carroll, 17 June 1808, Baltimore Cathedral Archives, as quoted in Clyde Crews, *An American Holy Land: A History of the Archdiocese of Louisville* (Wilmington, Del., 1987), 70. Peck, *American Baptist Magazine* (1817–1819), as quoted in Walter Brownlow Posey, *The Baptist Church in the Lower Mississippi Valley, 1776–1845* (Lexington, 1957), 136.

16. Carroll to Charles Plowden, 3 September 1800 and 26 November 1784, in *John Carroll Papers,* ed. Hanley, II, 317–18. Reported by Father Charles Nerinckx, 1807, as quoted in Maes, *The Life of Rev. Charles Nerinckx,* 156. Carroll to Charles Plowden, 12 February 1803, in *John Carroll Papers,* ed. Hanley, II, 408. Badin to cardinal prefect, 7 June 1805, Guilday Transcripts, in Duplicate Letter Book transcription (Sisters of Charity Archival Center, Nazareth, Ky.). "Reverend Charles Nerinckx's Pamphlet," ed. Agonito and Wellner, 8.

17. Badin to cardinal prefect of the Propaganda Fide, 7 June 1805, typescript trans. (Sisters of Charity Archival Center, Nazareth, Ky.). Flaget to Father Bruté, 28 October 1811, as quoted in Herman J. Schauinger, *Cathedrals in the Wilderness* (Milwaukee, 1952), 63. David Barrow Manuscript (Filson Historical Society, Louisville, Ky.). For Badin quote, see Schauinger, *Cathedrals in the Wilderness,* 137–38. For David, see letter of John Baptist David to fellow Sulpician priest, 26 October 1816, in typescript trans., Diocese of Bardstown Collection (Filson Historical Society, Louisville, Ky.). For further examples, see Badin, "Origin and Progress of the Mission of Kentucky, United States of America, By An Ocular Witness" (Paris, 1821), trans. William J. Howlett (Loretto Archives, Nerinx, Ky.).

2. A Central Role for Priests

1. Badin to Carroll, 17 December 1807, Letters to Archbishop Carroll, 1786–1815, Records of the Administration of John Carroll, Baltimore Cathedral Archives, Baltimore, Md. (microfilm, University of Notre Dame Archives).

2. Ibid.

3. Badin to Carroll, 11 April 1796, "Letters from the Baltimore Archives," ed. E. I. Devitt, *Records of the American Catholic Historical Society of Philadelphia* 19 (September 1908): 259–60. Badin asked for assistance many

times during his years in Kentucky. See, for example, Badin to Carroll, 6 November 1796.

4. Badin to Carroll, 2 March 1797, ibid. John Grassi, "The Catholic Religion in the United States in 1818," in Woodstock Letters 11 (1882), in Phillip Gleason, ed., *Documentary Reports on Early American Catholicism* (New York, 1978), 240.

5. Camillus P. Maes, *The Life of Rev. Charles Nerinckx* (Cincinnati, 1880), 62.

6. Gerald Shaughnessy, *Has the Immigrant Kept the Faith? A Study of Immigration and Catholic Growth in the United States, 1790–1920* (New York, 1925), 262.

7. Joseph William Ruane, *The Beginnings of the Society of St. Sulpice in the United States, 1791–1829* (Washington, D.C., 1935), 1–3, 22–26, 32–33, 39–44.

8. John Carroll, "Report for the Eminent Cardinal Antonelli Concerning the State of Religion in the United States of America, 1785," in Gleason, ed., *Documentary Reports on Early American Catholicism*, 153. Grassi, "The Catholic Religion in the United States in 1818," 235. Letter of Bishop Egan to Archbishop Carroll, 8 October 1811, CABA–Archdiocese of Baltimore, Original Documents 1717–1967, Archives of the University of Notre Dame, Notre Dame, Ind.

9. Jacob Dittoe to Carroll, 5 January 1805, Baltimore Archives, Case 3, D7, as cited in Victor Francis O'Daniel, *The Right Rev. Edward Dominic Fenwick, Founder of the Dominicans in the United States* (Washington, D.C., 1921), 195. For Rogers, see Felix Fellner, "Trials and Triumphs of Catholic Pioneers in Western Pennsylvania (As Revealed by the Correspondence)," *Records of the American Catholic Historical Society* 34 (September 1923): 305. For the infidels quote, see Maes, *Life of Rev. Charles Nerinckx*, 127.

10. Fellner, "Trials and Triumphs of Catholic Pioneers," 309–10.

11. Ibid., 310.

12. Letter from St. Francis congregation to Bishop Carroll, 1806, copy in St. Francis Archives, White Sulphur, Ky., as quoted in Ann Bolton Bevins and James R. O'Rourke, *That Troublesome Parish: St. Francis/St. Pius Church of White Sulphur, Kentucky* (White Sulfur, 1985), 70.

13. Ibid., 70.

14. Nerinckx to Carroll, 1806, Letters to Archbishop Carroll, Records of the Administration of John Carroll. For Gibault, see Andrew R. L. Cayton, *Frontier Indiana* (Bloomington, 1996), 45–46. Nerinckx to Carroll, 1806, Letters to Archbishop Carroll, Records of the Administration of John Carroll. Badin to Carroll, 10 June 1808, Letters to Archbishop Carroll, Records of the Administration of John Carroll.

15. Holy See, *Catechism of the Catholic Church* (Liguori, Mo., 1994), 381. Gibault quoted in Cayton, *Frontier Indiana,* 61–62.

16. Badin to Carroll, 28 June 1796 and 24 August 1796, "Letters from the Baltimore Archives," 265, 268, 270.

17. Gallitzin's concern about families in wilderness as recalled by friend and fellow priest Rev. Thomas Heyden, *A Memoir on the Life and Character of the Rev. Prince Demetrius A. de Gallitzin, Founder of Loretto and Catholicity in Cambria County, Pennsylvania, Apostle of the Alleghanies* (Baltimore, 1869), 64. Wolf quote recalled by another friend and fellow priest, Rev. Peter Henry Lemcke, *Life and Works of Prince Demetrius Augustine Gallitzin* (1861; London, 1940), 124–28. Gallitzin to Maréchal, 28 October 1823, quoted in Sarah M. Brownson, *Life of Demetrius Augustine Gallitzin, Prince and Priest* (New York, 1873), 345.

18. Patrick J. Carey suggests that most funds came from the plantations owned and operated by Jesuits in Maryland. See Carey, *People, Priests, and Prelates: Ecclesiastical Democracy and the Tensions of Trusteeism* (Notre Dame, 1985). Pastoral Letter, 28 May 1792, in Hugh J. Nolan, ed., *Pastoral Letters of the United States Catholic Bishops, Volume I, 1792–1940* (Washington, D.C., 1983), 22.

19. Herman J. Schauinger, *Cathedrals in the Wilderness* (Milwaukee, 1952), 13.

20. Fromm to Carroll, 9 March 1794, as quoted in Fellner, "Trials and Triumphs of Catholic Pioneers," 218.

21. Anthony Salmon to Bishop Carroll, 27 May 1799, Letters to Archbishop Carroll, Records of the Administration of John Carroll.

22. Badin to Carroll, 3 June 1799, ibid.

23. Badin to Carroll, 9 October 1799, ibid.

24. Badin to Carroll, 15 October 1805, ibid. Nerinckx to his parents, 1807, as quoted in Maes, *The Life of Rev. Charles Nerinckx,* 87–88. (Maes doesn't give any more information about this letter.)

25. Nerinckx to his parents, 1807, ibid.

26. Badin to Carroll, 29 August 1808, Letters to Archbishop Carroll, Records of the Administration of John Carroll.

27. Schauinger, *Cathedrals in the Wilderness,* 17. Carroll to Badin, Baltimore, 2 August 1794, RG-Spec. 13—Box, Badin, Rev. Stephen T. (Loretto Archives, Nerinx, Kentucky).

28. Badin to Carroll, 24 August, 1796, "Letters from the Baltimore Archives," 271–73.

29. Thomas D. Clark, *Frontier America: The Story of the Westward Movement* (New York, 1959), 168–70. See also Robert V. Remini, *The Life of Andrew Jackson* (New York, 1988), 20, and Jon Kukla, *A Wilderness So Immense: The Louisiana Purchase and America's Destiny* (New York, 2003).

30. Badin to Carroll, 28 June and 24 August 1796, "Letters from the Baltimore Archives," 267, 270. See also Bevins and O'Rourke, *That Troublesome Parish*, 63. Badin to Carroll, 4 March 1798 and 29 August 1808, Letters to Archbishop Carroll, Records of the Administration of John Carroll.

31. Carroll to Luis Penalver, 17 October 1798, in *The John Carroll Papers, 1755–1815*, ed. Thomas O'Brien Hanley (3 vols., Notre Dame, 1976), II, 246.

32. Excerpts of a Letter to the Cardinal Prefect of the Propaganda Fide from Father Stephen Badin, 7 June 1805, Guilday Transcripts, in Duplicate Letter Book transcription (Sisters of Charity Archival Center, Nazareth, Ky.).

33. Nerinckx to Carroll, circa August 1809, as quoted in Maes, *The Life of Rev. Charles Nerinckx*, 206.

34. Edward Fenwick to Jacob Dittoe, 25 May 1812, Archives of Saint Joseph's Priory, Somerset, Ohio, as cited in O'Daniel, *The Right Rev. Edward Dominic Fenwick*.

35. Schauinger, *Cathedrals in the Wilderness*, 3.

36. The election was officially contested because of his narrow margin of victory and because complaint was made that he had only become a U.S. citizen in June 1823. A Congressional committee determined, however, that the one-year citizenship rule for members of Congress did not apply to Richard because he was only a delegate. Frank B. Woodford and Albert Hyma, *Gabriel Richard: Frontier Ambassador* (Detroit, 1958), 48–70, 106–17.

37. Gallitzin to Carroll, 9 February 1800, in Brownson, *The Life of Demetrius Augustine Gallitzin*, 122. A. A. Lambing claims that Rev. J. A. Stillenger, Gallitzin's neighbor and friend for ten years, showed him the papers for this amount of land. Lambing cites Rev. Thomas Heyden, another colleague of Gallitzin's, for the dollar amount spent on Loretto. See Lambing, *A History of the Catholic Church in the Dioceses of Pittsburg and Allegheny from Its Establishment to the Present Time* (New York, 1880), 295–96, 311; Heyden, *A Memoir on the Life and Character of the Rev. Prince Demetrius A. de Gallitzin* (Baltimore, 1869).

38. Gallitzin to Archbishop Maréchal, 28 October 1823, Brownson, *The Life of Demetrius Augustine Gallitzin*, 345. Trustees quote recalled by his friend, fellow priest, and biographer, Rev. Peter Henry Lemcke, in *Life and Work of Prince Demetrius Augustine Gallitzin*, 102.

39. Heyden, *Memoir on the Life and Character of the Rev. Prince Demetrius A. de Gallitzin*, 48–49.

40. Badin to Carroll, 13 August 1798, Letters to Archbishop Carroll, Records of the Administration of John Carroll.

41. Badin to Carroll, 4 August 1800, ibid.

42. Grassi, "The Catholic Religion in the United States in 1818," 23.

43. Fellner, "Trials and Triumphs of Catholic Pioneers," 309–10.

44. Badin to Carroll, 17 December 1807, Letters to Archbishop Carroll, Records of the Administration of John Carroll. Letter of Father Charles Nerinckx, 1807, found at Bollandist Library, Brussels, Belgium, quoted in Maes, *The Life of Rev. Charles Nerinckx*, 127.

45. W. J. Howlett, ed., "Bishop Flaget's Diary," *Records of the American Catholic Historical Society of Philadelphia* 29 (September 1918): 246–49. V. F. O'Daniel, ed., "Bishop Flaget's Report of the Diocese of Bardstown to Pius VII, April 10, 1815," *Catholic Historical Review* 1 (October 1915): 317. "Reverend Charles Nerinckx's Pamphlet, 'A Look at the Present State of the Roman Catholic Religion in North America,'" ed. Joseph A. Agonito and Magdeleine Wellner, *Records of the American Catholic Historical Society of Philadelphia* 83 (March 1972): 9.

3. "Presumptuous Renegades"

1. Two influential studies of frontier religion in early America propose that Protestant denominations experience a long, gradual process of church cohesion as ecclesiastical authority increases. See Jon Butler, *Awash in a Sea of Faith: Christianizing the American People* (Cambridge, Mass., 1990) and Christine Leigh Heyrman, *Southern Cross: The Beginnings of the Bible Belt* (New York, 1997). Father Charles Nerinckx began his 1816 pamphlet "A Look at the Present State of the Roman Catholic Religion in North America" by focusing on the obstacles to Catholicism, the first of which appears in his opening sentence, "the deceits and wickedness of our presumptuous renegades." See "Reverend Charles Nerinckx's Pamphlet, 'A Look at the Present State of the Roman Catholic Religion in North America,'" (1816) ed. Joseph A. Agonito and Magdeleine Wellner, *Records of the American Catholic Historical Society of Philadelphia* 83 (March 1972): 3–35.

2. Father Ferdinand to Bishop Carroll, August 1785, as quoted in Felix Fellner, "Trials and Triumphs of Catholic Pioneers in Western Pennsylvania (As Revealed by the Correspondence)," *Records of the American Catholic Historical Society* 34 (September 1923): 198. Vincent Huber, "Sportsman's Hall," *Records of the American Catholic Historical Society of Philadelphia* 3 (1888–1891): 146. Carroll to Charles Plowden, in *The John Carroll Papers, 1755–1815*, ed. Thomas O'Brien Hanley (3 vols., Notre Dame, 1976), II, 22, 31.

3. Fellner, "Trials and Triumphs of Catholic Pioneers," 199–200.

4. James Hennesey, *American Catholics: A History of the Roman Catholic*

Community in the United States (New York, 1981), 77. Nathan O. Hatch, *The Democratization of American Christianity* (New Haven, 1989), argues that the Second Great Awakening was part of a tumultuous democratic revolution against elite domination, a period when a "wave of popular religious movements" upset traditional religious hierarchies and reinvigorated Christianity. See also Jay Dolan's *The American Catholic Experience* (Garden City, 1985); and Patrick Carey's *People, Priests, and Prelates: Ecclesiastical Democracy and the Tensions of Trusteeism* (Notre Dame, 1987), *The Roman Catholics* (Westport, 1993), "The Laity's Understanding of the Trustee System, 1785–1855," *Catholic Historical Review* 64 (July 1978): 357–76, and "Republicanism within American Catholicism, 1785–1860," *Journal of the Early Republic* 3 (Winter 1983): 413–37. These historians underscore the impact of trusteeism on the early American Catholic Church, though it is important to note that their studies focus on urban and eastern communities. Joseph Agonito's *The Building of an American Catholic Church: The Episcopacy of John Carroll* (New York, 1988) also emphasizes lay democratic impulses of trusteeism resisted by church hierarchy, though Agonito also begins to underscore the key role of troublemaking priests.

5. Thomas W. Spalding, *The Premier See: A History of the Archdiocese of Baltimore 1789–1989* (Baltimore, 1989), 76. Carey, *The Roman Catholics*, 29.

6. Hennesey, *American Catholics*, 77. See also Carey, *People, Priests, and Prelates*, 7–16. Carroll to Dominick Lynch and Thomas Stoughton, 24 January 1786, in *John Carroll Papers*, ed. Hanley, I, 203–4.

7. Patrick Carey, "Two Episcopal Views of Lay-Clerical Conflicts," *Records of the American Catholic Historical Society of Philadelphia* 87 (March–December 1976): 86. See Clyde F. Crews, *An American Holy Land: A History of the Archdiocese of Louisville* (Wilmington, Del., 1987).

8. Sydney E. Ahlstrom, *A Religious History of the American People* (New Haven, 1972), 537.

9. John Carroll, "Report for the Eminent Cardinal Antonelli Concerning the State of Religion in the United States of America, 1785," in Phillip Gleason, ed., *Documentary Reports on Early American Catholicism* (New York, 1978), 152–54.

10. Badin to Carroll, 28 June 1796, in "Letters from the Baltimore Archives," ed. E. I. Devitt, *Records of the American Catholic Historical Society of Philadelphia* 19 (September 1908): 265. See "Reverend Charles Nerinckx's Pamphlet, 'A Look at the Present State of the Roman Catholic Religion in North America,'" ed. Agonito and Wellner, 3–35. Regarding Flaget and Conwell, see Herman J. Schauinger, *Cathedrals in the Wilderness* (Milwaukee, 1952), 203.

11. James Flint, *Letters from America, Containing Observations on the*

Climate . . . 1818–1820 (Edinburgh, 1820), reprinted in Reuben Gold Thwaites, ed., *Early Western Travels, 1748–1846, Volume IX* (Cleveland, 1904), 167. On Burr and Wilkinson, see Thomas D. Clark, *Frontier America: The Story of the Westward Movement* (New York, 1959), 248–55. Karen Halttunen has described an analogous situation in mid-nineteenth-century cities, as the middle class faced the disorienting anxieties of the modern world and the comings and goings of unknown individuals, such as drifters and prostitutes, who seemed to represent all that threatens the social order. See her *Confidence Men and Painted Women: A Study of Middle-Class Culture in America, 1830–1870* (New Haven, 1982). For a close analysis of how settlers evaluated strangers in frontier regions, see Elizabeth A. Perkins, "Distinctions and Partitions amongst Us: Identity and Interaction in the Revolutionary Ohio Valley," in Andrew L. Cayton and Fredrika J. Teute, eds., *Contact Points: American Frontiers from the Mohawk Valley to the Mississippi, 1750–1830* (Chapel Hill, 1998), 205–34, especially 211–12.

12. Badin to Carroll, 24 August 1796, "Letters from the Baltimore Archives," 272.

13. Badin to cardinal prefect of Propaganda Fide, 7 June 1805, Guilday Transcripts, in Duplicate Letter Book transcription (Sisters of Charity Archival Center, Nazareth, Ky.). Badin to Carroll, 4 March 1798, Letters to Archbishop Carroll, 1786–1815, Records of the Administration of John Carroll, Baltimore Cathedral Archives, Baltimore, Md. (microfilm, University of Notre Dame Archives). Also in "Letters from the Baltimore Archives," 243–75. The latter, published, version of this letter omits mention of Barrieres's failure to deliver books or to return money with which he had been entrusted. See also Carroll to Badin, 2 August 1794, RG-Spec. 13—Box, Badin, Rev. Stephen T. (Loretto Archives, Nerinx, Ky.).

14. Badin to cardinal prefect of Propaganda Fide, 7 June 1805, Guilday Transcripts. For Carroll's description of de Rohan, see *John Carroll Papers*, ed. Hanley, I, 490. Badin to Carroll, 11 April 1796, "Letters from the Baltimore Archives," 259. About the possibility of transfer, see Badin to Carroll, 2 March 1797, Letters to Archbishop Carroll, Records of the Administration of John Carroll. Badin to Carroll, 29 August 1808, Letters to Archbishop Carroll, Records of the Administration of John Carroll. Catholic historian W. J. Howlett researched Father de Rohan's background and life in Kentucky, the gist of which he reported in a letter to Young Ewing Allison, 19 January 1920, Mss. A A439a, Young Ewing Allison, 1853–1932 (Filson Historical Society, Louisville, Ky.).

15. Spalding, *The Premier See*, 35, 43. See also *John Carroll Papers*, ed. Hanley, II, 166–67, 183, 415.

16. 1 March 1788, *John Carroll Papers*, ed. Hanley, I, 272–73. 16 June 1791, ibid., I, 507.

17. Tardiveau was taking revenge on Father Peter Huet de la Valinie're, who had written Congress that Tardiveau was a self promoter and not a true representative of the Illinois country in petitioning the government for land rights. Tardiveau to St. John de Crèvecoeur, 19 January 1789, in Howard C. Rice, *Barthelemi Tardiveau, A French Trader in the West* (Baltimore, 1938), 22–23.

18. Carroll to Luis Penalver, 17 October 1798 and 17 October 1799, *John Carroll Papers*, ed. Hanley, II, 246–47, 291.

19. *John Carroll Papers*, ed. Hanley, II, 448–49. Badin to Carroll, 4 December 1809, Letters to Archbishop Carroll, Records of the Administration of John Carroll.

20. Badin to Carroll, 3 October 1810, Letters to Archbishop Carroll, Records of the Administration of John Carroll.

21. Nerinckx to Carroll, 20 November 1803, Baltimore Archives, trans. copy by Sister Ann Patrick Ware, 1960 (Loretto Archives, Nerinx, Ky.).

22. Carroll to Leonard Neale, 20 June 1807, *John Carroll Papers*, ed. Hanley, III, 29. Regarding jejune documents, see Carroll to Simon Gallagher, September 1801, *John Carroll Papers*, II, 357–59. Carroll to Gallagher, 23 January 1799, *John Carroll Papers*, II, 258; Spalding, *The Premier See*, 44. Carroll to Gallagher, 14 July 1801, *John Carroll Papers*, II, 354.

23. V. F. O'Daniel, ed., "Bishop Flaget's Report of the Diocese of Bardstown to Pius VII, April 10, 1815," *Catholic Historical Review* 1 (October 1915): 314.

24. Flaget to Archbishop Maréchal, 8 March 1825, Folder 5, Letters of Rt. Rev. Benedict Joseph Flaget, 1764–1850, of Bardstown to Archbishop Maréchal, 3rd Archbishop of Baltimore, translations from documents in Archives of Archdiocese of Baltimore by Colomba E. Halsey, O.S.R (Filson Historical Society, Louisville, Ky.).

25. Archbishop Maréchal, "Archbishop Maréchal's Report to Propaganda, 1818," in Phillip Gleason, ed., *Documentary Reports on Early American Catholicism* (New York, 1978). Spalding, *The Premier See*, 87–89.

26. Flaget to Maréchal, 7 January 1820, Flaget to Maréchal, 8 March 1825, Folder 5, Letters of Rt. Rev. Benedict Joseph Flaget, 1764–1850, of Bardstown to Archbishop Maréchal, 3rd Archbishop of Baltimore.

27. Schauinger, *Cathedrals in the Wilderness*, 140–41.

28. Benjamin J. Webb, *The Centenary of Catholicity in Kentucky* (Louisville, 1884), 344–45; Schauinger, *Cathedrals in the Wilderness*, 212; and letter of J. B. M. David to Simon Bruté, 4 February 1823, Duplicate Letter Book XXIV (Sisters of Charity Archival Center, Nazareth, Ky.).

29. Augustin C. Wand and M. Lilliana Owens, eds., *Documents: Nerinckx—Kentucky—Loretto, 1804–1851, in Archives Propaganda Fide, Rome* (St. Louis, 1972), 238–39.

30. Carroll to Albinus Meister, 5 October 1799, *John Carroll Papers*, ed. Hanley, II, 284. Carroll chastised the acting prefect in Rome for having taken Reuter's side without waiting to hear the full story and for thereby "weakening the ordinary jurisdiction of the episcopal see." He sought a peaceful settlement with Reuter, but the German priest made another trip to Rome to complain, returned to the United States and was part of the trustee battle that consumed the German parish in Baltimore, and took a parishioner to court for assaulting him after the parishioner's wife accused the priest of a love affair. Carroll ultimately suspended and replaced Reuter, but the new priest was forced to seek a court order and quell a riot before the troublemaker departed in 1805. See Spalding, *The Premier See*, 32–33.

31. David to Bruté, 12 July 1813, Duplicate Letter Book XXIV, 77; and 31 October 1827, Duplicate Letter Book XXIV, 72.

32. David to Bruté, 31 October 1827, Duplicate Letter Book XXIV, 72.

33. Ibid., 73–75, 79.

34. Badin to Carroll, 3 June 1799, Letters to Archbishop Carroll, Records of the Administration of John Carroll. Hennesey, *American Catholics*, 75–79. Carroll to Plowden, 15 December 1785, *John Carroll Papers*, ed. Hanley, I, 197.

35. Carroll to Plowden, 22 February 1791, *John Carroll Papers*, ed. Hanley, I, 491, 494. Carroll to Rousselet, 10 March 1791, ibid., I, 497. Act of Submission for John Thayer (in Carroll's hand but signed and dated by Thayer), 13 June 1791, ibid., I, 506. Carroll to Thayer, 4 April 1795, ibid., II, 137.

36. Badin to Carroll, 3 June 1799 and 4 February 1800, Letters to Archbishop Carroll, Records of the Administration of John Carroll. Regarding Thayer and slavery, see Badin to Carroll, 5 July 1799 and 13 March 1800, Letters to Archbishop Carroll, Records of the Administration of John Carroll. See also Ann Bolton Bevins and James R. O'Rourke, *That Troublesome Parish: St. Francis/St. Pius Church of White Sulphur, Kentucky* (White Sulphur, 1985), 66–67. For the contradictory nature of Thayer's views on slavery, see C. Walker Gollar, "Father John Thayer: Catholic Antislavery Voice in the Kentucky Wilderness," *Register of the Kentucky Historical Society* (Summer 2003): 275–96, and his "Catholic Slaves and Slaveholders in Kentucky," *Catholic Historical Review* 83 (January 1998): 43–45.

37. Badin to Carroll, 25 February 1801, Special A-H-8, Baltimore Cathedral Archives, Baltimore, Md. (microfilm, University of Notre Dame Archives).

38. Carroll to Badin, January 1801, *John Carroll Papers*, ed. Hanley, II, 340–41. Badin to Carroll, 29 January 1801, Special A-H-10; James Twyman

to Carroll, 11 January 1801, Special A-H-9; and Henry Carivoe (?), 16 December 1800, Special A-H-11; and Badin to Carroll, 3 November 1801, Special A-H-12, Baltimore Cathedral Archives, Baltimore, Md. (microfilm, University of Notre Dame Archives).

39. Greed, cruelty, and carnality—especially that which resulted in the seduction of young women—were three main deviations that Anglo-American tradition attributed to priests in eighteenth-century anti-Catholic literature. See Francis D. Cogliano, *No King, No Popery: Anti-Catholicism in Revolutionary New England* (Westport, 1995), 10–12. According to David Brion Davis, "Some Themes of Counter-Subversion: An Analysis of Anti-Masonic, Anti-Catholic, and Anti-Mormon Literature," *Mississippi Valley Historical Review* 47 (September 1960): 217, "it was an ancient theme of anti-Catholic literature," which was often reprinted and imitated in America, that Catholic clergy were exceptionally sexually appealing and active, that they did not recognize Protestant marriages as legitimate, and they therefore were "astonishingly successful at seducing supposedly virtuous wives." Davis uses as an example of this genre Antonio Gavin, *A Master-Key to Popery, Giving a Full Account of All the Customs of the Priests and Friars, and the Rites and Ceremonies of Popish Religion* (n.p., 1812), 70–72. Regarding the travel expenses for a new priest, Badin to Carroll, 8 January 1801, Special A-H-10, Baltimore Cathedral Archives, Baltimore, Md. (microfilm, University of Notre Dame Archives).

40. Carroll to Badin, January 1801, *John Carroll Papers*, ed. Hanley, II, 340–41. See also Carroll to Badin, 18 March 1801, 349–50. Thayer was not the only priest whose personal life and allegations of sexual activity threatened the dignity of the church at this time. A former Jesuit named John Ashton in Maryland was dismissed from his position of managing the most profitable of the church plantations, White Marsh, a church estate then owned by the Corporation of the Roman Catholic Clergy of Maryland, the body of clerical trustees who controlled all the former Jesuit lands in the state.* He was reputed to be engaged in a "tasty arrangem[en]t" with a woman. When Bishop Carroll informed Ashton of the Corporation's decision, Ashton retorted that Carroll had no authority to remove him. "Let me cut my bread in peace or I will disturb the peace with a vengeance." Although Ashton later showed remorse, Carroll removed his faculties after the priest began slandering Bishop Neale, Carroll's coadjutator. Carroll explained to the Corporation trustees he had felt obligated to go "beyond the line" between his spiritual and their temporal responsibilities in this case because he was "anxious to put an end to discourses and an opinion generally prevailing, that clergymen might offend with impunity." Even after Ashton had agreed to give up his faculties, he remained at White Marsh and thwarted his replacement. Because Ashton and his successor

"could not live longer together without continually adding to the scandal," Carroll moved the latter to a nearby "asylum." In 1806 Ashton again was causing trouble. He had turned his attention to slandering Bishop Leonard Neale and his two brothers, Fathers Charles and Francis. "There is something not right in the heads of the Neales," he told Carroll, adding "What a woeful thing it would be to have a crazy Bi[sho]p." Three years later Ashton said he would sue Bishop Neale for defamation. The seemingly disturbed priest next claimed he had been attacked by nuns wearing men's clothing, implying that two of the Neale brothers, who directed convents, were resorting to nefarious means to silence him. The scenario he posited had, and was probably intended to have, all the flavor of the anti-Catholic rhetoric of the nativist attacks on the church in mid-century. It was, perhaps, symbolic of the degree of alienation he felt from episcopal authority and the community of church and fellow clergy. See Spalding, *The Premier See*, 43–44; Carroll to The Trustees of the Clergy, 1 September 1801, *John Carroll Papers*, ed. Hanley, II, 360–61. (*In December 1792 the Maryland legislature passed legislation creating the "Corporation of the Roman Catholic Clergy of Maryland," which was the board of elected representatives of the clergy that controlled all former Jesuits' land and Georgetown College. This board was dominated by ex-Jesuits. Carroll received an annual share of the revenues from the Corporation's several estates. Until 1802 Carroll carefully did not interfere in temporal powers exercised by the board and focused on his spiritual authority, though this changed due to trustee problems. See Spalding, *The Premier See*, 25–27, 38–39.)

41. Carroll to Fromm, 16 February 1801, *John Carroll Papers*, ed. Hanley, I, 493. Fellner, "Trials and Triumphs of Catholic Pioneers," 204.

42. Carroll to Fromm, 5 April 1791 and 23 August 1791, in Fellner, "Trials and Triumphs of Catholic Pioneers," 206–8. Fromm to Carroll, 9 April 1793, ibid., 209–11. Carroll to Fromm, 13 May 1793, *John Carroll Papers*, ed. Hanley II, 91.

43. Fromm to Carroll, 4 November 1793 and 9 March 1794, in Fellner, "Trials and Triumphs of Catholic Pioneers," 211–19. 18 to 30 April 1794, *John Carroll Papers*, ed. Hanley, II, 115.

44. Carroll to Fromm, 5 August 1795, and Phelan to Carroll, 5 October 1795, in Fellner, "Trials and Triumphs of Catholic Pioneers," 224–29.

45. Phelan to Carroll, 5 October 1795, in ibid., 230.

46. Phelan to Carroll, 17 October 1795, and 19 October 1795, in ibid., 229–30, 236–38.

47. Phelan to Carroll, 17 October 1795, in ibid., 230. Diary of Robert Ayres, 3 June 1795, MSS #23 (Historical Society of Western Pennsylvania, Pittsburgh, Pa.): "according to appointment, I fell in company with Doctor D[?]own, in Bedford we walked to the Jail and Court House, in which

was a poor condemned Malefactor, a German Clergyman for killing a man. The Clergyman's name was Spanzenberger! . . . Here I must not omit observing that the Jail Keepers Lady—showed us the knife, the aforesaid man was killed with." Phelan to Carroll, 19 October 1795, and 22 January 1796, in Fellner, "Trials and Triumphs of Catholic Pioneers," 238, 241.

48. Phelan to Carroll, 9 April 1796 and 26 May 1796, in Fellner, "Trials and Triumphs of Catholic Pioneers," 246–47, 256.

49. Phelan to Carroll, 19 October 1795 and 20 April 1796, in ibid., 237–38, 249–50.

50. Phelan to Carroll, [?] May 1796, in ibid., 252–53.

51. County docket, "Westmoreland County, December Term 1798, Lesse of the Executors of Theodorus Browers v. Franciscus Fromm," in Huber, "Sportsman's Hall," 154–55.

52. Ibid.

53. Carroll to secretary of the Propaganda Fide, Caesar Brancadoro, 9 February 1799, *John Carroll Papers*, ed. Hanley, II, 260, 265. County docket, "Westmoreland County, December Term 1798, Lesse of the Executors of Theodorus Browers v. Franciscus Fromm," in Huber, "Sportsman's Hall," 158–59.

54. Spalding, *The Premier See*, 45–46. Patrick Carey similarly shows that trusteeism battles in eastern cities ultimately resulted in the hierarchy taking a hard line with disobedient parishioners and priests, entrenching its own power with the help of Rome. See Carey, *People, Priests, and Prelates*, 1–4.

4. Making Sacred Place

1. 24–29 September 1821, John Brown Diary, Mss. A B 878a (Filson Historical Society, Louisville, Ky.). Brown was born in South Carolina on 1 December 1800 and died at Camden, Arkansas, on 4 May 1872.

2. 20 October 1821, ibid.

3. 24 October 1821, ibid.

4. 20 October 1821, ibid.

5. John Wrenshall Journal, Mss. #202, Schmeltzer Collection, Box 1, Folder 4, Wrenshall Journal #3, 1794–1799, 59–60 (Historical Society of Western Pennsylvania, Pittsburgh, Pa.).

6. John Adams to Abigail Adams, 9 October 1774, in L. H. Butterfield, ed., *The Adams Family Correspondence* (4 vols., Cambridge, Mass., 1963–1973), I, 166–67.

7. Jenny Franchot, *Roads to Rome: The Antebellum Protestant Encounter with Catholicism* (Berkeley, 1994), xii-xxii. Franchot begins her study in the early 1830s with the rise of American nativism, the first deluges of German

and Irish immigration, and attainment of suffrage by British Catholics in 1829. David Brion Davis has described rampant anti-Catholic stereotypes in the 1820s–1850s in which the enemy, who was seen as the "precise antithesis of American ideals," was nonetheless considered "frightening and fascinating." See Davis, "Some Themes of Counter-Subversion: An Analysis of Anti-Masonic, Anti-Catholic, and Anti-Mormon Literature," *Mississippi Valley Historical Review* 47 (September 1960): 208.

8. Jon Butler, *Awash in a Sea of Faith: Christianizing the American People* (Cambridge, Mass., 1990), 257–88, 291. John Breathitt Journal, 8 November 1804, Item 1121 (Kentucky Historical Society, Frankfort, Ky.). John Wrenshall Journal, 60. Nerinckx to his parents as quoted in letter from J. J. Peemans to Propaganda Fide, Louvain, 28 September 1806, in Augustin C. Wand and M. Lilliana Owens, eds., *Documents: Nerinckx—Kentucky—Loretto, 1804–1851, in Archives Propaganda Fide, Rome* (St. Louis, 1972). Ann Taves, *The Household of Faith: Roman Catholic Devotions in Mid-Nineteenth-Century America* (Notre Dame, 1986).

9. Badin to Carroll, 13 August 1798, Letters to Archbishop Carroll, 1786–1815, Records of the Administration of John Carroll, Baltimore Cathedral Archives, Baltimore, Md. (microfilm, University of Notre Dame Archives).

10. Altar stones were a "moveable altar," and the use of relics inside them was a "custom dating to the early Church when the liturgy was celebrated on the tombs of the martyrs." Richard P. McBrien, ed., *The HarperCollins Encyclopedia of Catholicism* (New York, 1995), 38.

11. Badin to Carroll, 13 August 1798, Box 1-E; 4 February 1800; 3 November 1801, Box Special A, H-12; and 20 May 1810; Letters to Archbishop Carroll, Records of the Administration of John Carroll.

12. See Stephen Aron, *How the West Was Lost: The Transformation of Kentucky from Daniel Boone to Henry Clay* (Baltimore, 1996), 131–32, 167–68; John Mack Faragher, *Sugar Creek: Life on the Illinois Prairie* (New Haven, 1986), 102–5, 134–36; and Jack Larkin, *The Reshaping of Everyday Life, 1790–1840* (New York, 1989), 38. Patrick W. Carey makes the point about salaries for priests versus church construction and emphasizes that "voluntaryism," or the voluntary support of one of many nonestablished churches, was a recurrent theme in Bishop John Carroll's administration. Most American Catholics, coming from Maryland, had been used to the Jesuits there supporting themselves with income from large, Jesuit-owned plantations. See Carey, *The Roman Catholics* (Westport, 1993), 22. Nerinckx to unknown recipient, November 1805, in Camillus P. Maes, *The Life of Rev. Charles Nerinckx* (Cincinnati, 1880), 114–15.

13. On Nerinckx's reputation, see letter of Rev. Walter H. Hill, S.J., December 1875, in Maes, *The Life of Rev. Charles Nerinckx*, 119; Nerinckx

to his parents as quoted in letter from J. J. Peemans to Propaganda Fide, Louvain, 28 September 1806, in Wand and Owens, eds., *Documents: Nerinckx—Kentucky—Loretto*. On 20 September 1824, Bishop Flaget wrote from Bardstown to John Nerinckx to announce his brother's death. Flaget made special note of the ten churches and six oratories that Nerinckx had built over the years. See typescript translation of letter, RG-Spec. 24, Box I-5 (Loretto Archives, Nerinx, Ky.). For Nerinckx's thoughts on how to get churches built, see "Reverend Charles Nerinckx's Pamphlet, 'A Look at the Present State of the Roman Catholic Religion in North America,'" ed. Joseph A. Agonito and Magdeleine Wellner, *Records of the American Catholic Historical Society of Philadelphia* 83 (March 1972): 16. Regarding the Bardstown cathedral, see John Baptist David to Simon Bruté, 11 July 1811, Notre Dame Archives, as quoted in Herman Schauinger, *Cathedrals in the Wilderness* (Milwaukee, 1952), 70; and Nerinckx's published journal of the events before and during his last trip to Europe, 1819–1820 (Flanders, 1825), quoted in Maes, *The Life of Rev. Charles Nerinckx*, 393.

14. Carroll to Bonaparte, 26 August 1803, in *The John Carroll Papers, 1755–1815*, ed. Thomas O'Brien Hanley (3 vols., Notre Dame, 1976), II, 423. Martin J. Spalding, *Life, Times, and Character of the Right Reverend Benedict Joseph Flaget* (1852; New York, 1969).

15. Nerinckx to Cardinal Michele de Pietro, prefect of the Congregation for the Propagation of the Faith, Feast of St. Martin 1813; and Congregation's reply, April 1816, in Wand and Owens, eds., *Documents: Nerinckx—Kentucky—Loretto*, 37, 141–54.

16. Badin to Carroll, 4 August 1800, Box 1-F, and Badin to Carroll, 2 January 1802, Box Special A-H, Letters to Archbishop Carroll, Records of the Administration of John Carroll; Charles Nerinckx journal, 1807, as quoted in Maes, *The Life of Rev. Charles Nerinckx*, 124. Nerinckx and Badin met similar generosity from non-Catholics near the rising structure of St. Clara's church in 1807, as well as in Christian County, where some 1,400 acres were pledged, and then in the town of Lexington in 1810, where a subscription list was started on St. Patrick's Day: Nerinckx, 27 June 1808. See Maes, *The Life of Rev. Charles Nerinckx*, 159. Badin, September 1810, as quoted in Mary Ramona Mattingly, *The Catholic Church on the Kentucky Frontier, 1785–1812* (Washington, D.C., 1936), 101; and Benjamin Webb, *The Centenary of Catholicity in Kentucky* (Louisville, 1884), 329.

17. Badin to Carroll, 7 January 1809 and 26 September 1810, Box 1-J, Letters to Archbishop Carroll, Records of the Administration of John Carroll. Badin to Carroll, 26 September 1810, Case 1-J9, Baltimore Cathedral Archives, Baltimore, Md. (microfilm, University of Notre Dame Archives). Typescript translation of Bishop Flaget's letter "to his countrymen in France . . . ," RG-Spec. 24, Box I-5 (Loretto Archives, Nerinx, Ky.).

18. Nerinckx to Carroll, May 1810, as quoted in Maes, *The Life of Rev. Charles Nerinckx*, 218. Regarding St. Hubert's, see Nerinckx's published journal, 1819–1820 (Flanders, 1825), as quoted in Maes, *The Life of Rev. Charles Nerinckx*, 401. For the Nashville situation, see Spalding, *Life, Times, and Character of the Right Reverend Benedict Joseph Flaget*, 236–37.

19. John Carroll to Joseph Edenshink, April–June 1785, *John Carroll Papers*, ed. Hanley, I, 186. Nerinckx to unnamed recipient in Belgium, September 1805–May 1806, as quoted in Maes, *The Life of Rev. Charles Nerinckx*, 79–80. Badin to Carroll, August 4, 1800, Box 1-F, Letters to Archbishop Carroll, Records of the Administration of John Carroll.

20. For more on land speculation and the tensions between elites and non-elites, see Andrew R. L. Cayton, *The Frontier Republic: Ideology and Politics in the Ohio Country, 1780–1825* (Kent, 1986), 1–32, 114–18; John Mack Faragher, *Daniel Boone: The Life and Legend of an American Pioneer* (New York, 1992), and *Sugar Creek: Life on the Illinois Prairie*, 53–55, 173–80; as well as Aron, *How the West Was Lost*, 15–21, 58–81, 82–101, 102–23. For another perspective on socioeconomic and cultural friction on a different frontier, see Alan Taylor, *Liberty Men and Great Proprietors: The Revolutionary Settlement on the Maine Frontier, 1760–1820* (Chapel Hill, 1990). Charles Nerinckx journal, 1807, as quoted in Maes, *The Life of Rev. Charles Nerinckx*, 124. Regarding St. Joseph's Cathedral, see Father John Baptist David to unknown recipient, 6 March 1820, Mss. BA B245, Diocese of Bardstown, Kentucky, Correspondence, 1808–1846, and Folder 3, Letters, 1814–1834, from Rt. Rev. John Baptist David, 1761–1841, of Bardstown to unknown recipients, trans. Colomba E. Halsey, O.S.R., from original documents in Archives of St. Sulpice in Paris, in 1968 (Filson Historical Society, Louisville, Ky.).

21. For a fascinating study of church construction and placement as expressions of a city's changing attitudes toward religion, commerce, and class, see Daniel Bluestone's "'A Parallel Moral Power': Churches, 1830–1895," in his *Constructing Chicago* (New Haven, 1991), 62–103. David to Bruté, 11 July 1811, and Flaget to Carroll, 21 August 1811, University of Notre Dame Archives, as quoted in Schauinger, *Cathedrals in the Wilderness*, 70.

22. David to Bruté, 17 June 1811, Letters of Bishop J. B. M. David to Father Simon Bruté, St. Louis Archdiocesan Archives, 12; copy in Duplicate Letter Book XXIV (Sisters of Charity Archival Center, Nazareth, Ky.).

23. Flaget to Bishop Plessis of Quebec, 18 June 1816, printed in *Records of the American Catholic Historical Society of Philadelphia* 18 (March 1907). Father Nerinckx later estimated the total cost at $20,000 in his journal (Flanders, 1825); see Maes, *The Life of Rev. Charles Nerinckx*, 393. David to unnamed fellow Sulpician priest, 26 October 1816, trans. Colomba E.

Halsey, O.S.R., from original documents in Baltimore, Rome, or Paris, in 1968, Mss. BA B245 Diocese of Bardstown, Kentucky (Filson Historical Society, Louisville, Ky.).

24. Colleen McDannell, *Material Christianity: Religion and Popular Culture in America* (New Haven, 1995), 133, 154–55.

25. Ibid., 18. Taves, *The Household of Faith*, viii, 89–95, 102–11.

26. McDannell, *Material Christianity*, 45–48.

27. Pastoral Letter of Bishop John Carroll, 28 May 1792, in Hugh J. Nolan, ed., *Pastoral Letters of the United States Catholic Bishops, Volume I, 1792–1940* (Washington, D.C., 1983), 20–23.

28. Badin to Carroll, 26 September 1796, "Letters from the Baltimore Archives," ed. E. I. Devitt, *Records of the American Catholic Historical Society of Philadelphia* 19 (September 1908), 274. Badin to Carroll, 4 February 1800, Letters to Archbishop Carroll, Records of the Administration of John Carroll. Badin expected to receive a new supply of oils at least annually. See, for example, Badin to Carroll, 2 March 1797, 3 June 1799, 9 October 1799, and 4 December 1809, Letters to Archbishop Carroll, Records of the Administration of John Carroll.

29. "Reverend Charles Nerinckx's Pamphlet," ed. Agonito and Wellner, 16. Fenwick to an unnamed friend, 8 November 1818, as quoted in Diario di Roma, 23 January 1819, cited in V. F. O'Daniel, *The Right Rev. Edward Dominic Fenwick, O.P., Founder of the Dominicans in the United States* (Washington, D.C., 1921), 216. Stephen T. Badin, "Origin and Progress of the Mission of Kentucky, United States of America, By An Ocular Witness" (Paris, 1821), trans. William J. Howlett (Loretto Archives, Nerinx, Ky.).

30. Nerinckx to Carroll, 14 February 1805, in Maes, *The Life of Rev. Charles Nerinckx*, 58.

31. Nerinckx to his parents, 16 January 1806, and to John Joseph Peemans, October 1806, in Wand and Owens, eds., *Documents: Nerinckx—Kentucky—Loretto*, 29–30. Nerinckx to Mr. C. M. J. DeWolff of Antwerp, 1 October 1806, ibid., 29.

32. Nerinckx to John Joseph Peemans, October 1806, in Wand and Owens, eds., *Documents: Nerinckx—Kentucky—Loretto*, 29–30. Nerinckx to his parents, as quoted in letter from J. J. Peemans to the Propaganda Fide, 28 September 1806, ibid., 22. Regarding good models and sketches, see Nerinckx to unknown recipient, 1807, in Maes, *The Life of Rev. Charles Nerinckx*, 349.

33. David to Bruté, 7 May 1815, Letters of Bishop J. B. M. David to Father Simon Bruté.

34. Cost in 1819 from Nerinckx's published journal of the events before and during his last trip to Europe, 1819–1820 (Flanders, 1825), quoted in Maes, *The Life of Rev. Charles Nerinckx*, 393. On the desire for an organ,

see ibid. See also David to unknown recipient, 6 March 1820, and Flaget to Maréchal, 7 January 1820, Folder 5, Correspondence of the Diocese of Bardstown, 1808–1846 (Filson Historical Society, Louisville, Ky.). On the sale of the organ from Maréchal's cathedral, see Flaget to Maréchal, 7 January 1820, ibid.

35. Flaget to Nerinckx's brother, Father John Nerinckx, 20 September 1824, from typescript translation, RG-Spec. 24, Box I-5 (Sisters of Loretto Archives, Loretto, Ky.). Nerinckx quoted from letter of recommendation from Bishop Flaget that he carried with him, sent from Kentucky on 14 September 1815, in "Reverend Charles Nerinckx's Pamphlet," ed. Agonito and Wellner, 20.

36. Nerinckx to Sisters of Loretto, 2 November 1820, in Maes, *The Life of Rev. Charles Nerinckx*, 440.

37. *The Catholic Almanac* for 1848, as quoted in O'Daniel, *The Right Rev. Edward Dominic Fenwick*, 260.

38. Nerinckx to Sisters of Loretto, 2 November 1820, in Maes, *The Life of Rev. Charles Nerinckx*, 440. McDannell, *Material Christianity*, 25–43.

39. Letters from Nerinckx to unnamed recipient, 1807, and to his parents, Ash Wednesday, 1807, as quoted in Maes, *The Life of Rev. Charles Nerinckx*, 121–22.

40. Carroll to William Vousdan, 1801, *John Carroll Papers*, ed. Hanley, II, 362–63.

41. For politicking at Protestant houses of worship, see, for example, Rhys Isaac, *The Transformation of Virginia* (Chapel Hill, 1982), 60–61, and Nathan O. Hatch, *The Democratization of American Religion* (New Haven, 1989). Badin to Carroll, 29 August 1808, Letters to Bishop Carroll, Records of the Administration of John Carroll.

42. John Rothensteiner, *History of the Archdiocese of St. Louis, Vol. I* (St. Louis, 1928), 256–57, as quoted in Schauinger, *Cathedrals in the Wilderness*, 151.

43. 20 October 1821, John Brown Diary.

44. Nerinckx to unnamed recipient, 1818, as quoted in Maes, *The Life of Rev. Charles Nerinckx*, 353.

45. B. Martial, "Survey of the Diocese of Kentucky" (1827), Sacred Congregation of Propaganda Fide Archives, typescript trans. Sister Edward Barnes, Duplicate Letter Book (Sisters of Charity Archival Center, Nazareth, Ky.).

46. John Brown Diary, 20 October 1821.

5. The Promise and Risks of Proximity on the Frontier

1. Gallitzin's report ultimately was lost. See Sarah Brownson, *Life of Demetrius Augustine Gallitzin, Prince and Priest* (New York, 1873), 100–107.

See also Daniel Sargent, *Mitri* (New York, 1945), and Peter H. Lemcke, *Life and Work of Prince Demetrius Augustine Gallitzin*, trans. J. Plumpe (1861; New York, 1940), 124–26. See also the detailed account by Joseph M. Finotti, *The Mystery of the Wizard Clip (Smithfield, W. Va.): A Monograph* (Baltimore, 1879).

2. On frontier dissolution and immorality, see John Mack Faragher, *Sugar Creek: Life on the Illinois Prairie* (New Haven, 1986), 51–52; and for early nineteenth-century commentary on the matter, Frances M. Trollope's *Domestic Manners of the Americans* (London, 1832). Badin to Carroll, 28 June 1796, "Letters from the Baltimore Archives," ed. E. I. Devitt, *Records of the American Catholic Historical Society of Philadelphia* 19 (September 1908): 266–67; and Badin to Propaganda, 7 June 1805, Excerpts of a Letter to the Cardinal Prefect of the Propaganda Fide from Father Stephen Badin, Guilday Transcripts, in Duplicate Letter Book transcription (Sisters of Charity Archival Center, Nazareth, Ky.). Andrew R. L. Cayton, *Frontier Indiana* (Bloomington, 1996), 46, 62.

3. Badin to Carroll, 9 October 1799, Letters to Archbishop Carroll, 1786–1815, Records of the Administration of John Carroll, Baltimore Cathedral Archives, Baltimore, Md. (microfilm, University of Notre Dame Archives). Nerinckx to Carroll, as quoted in Camillus P. Maes, *The Life of Rev. Charles Nerinckx* (Cincinnati, 1880), 92. John Mason Peck, *Forty Years of Pioneer Life: Memoir of John Mason Peck, D. D., Edited from His Journals and Correspondence by Rufus Babcock* (1864; Carbondale, Ill., 1965), 88.

4. Carroll, "Report for the Eminent Cardinal Antonelli Concerning the State of Religion in the United States of America, 1785," in Phillip Gleason, ed., *Documentary Reports on Early American Catholicism* (New York, 1978), 153–54. Regarding the situation in southwestern Pennsylvania, see Father Helbron to Carroll, 11 December 1806, in Felix Fellner, "Trials and Triumphs of Catholic Pioneers in Western Pennsylvania (As Revealed by the Correspondence)," *Records of the American Catholic Historical Society* 34 (September 1923): 318. Badin to Carroll, 3 November 1810, Box Special A, H-12, Letters to Archbishop Carroll, Records of the Administration of John Carroll.

5. Lemcke, *Life and Works of Prince Demetrius Augustine Gallitzin*, 102, 220–21. For Badin, see letter of 3 November 1801, Case A Special, Baltimore Cathedral Archives, as quoted in Mary Ramona Mattingly, *The Catholic Church on the Kentucky Frontier, 1785–1812* (Washington, D.C., 1936), 191.

6. On American Tract Society, see Sydney E. Ahlstrom, *A Religious History of the American People* (New Haven, 1972), 423–25. For Bible Society of Philadelphia, see Samuel J. Mills and Daniel Smith, "Report of a Missionary Tour Through That Part of the United States Which Lies

West of the Allegany Mountains" (1815), in Edwin S. Gaustad, ed., *To Win the West: Missionary Viewpoints 1814–1815* (New York, 1972), 6.

7. Jay P. Dolan briefly compares the millennial missions with which Catholicism and Protestantism founded their respective churches in America in *The American Catholic Experience: A History from Colonial Times to the Present* (Garden City, 1985), 18.

8. "Reverend Charles Nerinckx's Pamphlet, 'A Look at the Present State of the Roman Catholic Religion in North America,'" ed. Joseph A. Agonito and Magdeleine Wellner, *Records of the American Catholic Historical Society of Philadelphia* 83 (March 1972): 17.

9. Martin J. Spalding, *Life, Times, and Character of the Right Reverend Benedict Joseph Flaget* (1852; New York, 1969), 30–32.

10. Brownson, *The Life of Demetrius Gallitzin*, 98–99.

11. Stephen Theodore Badin, "Origin and Progress of the Mission of Kentucky, United States of America, By An Ocular Witness" (Paris, 1821), trans. William J. Howlett (Loretto Archives, Nerinx, Ky.). See also Mattingly, *The Catholic Church on the Kentucky Frontier*, 110.

12. Badin to Carroll, 5 October 1805, Letters to Archbishop Carroll, Records of the Administration of John Carroll. For Badin's views of the Protestant revivals, see Badin to cardinal prefect of the Propaganda Fide, P.F.A., Amer. III, 228, Guilday Transcripts: 1624, as cited in Mattingly, *The Catholic Church on the Kentucky Frontier*, 192–93. The "Twelve Apostles" quote is from Badin to Carroll, 5 October 1805, Letters to Archbishop Carroll, Records of the Administration of John Carroll.

13. David to Bruté, 16 September 1811, Letters of Bishop J. B. M. David to Father Simon Bruté, St. Louis Archdiocesan Archives; copy in Duplicate Letter Book XXIV (Sisters of Charity Archival Center, Nazareth, Ky.).

14. "Bishop Flaget's Report of the Diocese of Bardstown to Pius VII, April 10, 1815," in Gleason, ed., *Documentary Reports on Early American Catholicism*, 318.

15. David to unnamed recipient, 14 July 1817, Diocese of Bardstown Correspondence (Filson Historical Society, Louisville, Ky.).

16. "Archbishop Maréchal's Report to Propaganda, 1818," in Gleason, ed., *Documentary Reports on Early American Catholicism*, 213–17.

17. Gerald Shaughnessy, *Has the Immigrant Kept the Faith? A Study of Immigration and Catholic Growth in the United States, 1790–1920* (New York, 1925), 71. Shaughnessy's estimate seems to agree with the number of conversions (23) that Archbishop Maréchal counted for the diocese of Baltimore in 1824, given the number of clergy there. See diary of Maréchal, 1818–1827, in Baltimore Archdiocese (Original Documents), 1717–1967 (University of Notre Dame Archives, Notre Dame, Ind.).

18. Mattingly, *The Catholic Church on the Kentucky Frontier*, 110; Badin to Carroll, 17 December 1807, Letters to Archbishop Carroll, Records of the Administration of John Carroll. W. J. Howlett, ed., "Bishop Flaget's Diary," *Records of the American Catholic Historical Society of Philadelphia* 29 (March and June 1918): 46, 48, 160. 28 May 1818, in Spalding, *Life, Times, and Character of the Right Reverend Benedict Joseph Flaget*, 185.

19. Maes, *The Life of Rev. Charles Nerinckx*, 416. David to Bruté, 6–18 May 1822, Letters of Bishop J. B. M. David to Father Simon Bruté.

20. *The John Carroll Papers, 1755–1815*, ed. Thomas O'Brien Hanley (3 vols., Notre Dame, 1976), II, 408.

21. Robert F. McNamara, "John Carroll and Interfaith Marriages: The Case of the Belle Vue Carrolls," in Nelson H. Minnich et al., eds., *Studies in Catholic History in Honor of John Tracy Ellis* (Wilmington, Del., 1985), 29. For definition of blood relationships (i.e., consanguinity, permitted in Catholic marriages), see Richard P. McBrien, ed., *The HarperCollins Encyclopedia of Catholicism* (New York, 1995), 356. Robert F. McNamara has suggested that perhaps mixed marriages did not require dispensation because "the matrimonial legislation of the Council of Trent was not considered binding in British and Anglo-American territories." See McNamara, "John Carroll and Interfaith Marriages," 29–30. This is likely the case, because in 1813 Father Charles Nerinckx had to write to the prefect of the Congregation for the Propagation of the Faith to inquire about a ruling, "Does Tridentine law in matrimonial cases bind in this part of North America? If not, will the pope be promulgating it here?" He also wrote to the Congregation in 1821 more directly stating, "Tridentine law has not been promulgated in the States." Nerinckx to Cardinal Michele de Pietro (1813) and to Cardinal Francesco Luigi Fontana (1821), in Augustin C. Wand and M. Lilliana Owens, eds., *Documents: Nerinckx—Kentucky—Loretto, 1804–1851, in Archives Propaganda Fide, Rome* (St. Louis, 1972), 35–36, 49.

22. Undated sermon, *John Carroll Papers*, ed. Hanley, III, 430; and II, 310–11.

23. Ibid., I, 530–31; see also Peter Guilday, *A History of the Councils of Baltimore, 1791–1884* (New York, 1932), 67.

24. McNamara, "John Carroll and Interfaith Marriages," 34–35; Carroll to Charles Plowden, 12 February 1803, *John Carroll Papers*, ed. Hanley, II, 408.

25. Badin to Carroll, 11 April 1796 (from typescript translation from French by Sister Edward Barnes, labeled "BCA" at the top) and 13 August 1798, Letters to Archbishop Carroll, Records of the Administration of John Carroll.

26. Badin to Carroll, 20 February 1799, ibid. Nerinckx letter from

1807, in Maes, *The Life of Rev. Charles Nerinckx*, 149–50. Badin to Carroll, 13 March 1800, Letters to Archbishop Carroll, Records of the Administration of John Carroll.

27. Badin to Carroll, 26 December 1810 and 29 August 1808, ibid.

28. Badin to Carroll, 29 August 1808, ibid.

29. Spalding, *Life, Times, and Character of the Right Reverend Benedict Joseph Flaget*, 242, 197. Nerinckx's letter to Cardinal Lorenzo Litta, 24 June 1816, in Wand and Owens, eds., *Documents: Nerinckx—Kentucky—Loretto*, 170. For another case, see Flaget to Archbishop Maréchal, 23 January 1816, Letters of Rt. Rev. Benedict Joseph Flaget, 1764–1850, Correspondence 1808–1846, Diocese of Bardstown, Kentucky, trans. Colomba E. Halsey, O.S.R., 1968 (Filson Historical Society, Louisville, Ky.).

30. Nerinckx to Cardinal Michele de Pietro, Feast of St. Martin 1813, in Wand and Owens, eds., *Documents: Nerinckx—Kentucky—Loretto*, 35–36.

31. Ibid. Regarding Nerinckx's financial difficulties with parishioners, see chapter 2. For the diocesan synod of 1791, see Pastoral Letter, 28 May 1792, in Hugh J. Nolan, ed., *Pastoral Letters of the United States Catholic Bishops, Volume I, 1792–1940* (Washington, D.C., 1983), 22.

32. Nerinckx to Cardinal Michele de Pietro, Feast of St. Martin 1813, in Wand and Owens, eds., *Documents: Nerinckx—Kentucky—Loretto*, 36–37, 143–45; Badin to Carroll, 4 March 1798, Letters to Archbishop Carroll, Records of the Administration of John Carroll.

33. Wand and Owens, eds., *Documents: Nerinckx—Kentucky—Loretto*, 141–54. John Grassi, "The Catholic Religion in the United States in 1818," in Gleason, ed., *Documentary Reports on Early American Catholicism*, 239. B. Martial, "Survey of the Diocese of Kentucky" (1827), Sacred Congregation of Propaganda Fide Archives, typescript trans. Sister Edward Barnes, Duplicate Letter Book (Sisters of Charity Archival Center, Nazareth, Ky.).

34. Wand and Owens, eds., *Documents: Nerinckx—Kentucky—Loretto*, 127–29, 145–52.

35. Ibid., 152. The definition of simony is from *The Random House College Dictionary, Revised Edition*, ed. Jess Stein (New York, 1980), 1226.

36. Nerinckx to Cardinal Francesco Luigi Fontana, 1821, in Wand and Owens, eds., *Documents: Nerinckx—Kentucky—Loretto*, 47–49.

37. Letter of Father Charles Nerinckx, 1807, found at Bollandist Library, Brussels, Belgium, quoted in Maes, *The Life of Rev. Charles Nerinckx*, 127.

38. David to Bruté, 13 November 1826 and 14 June 1830, Duplicate Letter Book XXIV (Sisters of Charity Archival Center, Nazareth, Ky.).

6. Emphatic Persuasion

1. Badin to John Carroll, 14 March 1807, Case C, Special L, Baltimore Cathedral Archives, Baltimore, Md. (microfilm, University of Notre Dame Archives).

2. Mary Ramona Mattingly, *The Catholic Church on the Kentucky Frontier, 1785–1812* (Washington, D.C., 1936), 145. Badin to Carroll, 2 March 1797, Letters to Archbishop Carroll, 1786–1815, Records of the Administration of John Carroll, Baltimore Cathedral Archives, Baltimore, Md. (microfilm, University of Notre Dame Archives).

3. Badin to Carroll, 4 February 1800, Letters to Archbishop Carroll, 1786–1815, Records of the Administration of John Carroll. John B. Boles, *Religion in Antebellum Kentucky* (Lexington, 1976), 63; Badin to Carroll, 15 October 1805, Letters to Archbishop Carroll, 1786–1815, Records of the Administration of John Carroll.

4. Benedict Flaget and Jean Baptiste Marie David, "An Abbreviated History of the Sisters of Charity of Nazareth, Kentucky, United States of America," in Augustin C. Wand and M. Lilliana Owens, eds., *Documents: Nerinckx—Kentucky—Loretto, 1804–1851, in Archives Propaganda Fide, Rome* (St. Louis, 1972), 52. Nerinckx to his parents, September 1805, quoted in Camillus P. Maes, *The Life of Rev. Charles Nerinckx* (Cincinnati, 1880), 135–36, 138–39. For Nerinckx's thoughts on mixed schooling, see typescript of his journal, RG-Spec. 1, Box I-5 (Loretto Archives, Nerinx, Ky.). For his comments on Catholic schools used to win over non-Catholics, see Nerinckx to Cardinal Michele de Pietro, Feast of St. Martin 1813, in Wand and Owens, eds., *Documents: Nerinckx—Kentucky—Loretto*, 33.

5. Maes, *The Life of Rev. Charles Nerinckx*, 245–54, 288–89; and Nerinckx to Cardinal Michele de Pietro, Feast of St. Martin 1813, in Wand and Owens, eds., *Documents: Nerinckx—Kentucky—Loretto*, 33. Herman J. Schauinger, *Cathedrals in the Wilderness* (Milwaukee, 1952), 128.

6. David to Simon Bruté, 12 April 1814, as quoted in Schauinger, *Cathedrals in the Wilderness*, 103. David to Carroll, 17 September 1814, in Letters of J. B. M. David to Archbishop Carroll, Duplicate Letter Book XXIV (Sisters of Charity Archival Center, Nazareth, Ky.).

7. Maes, *The Life of Rev. Charles Nerinckx*, 266–70, 377.

8. "Archbishop Maréchal's Report to Propaganda, 1818," in Philip Gleason, ed., *Documentary Reports on Early American Catholicism* (New York, 1978), 213–17. For Flaget's and David's comments, see Wand and Owens, eds., *Documents: Nerinckx—Kentucky—Loretto*, 55–56.

9. Typescript translation of Bishop Flaget epistle "to his countrymen in France . . . ," RG-Spec. 24, Box I-5 (Loretto Archives, Nerinx, Ky.); and Benjamin Webb, *The Centenary of Catholicity in Kentucky* (Louisville, 1884),

341. See Nerinckx's journal of the events before and during his last journey to Europe, 1819–1820 (Flanders, 1825), as quoted in Maes, *The Life of Rev. Charles Nerinckx*, 395.

10. David to Bruté, 17 September 1822, 27 November 1827, and 27 January 1828, Duplicate Letter Book XXIV (Sisters of Charity Archival Center, Nazareth, Ky.).

11. Mary J. Oates, "Catholic Female Academies on the Nineteenth-Century Frontier," *U.S. Catholic Historian* 12 (Fall 1994): 121–36.

12. Peter Henry Lemcke, *Life and Works of Prince Demetrius Augustine Gallitzin* (1861; London, 1940), 244, 102.

13. Nerinckx, 6 December 1805, quoted in Maes, *The Life of Rev. Charles Nerinckx*, 90. Badin to Carroll, 25 May 1807, Case 1, J-4, Baltimore Cathedral Archives, as quoted in Mattingly, *The Catholic Church on the Kentucky Frontier*, 126.

14. Badin's notes for a procession (date unknown), found on scrap of paper in "Bible presented to Father Badin by Bishop Carroll (1790)" in RG-Spec. 13—Box, Badin, Rev. Stephen T. (Loretto Archives, Nerinx, Ky.). David to Bruté, 2 July 1812, Letters of Bishop J. B. M. David to Father Simon Bruté, St. Louis Archdiocesan Archives; copy in Duplicate Letter Book XXIV. Badin, Loretto Archives, Nerinx, Ky., as cited by Mattingly, *The Catholic Church on the Kentucky Frontier*, 127–28.

15. B. Martial, "Survey of the Diocese of Kentucky" (1827), Sacred Congregation of Propaganda Fide Archives, typescript trans. Sister Edward Barnes, Duplicate Letter Book (Sisters of Charity Archival Center, Nazareth, Ky.). David to Bruté, 5 June 1826, Notre Dame Archives; translated copies in Duplicate Letter Book XXIV.

16. Loretto Archives, Nerinx, Ky., as quoted in Mattingly, *The Catholic Church on the Kentucky Frontier*, 127–28. During a session at the 1997 conference of the Society for Historians of the Early Republic, A. G. Roeber suggested that Badin's precept regarding deference from Protestant observers had larger ramifications in light of the Reformation.

17. David to Bruté, June 1816, Notre Dame Archives, Duplicate Letter Book XXIV.

18. Flaget to Bruté, 1 August 1816, Notre Dame Archives, typescript trans. Sister Edward Barnes, Duplicate Letter Book (Sisters of Charity Archives, Nazareth, Ky.).

19. Quoted in Maes, *The Life of Rev. Charles Nerinckx*, 318–21.

20. Badin to Carroll, November 1801, as quoted in Mattingly, *The Catholic Church on the Kentucky Frontier*, 191. Badin to cardinal prefect of the Propaganda Fide, 7 June 1805, Guilday Transcripts, in Duplicate Letter Book transcription (Sisters of Charity Archival Center, Nazareth, Ky.).

21. "Reverend Charles Nerinckx's Pamphlet, 'A Look at the Present

State of the Roman Catholic Religion in North America,'" ed. Joseph A. Agonito and Magdeleine Wellner, *Records of the American Catholic Historical Society of Philadelphia* 83 (March 1972): 17. Nerinckx reported on 28 October 1807 that Badin wrote this to him; see Maes, *The Life of Rev. Charles Nerinckx*, 154–55. V. F. O'Daniel, ed., "Bishop Flaget's Report of the Diocese of Bardstown to Pius VII, April 10, 1815," *Catholic Historical Review* 1 (October 1915): 310–19.

22. Phelan to Carroll, 26 May 1796, in Felix Fellner, "Trials and Triumphs of Catholic Pioneers in Western Pennsylvania (As Revealed by the Correspondence)," *Records of the American Catholic Historical Society* 34 (September 1923): 255–56. For examples of Catholic clergy reporting on curious Protestants, see Martin J. Spalding, *Life, Times, and Character of the Right Reverend Benedict Joseph Flaget* (1852; New York, 1969), and Victor Francis O'Daniel, *The Right Rev. Edward Dominic Fenwick, O.P., Founder of the Dominicans in the United States, Pioneer Missionary in Kentucky, Apostle of Ohio, First Bishop of Cincinnati* (Washington, D.C., 1921). David to Bruté, 2 July 1812, Duplicate Letter Book XXIV. On De Andreis's observations, see Schauinger, *Cathedrals in the Wilderness*, 151.

23. Ella M. E. Flick, ed. and trans., "Epistle or Diary of the Reverend Father Marie Joseph Dunand," *Records of the American Catholic Historical Society of Philadelphia* 26 (December 1915): 329–31. Paul J. Foik, *Pioneer Catholic Journalism* (New York, 1930), 15–16, Monograph Series XI, United States Catholic Historical Society, quoting from *The Shamrock of Hibernian Chronicle*, 27 April 1811.

24. 13 and 14 September and 4 October 1812, as quoted in W. J. Howlett, ed., "Bishop Flaget's Diary," *Records of the American Catholic Historical Society of Philadelphia* 29 (September 1918): 232–34.

25. Spalding, *Life, Times, and Character of the Right Reverend Benedict Joseph Flaget*, 198. Badin as quoted in Mattingly, *The Catholic Church on the Kentucky Frontier*, 106; and as translated by William J. Howlett from Badin, "Origin and Progress of the Mission of Kentucky, United States of America, By An Ocular Witness" (Paris, 1821) (Loretto Archives, Nerinx, Ky.).

26. Letter from Flaget extracted in letter of Father J. B. M. David to Father Simon Bruté, 14 June 1830, Duplicate Letter Book XXIV.

27. According to historian Robert Gorman, for American apologetics—i.e., works "that deal with the justification and defense of religion"—the period 1784–1800 was only a "period of beginnings," and 1801–1812 a time of "relative scarcity of native works." American clergy actively began to defend the faith in print after 1813, when the nation as a whole was decidedly antiforeign and caught up in Protestant revivalism. Gorman, *Catholic Apologetical Literature in the United States, 1784–1858* (Washington, D.C., 1939), 14, 25, 27–28.

28. Father Badin to Bishop Neale, 2 September 1808, Baltimore Cathedral Archives, as quoted in Schauinger, *Cathedrals in the Wilderness*, 29–30. Regarding McHenry's challenge, see Martin John Spalding, *Sketches of the Early Catholic Missions of Kentucky from their Commencement in 1787, to the Jubilee of 1826–1827* (Louisville, 1844), 121. Regarding Washington Academy, the governor of Kentucky approved the act of the legislature that made its founding official on 22 December 1798. See Mattingly, *The Catholic Church on the Kentucky Frontier*, 145.

29. Badin 1798 quote in Mattingly, *The Catholic Church on the Kentucky Frontier*, 114. The confrontational style of Thayer's *An Account of the Conversion of the Rev. Mr. John Thayer* (London, 1788), as well as the fact that it was printed in the U.S. even before his return from Europe, appeared in four languages, and was an extremely popular tract, indicated that his was not a voice easily quieted. Gorman, *Catholic Apologetical Literature*, 11–12. For Thayer's criticisms of Methodists in Kentucky, see Badin to Carroll, 4 February 1800, Letters to Archbishop Carroll, 1786–1815, Records of the Administration of John Carroll.

30. On Badin's book, see Spalding, *Sketches of the Early Catholic Missions of Kentucky*, 125. Regarding the Trappists, see Mattingly, *The Catholic Church on the Kentucky Frontier*, 110.

31. Mattingly, *The Catholic Church on the Kentucky Frontier*, 183. Badin, "Origin and Progress of the Mission of Kentucky, United States of America, By An Ocular Witness" (Paris, 1821), trans. Howlett.

32. Gorman, *Catholic Apologetical Literature*, 29–30. Lemcke, *Life and Works of Prince Demetrius Augustine Gallitzin*, 170–72; Gorman, *Catholic Apologetical Literature*, 30–32.

33. Spalding, *Life, Times, and Character of the Right Reverend Benedict Joseph Flaget*, 144–46.

34. Ibid., 221–42.

35. Ibid., 98. David to Bruté, 15 October 1816, Duplicate Letter Book XXIV.

36. David to Bruté, 9 April 1821, Duplicate Letter Book XXIV.

37. Ibid. The controversy between David and Hall is described in Columba Fox, "The Life of the Right Reverend John Baptist Mary David (1761–1841) Bishop of Bardstown and Founder of the Sisters of Charity of Nazareth," MS IX (M.A. thesis, Catholic University of America, 1925). Regarding Flaget's order for public prayers, see Spalding, *Life, Times, and Character of the Right Reverend Benedict Joseph Flaget*, 235. David to Bruté, 9 April 1821, and 4 June to 4 September 1821, Duplicate Letter Book XXIV.

38. David to Bruté, 4 June to 4 September 1821, and 26 February 1822, Duplicate Letter Book XXIV.

39. Ibid., 17 September 1822. O'Daniel, *The Right Rev. Edward Dominic Fenwick*, 250. David to Bruté, 4 February 1823, Duplicate Letter Book XXIV. Flaget to Maréchal, 14 April 1823, Letters of Rt. Rev. Benedict Joseph Flaget, 1764–1850, of Bardstown to Archbishop Maréchal, 3rd Bishop of Baltimore, Mss. BA B245 Diocese of Bardstown, Kentucky, Correspondence, 1808–1846, trans. Columba E. Hasley, O.S.R., from copies of documents in Archives of the Archdiocese of Baltimore, in 1968 (Filson Historical Society, Louisville, Ky.).

40. For more on missions, see Jay P. Dolan, *Catholic Revivalism: The American Experience, 1830–1900* (Notre Dame, 1978).

41. Ray Allen Billington, *The Protestant Crusade, 1800–1860: A Study of the Origins of American Nativism* (New York, 1938), 32–52; Gorman, *Catholic Apologetical Literature*, 40–52.

42. See "Jubilee" and "Holy Year" in Richard P. McBrien, ed., *The HarperCollins Encyclopedia of Catholicism* (New York, 1995), 720, 637; O'Daniel, *The Right Rev. Edward Dominic Fenwick*, 320. Spalding, *Life, Times, and Character of the Right Reverend Benedict Joseph Flaget*, 258–59; O'Daniel, *The Right Rev. Edward Dominic Fenwick*, 321.

43. O'Daniel, *The Right Rev. Edward Dominic Fenwick*, 320–27.

44. David to Bruté, 13 November 1826, Duplicate Letter Book XXIV. For reference to Methodist, see letter from unknown author, 7 December 1826, quoted at length in B. Martial's "Survey of the Diocese of Kentucky" (1827), in Duplicate Letter Book, trans. Sister Edward Barnes from the Sacred Congregation of Propaganda Fide Archives (Sisters of Charity Archival Center, Nazareth, Ky.).

45. David to Bruté, 13 November 1826, 9 October 1827, and 13 November 1826, Duplicate Letter Book XXIV.

46. Letter from unknown author, 7 December 1826, quoted in Martial, "Survey of the Diocese of Kentucky." David to Bruté, 9 October 1827, Duplicate Letter Book XXIV.

47. Schauinger, *Cathedrals in the Wilderness*, 225.

Conclusion

1. Nerinckx to Cardinal Francesco Luigi Fontana, 1821, in Augustin C. Wand and M. Lilliana Owens, eds., *Documents: Nerinckx—Kentucky—Loretto, 1804–1851, in Archives Propaganda Fide, Rome* (St. Louis, 1972), 47–49.

2. Ray Allen Billington, *The Protestant Crusade, 1800–1860: A Study of the Origins of American Nativism* (New York, 1938), 32–37.

3. John Carroll, "Report for the Eminent Cardinal Antonelli Concerning the State of Religion in the United States of America, 1785," in

Phillip Gleason, ed., *Documentary Reports on Early American Catholicism* (New York, 1978), 153.

4. The shift from an accommodating, Americanized Catholicism to a conservative, European form in the 1830s, particularly the episcopal crackdown on lay trustees' attempts to control church properties and policies, provoked a "violent nativism" among Protestants, according to Patrick Carey, *The Roman Catholics* (Westport, 1993), 31–34. Nerinckx's journal, 14 July 1824, in Camillus P. Maes, *The Life of Rev. Charles Nerinckx* (Cincinnati, 1880), 396–97. Rev. Joshua L. Wilson to Rev. A. Cameron, 12 September 1828, as quoted in William Warren Sweet, *Religion on the Frontier, 1783–1830, Volume II, The Presbyterians* (New York, 1964), 733–34.

5. David Brion Davis, "Some Themes of Counter-Subversion: An Analysis of Anti-Masonic, Anti-Catholic, and Anti-Mormon Literature," *Mississippi Valley Historical Review* 47 (September 1960): 205–24.

6. Bryan Le Beau has argued that antebellum Protestant propaganda literature generated by easterners clearly demonstrated that they would not entrust to westerners the battle against Catholicism. The sturdy values of New England had not been transplanted successfully, so the struggle to save the West belonged to the East. Le Beau, "Saving the West from the Pope: Anti-Catholic Propaganda and the Settlement of the Mississippi River Valley," *American Studies* 32 (Spring 1991): 104–14. Missionary society quote is from Sweet, *Religion on the Frontier, 1783–1830, Volume II, The Presbyterians,* 668–69. Billington, *The Protestant Crusade, 1800–1860,* 72–76.

7. Quoted in Martin E. Marty, *Pilgrims in Their Own Land: 500 Years of Religion in America* (Boston: Little, Brown, 1984). Lyman Beecher, *Plea for the West* (Cincinnati, 1835), 117.

8. "Letters from Bishop Benedict Joseph Flaget to Bishop Joseph Rosati, St. Louis, Mo.," *Social Justice Review* (June 1970): 1–3. Nerinckx to unnamed recipient, 1818, as quoted in Maes, *The Life of Rev. Charles Nerinckx,* 353. B. Martial, "Survey of the Diocese of Kentucky" (1827), Sacred Congregation of Propaganda Fide Archives, typescript trans. Sister Edward Barnes, Duplicate Letter Book (Sisters of Charity Archival Center, Nazareth, Ky.).

Works Cited

Manuscript Sources

Allison, Young Ewing. Papers, 1853–1932. Filson Historical Society, Louisville, Kentucky.

Archdiocese of Baltimore. Original Documents 1717–1967. University of Notre Dame Archives, Notre Dame, Indiana.

Ayres, Robert. Diary. Historical Society of Western Pennsylvania, Pittsburgh, Pennsylvania.

Badin, Stephen Theodore. Papers. Sisters of Loretto Archives, Nerinx, Kentucky.

Badin, Stephen Theodore. "Origin and Progress of the Mission of Kentucky, United States of America, By An Ocular Witness" (Paris, 1821). Trans. William J. Howlett. Loretto Archives, Nerinx, Kentucky.

Barrow, David. Manuscript. Filson Historical Society, Louisville, Kentucky.

Breathitt, John. Journal. Kentucky Historical Society, Frankfort, Kentucky.

Brown, John. Diary. Filson Historical Society, Louisville, Kentucky.

Carroll, John. Administration Records. Baltimore Cathedral Archives, Baltimore, Maryland. Microfilm, University of Notre Dame Archives, Notre Dame, Indiana.

David, John Baptist. Letters, Duplicate Letter Book XXIV. Sisters of Charity Archival Center, Nazareth, Kentucky.

David, John Baptist. Letters, 1814–34, to unknown recipients. Trans. Colomba E. Halsey from original documents in Archives of St. Sulpice, Paris. Filson Historical Society, Louisville, Kentucky.

Diocese of Bardstown, Kentucky. Correspondence, 1808–1846, Filson Historical Society, Louisville, Kentucky.

Flaget, Benedict Joseph. Letters, 1764–1850. Trans. Colomba E. Halsey from documents in Archives of Archdiocese of Baltimore. Filson Historical Society, Louisville, Kentucky.

Guilday, Peter. Transcripts from the Propaganda Archives, Duplicate Letter Book transcription. Sisters of Charity Archival Center, Nazareth, Kentucky.

Nerinckx, Charles. Papers. Typescript trans. Sisters of Loretto Archives, Loretto, Kentucky.

Martial, B. "Survey of the Diocese of Kentucky" (1827). Trans. Sister Edward Barnes from Sacred Congregation of Propaganda Fide Archives. Sisters of Charity Archival Center, Nazareth, Kentucky.

Wrenshall, John. Journal, 1794–1799. Schmelzer Collection. Historical Society of Western Pennsylvania, Pittsburgh, Pennsylvania.

Published Letters, Diaries, and Other Primary Sources

Badin, Stephen Theodore. "Origin and Progress of the Mission of Kentucky, United States of America" (1821). In *Documentary Reports on Early American Catholicism*, ed. Phillip Gleason. New York: Arno Press, 1978.

Beecher, Lyman. *Plea for the West*. Cincinnati: Truman & Smith, 1835.

Butterfield, L. H., ed. *The Adams Family Correspondence*. 4 vols. Cambridge, Mass.: Belknap Press of Harvard University Press, 1963–73.

Carroll, John. "Report for the Eminent Cardinal Antonelli Concerning the State of Religion in the United States of America, 1785." In *Documentary Reports on Early American Catholicism*, ed. Phillip Gleason. New York: Arno Press, 1978.

Devitt, E. I., ed. "Letters from the Baltimore Archives [Carroll Administration, Case 1]." *Records of the American Catholic Historical Society of Philadelphia* 19 (June–September 1908): 214–38 and 243–75.

Fellner, Felix, trans. and ed. "Trials and Triumphs of Catholic Pioneers in Western Pennsylvania (As Revealed by the Correspondence)." *Records of the American Catholic Historical Society* 34 (September–December 1923): 195–261 and 287–343.

Finotti, Joseph M. *The Mystery of the Wizard Clip (Smithfield, W. Va.): A Monograph*. Baltimore: Piet Kelly, 1879.

Flaget, Benedict. "Bishop Flaget's Report of the Diocese of Bardstown to Pius VII, April 10, 1815." In *Documentary Reports on Early American Catholicism*, ed. Phillip Gleason. New York: Arno Press, 1978.

Flick, Ella M. E., trans. and ed. "Epistle or Diary of the Reverend Father Marie Joseph Dunand." *Records of the American Catholic Historical Society of Philadelphia* 26 (December 1915): 328–46, and 27 (March 1916): 45–64.

Flint, James. *Letters from America, Containing Observations on the Climate . . . 1818–1820*. 1820. Reprinted in Reuben Gold Thwaites, ed., *Early*

Western Travels, 1748–1846, Volume IX. Cleveland: A. H. Clark Company, 1904.

Grassi, John. "The Catholic Religion in the United States in 1818." In *Documentary Reports on Early American Catholicism*, ed. Phillip Gleason. New York: Arno Press, 1978.

Hanley, Thomas O'Brien, ed. *The John Carroll Papers, 1755–1815.* 3 vols. Notre Dame, Ind.: University of Notre Dame Press, 1976.

Holy See. *Catechism of the Catholic Church.* Liguori, Mo.: Liguori Publishing, 1994.

Howlett, W. J., ed. "Bishop Flaget's Diary." *Records of the American Catholic Historical Society of Philadelphia* 29 (March, June, and September 1918): 36–59, 153–69, and 231–49.

"Letters from Bishop Benedict Joseph Flaget to Bishop Joseph Rosati, St. Louis, Mo.," *Social Justice Review* (June 1970): 1–3.

Maréchal, Ambrose. "Archbishop Maréchal's Report to Propaganda, 1818." In *Documentary Reports on Early American Catholicism*, ed. Phillip Gleason. New York: Arno Press, 1978.

Mills, Samuel J., and Daniel Smith. "Report of a Missionary Tour Through That Part of the United States Which Lies West of the Allegany Mountains" (1815). In *To Win the West: Missionary Viewpoints 1814–1815*, ed. Edwin S. Gaustad. New York: Arno Press, 1972.

Nerinckx, Charles. "Reverend Charles Nerinckx's Pamphlet, 'A Look at the Present State of the Roman Catholic Religion in North America,'" trans. and ed. Joseph A. Agonito and Magdeleine Wellner. *Records of the American Catholic Historical Society of Philadelphia* 83 (March 1972): 3–35.

Nolan, Hugh J., ed. *Pastoral Letters of the United States Catholic Bishops, Volume I, 1792–1940.* Washington, D.C.: National Conference of Catholic Bishops, United States Catholic Conference, 1983.

O'Daniel, V. F., ed. "Bishop Flaget's Report of the Diocese of Bardstown to Pius VII, April 10, 1815." *Catholic Historical Review* 1 (October 1915): 310–19.

Peck, John Mason. *Forty Years of Pioneer Life: Memoir of John Mason Peck, D. D., Edited from His Journals and Correspondence by Rufus Babcock*, ed. Rufus Babcock. 1864. Reprint, Carbondale: Southern Illinois University Press, 1965.

Schermerhorn, John F., and Samuel J. Mills. "A Correct View of That Part of the United States Which Lies West of the Allegany Mountains, With Respect to Religion and Morals." In *To Win the West: Missionary Viewpoints 1814–1815*, ed. Edwin S. Gaustad. New York: Arno Press, 1972.

U.S. Bureau of the Census. *Historical Statistics of the United States, Colonial*

Times to 1957. Washington, D.C.: U.S. Government Printing Office, 1960.

Wand, Augustin C., and M. Lilliana Owens, eds. *Documents: Nerinckx— Kentucky—Loretto, 1804–1851, in Archives Propaganda Fide, Rome*. St. Louis: Mary Loretto Press, 1972.

Secondary Sources

Agonito, Joseph A. "Ecumenical Stirrings: Catholic-Protestant Relations during the Episcopacy of John Carroll." *Church History* 45 (September 1976): 358–73.

———. *The Building of an American Catholic Church: The Episcopacy of John Carroll*. New York: Garland Publishing, 1988.

Ahlstrom, Sydney E. *A Religious History of the American People*. New Haven: Yale University Press, 1972.

Aron, Stephen. "The Significance of the Kentucky Frontier." *Register of the Kentucky Historical Society* 91 (1993): 298–323.

———. *How the West Was Lost: The Transformation of Kentucky from Daniel Boone to Henry Clay*. Baltimore: Johns Hopkins University Press, 1996.

Bevins, Ann Bolton, and James R. O'Rourke. *That Troublesome Parish: St. Francis/St. Pius Church of White Sulphur, Kentucky*. White Sulfur, Ky.: St. Francis Parish, 1985.

Billington, Ray Allen. *The Protestant Crusade, 1800–1860: A Study of the Origins of American Nativism*. New York: Macmillan Company, 1938.

Bishop, Robert. *An Outline of the History of the Church in the State of Kentucky during a Period of Forty Years: Containing the Memoirs of Rev. David Rice, and Sketches*. Lexington: Thomas T. Skillman, 1824.

Bluestone, Daniel. *Constructing Chicago*. New Haven: Yale University Press, 1991.

Boles, John B. *Religion in Antebellum Kentucky*. Lexington: University Press of Kentucky, 1976.

Brownson, Sarah. *Life of Demetrius Augustine Gallitzin, Prince and Priest*. New York: Fr. Pustet & Co., 1873.

Butler, Anne M., Michael E. Engh, and Thomas W. Spalding. *The Frontiers and Catholic Identities*. New York: Orbis Books, 1999.

Butler, Jon. *Awash in a Sea of Faith: Christianizing the American People*. Cambridge, Mass.: Harvard University Press, 1990.

Carey, Patrick. "Two Episcopal Views of Lay-Clerical Conflicts." *Records of the American Catholic Historical Society of Philadelphia* 87 (March–December 1976): 85–98.

———. "The Laity's Understanding of the Trustee System, 1785–1855." *Catholic Historical Review* 64 (July 1978): 357–76.

———. "Republicanism within American Catholicism, 1785–1860." *Journal of the Early Republic* 3 (Winter 1983): 413–37.

———. *People, Priests, and Prelates: Ecclesiastical Democracy and the Tensions of Trusteeism.* Notre Dame, Ind.: University of Notre Dame Press, 1987.

———. *The Roman Catholics.* Westport, Conn.: Greenwood Press, 1993.

———. *Catholics in America: A History.* Westport, Conn.: Praeger Publishers, 2004.

Cayton, Andrew R. L., *The Frontier Republic: Ideology and Politics in the Ohio Country, 1780–1825.* Kent, Ohio: Kent State University Press, 1986.

———. *Frontier Indiana.* Bloomington: Indiana University Press, 1996.

Cayton, Andrew R. L., and Fredrika J. Teute, eds. *Contact Points: American Frontiers from the Mohawk Valley to the Mississippi, 1750–1830.* Chapel Hill: University of North Carolina Press, 1998.

Chinnici, Joseph P. "American Catholics and Religious Pluralism 1775–1820." *Journal of Ecumenical Studies* 16 (Fall 1977): 727–46.

Clark, Thomas D. *Frontier America: The Story of the Westward Movement.* New York: Charles Scribner's Sons, 1959.

Cogliano, Francis D. *No King, No Popery: Anti-Catholicism in Revolutionary New England.* Westport, Conn.: Greenwood Press, 1995.

Crews, Clyde F. *An American Holy Land: A History of the Archdiocese of Louisville.* Wilmington, Del.: Michael Glazier, 1987.

———. "Holy Valleys and Holy Lands: Selected Historic Catholic Sites along the Lower Ohio and Middle Mississippi Rivers." *U.S. Catholic Historian* 18 (Fall 2000): 50–63.

Davidson, Robert. *History of the Presbyterian Church in the State of Kentucky.* New York: Robert Carter, 1847.

Davis, David Brion. "Some Themes of Counter-Subversion: An Analysis of Anti-Masonic, Anti-Catholic, and Anti-Mormon Literature." *Mississippi Valley Historical Review* 47 (September 1960): 205–24.

Dolan, Jay P. *Catholic Revivalism: The American Experience, 1830–1900.* Notre Dame, Ind.: University of Notre Dame Press, 1978.

———. *The American Catholic Experience: A History from Colonial Times to the Present.* Garden City, N.Y.: Doubleday, 1985.

———. "Catholic Attitudes toward Protestants." In *Uncivil Religion: Interreligious Hostility in America*, ed. Robert N. Bellah and Frederick E. Greenspahn. New York: Crossroad Press, 1987: 72–85.

Faragher, John Mack. *Sugar Creek: Life on the Illinois Prairie.* New Haven: Yale University Press, 1986.

———. *Daniel Boone: The Life and Legend of an American Pioneer.* New York: Henry Holt, 1992.

Finke, Roger, and Rodney Stark. *The Churching of America, 1776–1900:*

Winners and Losers in Our Religious Economy. New Brunswick, N.J.: Rutgers University Press, 1992.

Flick, Lawrence F. "Gallitzin." *Catholic Historical Society Review* New Series 7 (1927): 394–469.

Foik, Paul J. "Anti-Catholic Parties in American Politics, 1776–1860." *Records of the American Catholic Historical Society of Philadelphia* 36 (March 1925): 41–69.

———. *Pioneer Catholic Journalism.* New York: Greenwood Press, 1930.

Fox, Columba. "The Life of the Right Reverend John Baptist Mary David (1761–1841) Bishop of Bardstown and Founder of the Sisters of Charity of Nazareth." Masters thesis, Catholic University of America, 1925.

Franchot, Jenny. *Roads to Rome: The Antebellum Protestant Encounter with Catholicism.* Berkeley: University of California Press, 1994.

Gaustad, Edwin S. *Historical Atlas of Religion in America.* New York: Harper & Row, 1962.

———, ed. *To Win the West: Missionary Viewpoints 1814–1815.* New York: Arno Press, 1972.

Gollar, C. Walker. "Catholic Slaves and Slaveholders in Kentucky." *Catholic Historical Review* 83 (January 1998): 42–62.

———. "John Thayer and Early Catholic Opposition to Slavery." Unpublished manuscript for the *Register of the Kentucky Historical Society* (May 2000).

———. "Father John Thayer: Catholic Antislavery Voice in the Kentucky Wilderness," *Register of the Kentucky Historical Society* (Summer 2003): 275–96.

Gorman, Robert. *Catholic Apologetical Literature in the United States, 1784–1858.* Washington, D.C.: Catholic University of America, 1939.

Guilday, Peter. *A History of the Councils of Baltimore, 1791–1884.* New York: Macmillan Company, 1932.

Halttunen, Karen. *Confidence Men and Painted Women: A Study of Middle-Class Culture in America, 1830–1870.* New Haven: Yale University Press, 1982.

Hatch, Nathan O. *The Democratization of American Christianity.* New Haven: Yale University Press, 1989.

Haydon, Colin. *Anti-Catholicism in Eighteenth-Century England, c. 1714–1780, A Political and Social Study.* Manchester, England: Manchester University Press, 1993.

Hennesey, James. *American Catholics: A History of the Roman Catholic Community in the United States.* New York: Oxford University Press, 1981.

Heyden, Thomas. *A Memoir on the Life and Character of the Rev. Prince Demetrius A. de Gallitzin, Founder of Loretto and Catholicity in Cambria*

County, Pennsylvania, Apostle of the Alleghanies. Baltimore: John Murphy & Co., 1869.

Heyrman, Christine Leigh. *Southern Cross: The Beginnings of the Bible Belt.* New York: Alfred A. Knopf, 1997.

Huber, Vincent. "Sportsman's Hall." *Records of the American Catholic Historical Society of Philadelphia* 3 (1888–91): 142–73.

Isaac, Rhys. *The Transformation of Virginia.* Chapel Hill: University of North Carolina Press, 1982.

Johnson, Roy H. "The Lutheran Church and the Western Frontier, 1789 to 1830." *Lutheran Church Quarterly* (July 1930): 225–48.

Kenney, Lawrence J. "The Gallipolis Colony." *Catholic Historical Review* 4 (October 1918): 415–51.

Kukla, Jon. *A Wilderness So Immense: The Louisiana Purchase and America's Destiny.* New York: Alfred A. Knopf, 2003.

Lambing, Andrew Arnold. *A History of the Catholic Church in the Dioceses of Pittsburg and Allegheny from Its Establishment to the Present Time.* New York: Benziger Brothers, 1880.

Larkin, Jack. *The Reshaping of Everyday Life, 1790–1840.* New York: Harper Perennial, 1989.

Le Beau, Bryan. "Saving the West from the Pope: Anti-Catholic Propaganda and the Settlement of the Mississippi River Valley." *American Studies* 32 (Spring 1991): 104–14.

Lemcke, Peter Henry. *Life and Work of Prince Demetrius Augustine Gallitzin,* trans. J. Plumpe. 1861. Reprint, London: Longmans, Green and Co., 1940.

Leonard, Ira M., and Robert D. Parmet. *American Nativism, 1830–1860.* New York: Van Nostrand Reinhold Company, 1971.

Light, Dale. *Rome and the New Republic: Conflict and Community in Philadelphia Catholicism between the Revolution and the Civil War.* Notre Dame, Ind.: University of Notre Dame Press, 1996.

Maes, Camillus P. *The Life of Rev. Charles Nerinckx.* Cincinnati: Robert Clarke & Co., 1880.

Marty, Martin E. *Pilgrims in Their Own Land: 500 Years of Religion in America.* Boston: Little, Brown, 1984.

Mattingly, Mary Ramona. *The Catholic Church on the Kentucky Frontier, 1785–1812.* Washington, D.C.: Catholic University of America, 1936.

McAvoy, Thomas. "Americanism and Frontier Catholicism." *Review of Politics* 5 (July 1943): 275–301.

———. "The Formation of the Catholic Minority in the United States, 1820–1860." *Review of Politics* 10 (January 1948): 13–34.

McBrien, Richard P., ed. *The HarperCollins Encyclopedia of Catholicism.* New York: HarperCollins, 1995.

McDannell, Colleen. *Material Christianity: Religion and Popular Culture in America.* New Haven: Yale University Press, 1995.

McGill, Anna Blanche. *The Sisters of Charity of Nazareth Kentucky.* New York: Encyclopedia Press, 1917.

McNamara, Robert F. "John Carroll and Interfaith Marriages: The Case of the Belle Vue Carrolls." In *Studies in Catholic History in Honor of John Tracy Ellis*, ed. Nelson H. Minnich et al. Wilmington, Del.: Michael Glazier, 1985: 26–59.

Nobles, Gregory H. "Breaking into the Backcountry: New Approaches to the Early American Frontier, 1750–1800." *William and Mary Quarterly* 46 (1989): 641–70.

———. *American Frontiers: Cultural Encounters and Continental Conquest.* New York: Hill and Wang, 1997.

Oates, Mary J. "Catholic Female Academies on the Nineteenth-Century Frontier." *U.S. Catholic Historian* 12 (Fall 1994): 121–36.

O'Daniel, Victor Francis. *The Right Rev. Edward Dominic Fenwick, O.P.: Founder of the Dominicans in the United States, Pioneer Missionary in Kentucky, Apostle of Ohio, First Bishop of Cincinnati.* Washington, D.C.: Dominicana, 1921.

Posey, Walter Brownlow. *The Baptist Church in the Lower Mississippi Valley, 1776–1845.* Lexington: University of Kentucky Press, 1957.

Remini, Robert V. *The Life of Andrew Jackson.* New York: Penguin Books, 1988.

Rice, Howard C. *Barthelemi Tardiveau, A French Trader in the West.* Baltimore: Johns Hopkins Press, 1938.

Ruane, Joseph William. *The Beginnings of the Society of St. Sulpice in the United States, 1791–1829.* Washington, D.C.: Catholic University of America, 1935.

Ruskowski, Leo F. *French Émigré Priests in the United States, 1791–1815.* Washington, D.C.: Catholic University of America, 1940.

Sargent, Daniel. *Mitri.* New York: Longmans, Green, and Co., 1945.

Schauinger, Herman J. *Cathedrals in the Wilderness.* Milwaukee: Bruce Publishing Company, 1952.

Shaughnessy, Gerald. *Has the Immigrant Kept the Faith? A Study of Immigration and Catholic Growth in the United States, 1790–1920.* New York: Macmillan Company, 1925.

Shea, John Gilmary. *History of the Catholic Church in the United States, 1763–1815.* Akron: D. H. McBride & Co., 1888.

Slosser, Gaius Jackson. "A Chapter from the Religious History of Western Pennsylvania." *Journal of the Department of History of the Presbyterian Church in the U.S.A.* 16 (September 1934): 97–125.

Spalding, Martin John. *Sketches of the Early Catholic Missions of Kentucky from their Commencement in 1787, to the Jubilee of 1826–1827.* Louisville: B. J. Webb & Brother, 1844.

———. *Life, Times, and Character of the Right Reverend Benedict Joseph Flaget.* 1852. Reprint, New York: Arno Press and the New York Times, 1969.

———. "Bardstown Kentucky." *U.S. Catholic Historian* 18 (Fall 2000): 40–49.

Spalding, Thomas W. *The Premier See: A History of the Archdiocese of Baltimore 1789–1989.* Baltimore: Johns Hopkins University Press, 1989.

———. "Frontier Catholicism." *Catholic Historical Review* 77 (July 1991): 470–84.

———. "The Catholic Frontiers." *U.S. Catholic Historian* 12 (Fall 1994): 1–15.

Sweet, William Warren. *Religion on the Frontier, 1783–1830, Volume II, The Presbyterians.* 1936. Reprint, New York: Cooper Square Publishers, 1964.

Taves, Ann. *The Household of Faith: Roman Catholic Devotions in Mid-Nineteenth-Century America.* Notre Dame, Ind.: University of Notre Dame Press, 1986.

Taylor, Alan. *Liberty Men and Great Proprietors: The Revolutionary Settlement on the Maine Frontier, 1760–1820.* Chapel Hill: University of North Carolina Press, 1990.

Tentler, Leslie Woodcock. "'How I would save them all': Priests on the Michigan Frontier." *U.S. Catholic Historian* 12 (Fall 1994): 17–35.

Thompson, Leonard, and Howard Lamar, eds. *The Frontier in History: North America and Southern Africa Compared.* New Haven: Yale University Press, 1981.

Trollope, Frances M. *Domestic Manners of the Americans.* London, 1832.

Webb, Benjamin. *The Centenary of Catholicity in Kentucky.* Louisville: C. A. Rogers, 1884.

West, Elliott. *The Contested Plains: Indians, Goldseekers, and the Rush to Colorado.* Lawrence: University Press of Kansas, 1998.

Woodford, Frank B., and Albert Hyma. *Gabriel Richard: Frontier Ambassador.* Detroit: Wayne State University Press, 1958.

Index

Nerinckx *(cont)*
  and education, 147–48, 149–50
  on immorality on the frontier,
    117–18
  on intermarriage, 131
  on lack of financial support from
    parishes, 34, 136
  on marriage preparation, 131
  on Native Americans, 120
  on need for more priests, 47–48
  preparation for departure to
    Bardstown, 104
  on processions, 153
  and religious objects, 105–6,
    109–10
  on renegade priests, 57
  request for guidance from
    Rome, 133, 134–36, 139–42
  request for transfer from
    Kentucky, 40–41
  on shortage of priests, 21–22
  solicitation for help from
    abroad, 103, 104–5, 107–8,
    125, 156–57
  and St. Joseph's College, 151
  in Vincennes (Indiana
    Territory), 27–28
  on western expansion, 15
non-Catholics, preaching to, 157–62
Nugent, Andrew, 45–55, 61
nuns, 14, 15, 71–72, 147–48, 149,
  178

Ohio, Catholic settlement in,
  12–13
orthodoxy
  Charles Nerinckx on, 134
  Congregation for the
    Propagation of the Faith on,
    136
  Demetrius Augustus Gallitzin
    on, 11, 44

flexibility in new frontier, 136,
  181
  and interaction between
    Catholics and non-Catholics,
    134
  John Carroll on, 10, 85, 129
  and non-Catholics, 53, 113
  religious objects and, 113
  Stephen Theodore Badin on, 11
outreach, 146, 174, 179

Pellentz, James, 78, 81
Penalver, Luis, 39
personal gain, priests using their
  position for, 49
Phelan, Sylvester, 80, 81, 158
polemics, 74, 145, 162–70, 175, 179
politics, 41, 42–43, 110, 171, 179
power. *See* authority, clerical/
  episcopal
preaching, 6, 69, 157–62
Presbyterians, 12, 15, 16, 28, 81,
  82, 87, 97, 107, 119, 122,
  125, 146, 155, 157, 161, 167,
  168–69, 170, 173, 174, 182,
  183
priests
  characteristics needed for
    frontier, 19–20, 47
  as community leaders, 36
  criticism of Protestant ministers,
    157–58, 174
  demand for, 40
  emigration of, 36, 39, 62–63
  European, 10–15
  financial support for, 31–35, 135
  and loneliness, 21
  number of in Kentucky, 15
  number of in United States, 22
  as peace-keepers, 98
  personal gain, using position
    for, 49